Fair and Justice-Oriented Assessment

Fair and Justice-Oriented Assessment

Developing Teachers' Knowledge and Skills

MARGARET HERITAGE
E. CAROLINE WYLIE

HARVARD EDUCATION PRESS
CAMBRIDGE, MASSACHUSETTS

Paperback ISBN 979-8-89557-012-8

The Library of Congress Cataloging-in-Publication Data is on file.

Published by Harvard Education Press,
an imprint of the Harvard Education Publishing Group

Harvard Education Press
8 Story Street
Cambridge, MA 02138

Cover Design: Patrick Ciano
Cover Image: ljubaphoto via Getty Images

The typefaces in this book are Adobe Garamond Pro and Myriad Pro.

Contents

Preface

The primary purpose of classroom assessment is to improve student learning.[1] At face value this statement appears straightforward. Yet, the effective use of assessment harbors considerable complexities. By focusing on assessment literacy, in this book we aim to untangle some of these complexities. We consider the knowledge and skills that teachers need to acquire so that they can maximize the benefit of assessment for each student's learning in a way that is fair and just. In this preface, we lay out the main topics and themes that will be explored throughout the book as we examine what it means for teachers to become assessment literate.

In general, there are two forms of classroom assessment: summative and formative. It is important to note that the terms *summative* and *formative* indicate the purpose of the assessment and not the method of how students are assessed. Summative assessment is implemented at the end of a period of learning—for example, at the end of a unit or a course of study—and is concerned with "summing up" student learning relative to intended longer-term learning outcomes. Summative assessment may be thought of as a point-in-time view of achievement. Teachers can use results to assign grades or otherwise certify achievement, examine patterns of performance in their classes or across classes, and reflect on their teaching and plan for future modifications in content and pedagogy.[2]

Formative assessment provides a steady stream of information about how student learning is progressing toward the intended longer-term outcomes.[3] Formative assessment is conducted at the point of learning and is intended to reveal what students' next steps might be, so that both teachers and students can take continuous action to secure progress.[4] Its primary purpose is to keep student learning on track toward meeting the longer-term outcomes that are the focus of summative assessment.

Again, using assessment for summative and formative purposes might seem fairly uncomplicated. However, when we think about the body of knowledge and skills that teachers require, the picture becomes more complex. This skill set includes

- understanding the purposes of assessments and being able to discriminate among them;
- the ability to establish substantive learning goals;
- the methods by which to assess those goals, such as developing the tasks or situations that prompt students to say, do, or create something that shows the status of their learning; and
- the skills to interpret assessment information in relation to those goals, for both formative and summative purposes, in order to develop an explanation that will guide decisions about action intended to advance the learning of each student.[5]

Indeed, in the absence of such knowledge and skills, the promise of assessment to bolster student learning is significantly reduced.

In addition to specific knowledge and skills, teachers' dispositions toward assessment will also have a bearing on the effectiveness of assessment use. If teachers do not value assessment as an integral part of their professional practice and lack the motivation and confidence to use assessment information constructively, then the potential of assessment to benefit student learning is further undermined.

While there are a range of definitions of assessment literacy, we adopt the view that being assessment literate is having the ability to engage in a chain of reasoning from evidence, a process that is always applicable regardless of the differing contexts, purposes, and timescales of assessment.[6] A chain of reasoning begins with identifying learning goals—what is to be assessed—followed by a means to elicit evidence of learning in relation to the goal, and ends with interpreting evidence to guide asset-based and future-oriented actions to advance student learning.[7] This process characterizes all classroom assessment, whether for summative or formative purposes.[8] Across the chapters, we will unpack the details of this process and situate assessment knowledge and use within ambitious teaching, an umbrella term for teaching that is grounded in sociocultural theory and centers on each student's participation in rigorous learning opportunities that attend to their prior knowledge from their homes, communities and lived experiences.[9] As a result, ambitious teaching addresses not only the cognitive dimension of learning but the cultural and social/emotional dimensions as well. For this reason, classroom assessment has to take account of a broader view of learning and development.[10]

When assessment is positioned in the context of ambitious teaching, assessment literacy competencies are not conceived as a fixed, isolated body of knowledge, nor a discrete set of skills. Rather, assessment literacy practices are shaped by the students' cultural, ethnic, and linguistic environments and the assets they embody that can be leveraged for learning and assessment; for example, assessment literate teachers know how to create lesson-sized learning goals that address the "complex interplay among learners' prior knowledge, experiences, motivations, interests, and language and cognitive skills," while still being concerned about the longer-term goals of mandated curricula or standards.[11] In this vein, Australian researcher Dr. Jill Willis and colleagues propose the term "assessment literacies" instead of "assessment literacy" to reflect the dynamic, context-dependent, and social nature of teachers' processes and practices in their local situations and policy environments.[12] In short, none of the knowledge and skills associated with assessment literacy exist in a vacuum.

A corollary to the perspective that assessment practices are not static but influenced by local circumstances is *fair and justice-oriented assessment literacy*. By this we mean that all students have the right to be advantaged by assessment use regardless of any racial, social, economic, cultural, or linguistic factors.[13] Fair and justice-oriented assessment literacy is a theme that will be woven through all the book's chapters.

Ambitious teaching goes a long way toward laying the groundwork for fair and justice-oriented assessment literacy by promoting pedagogy that requires teachers to understand their students and take account of who they are and what they bring to the classroom from their homes and communities. This understanding provides the foundation for teachers to create assessment tasks that are reflective of the learning goals the students must meet—for instance, state standards—and also of students' own lives, which gives a personal meaning to them. Teachers then engage in equitable and just data interpretations informed by local insights and understandings about students' cultural background and lived experiences—for example, if performance could be impacted by students' perception of learning as irrelevant to their lives and concerns, if the student is experiencing anxiety about school or home, or if the discourse patterns of instruction and assessment are not accessible to students. Interpretation of evidence based on teachers' deep knowledge of their students optimizes the potential for sensitive action which builds on students' current strengths and sustains their learning within the context of their language and cultural ways of being.[14]

A core feature of the book is the inclusion of classroom examples to illustrate ambitious teaching and assessment design and use from teachers who represent a range of ethnic backgrounds, grade levels, geographic locations, subject-matter content, and student populations. In addition to spotlighting assessment literacy knowledge and skills in the context of ambitious teaching, the teachers also provide reflections about how they developed these competencies and put them into action in their classrooms. The quotations in the book are from these teachers, unless otherwise stated. Common among the teachers is the idea that teaching ambitiously and becoming assessment literate takes time, commitment, and support from colleagues and administrators. These teachers' experiences complement our focus on practical professional learning opportunities through which teachers can develop assessment literacy competencies over the course of their careers.

OVERVIEW OF CHAPTERS

Chapter 1 focuses on ambitious teaching as the context for justice and equity-oriented classroom assessment. We describe what constitutes ambitious teaching and provide extended illustrative examples of practice. Chapter 2 provides a brief overview of the historical assessment reforms that gave the impetus to ambitious teaching and justice-oriented and equity-focused assessment at the classroom level and develops the theme of fair and social-justice outcomes for all students in relation to teaching and assessment practices. Chapter 3, drawing on a framework that conceptualizes assessment as convergent and divergent,[15] gives a thorough account of the types of assessment that teachers have available to them and their respective purposes. In chapter 4, we provide a grounding for the professional learning opportunities across three main phases of development during the course of a teacher's career within the areas of learning supports, deliberate practice, and ownership and agency.

Chapters 5, 6, and 7 focus on three assessment components: learning goals, assessment evidence, and interpretation of action, addressing each one in turn. These components are considered in the context of ambitious teaching, which takes account of three dimensions of learning: cognitive, cultural, and socio-emotional. We also discuss these components in relation to expanded goals of schooling—for instance, the need for students to develop metacognition, take responsibility for their learning, and develop self-awareness.[16] Each chapter details the particular knowledge, and skills for assessment literacy in relation to the specific assessment component, along with practical suggestions for how it can be developed across the three phases outlined in chapter 4.

Chapters 8 and 9 go beyond classroom assessment. Chapter 8 considers the assessments that teachers may have to use as a result of state, district, or school policy, how they can complement or distort classroom assessment, and the assessment literacy competencies they need to use these assessments effectively in support of student learning. Chapter 9 concludes the book by outlining specific actions that leaders can employ to realize a vision of assessment literacy. These actions include promoting collaborative learning among teachers, generating buy-in for sustained teacher learning, creating time and space for teacher learning, and ensuring alignment with school and district policies.

WHO SHOULD READ THIS BOOK?

Our hope is that the book will encourage conversations and actions among professionals who desire to promote assessment practices that are consistent with contemporary ideas about teaching and learning and who are concerned with issues of fairness and equity in assessment design and use, particularly at the classroom level.

We believe the book will be useful for all educators who wish to understand what constitutes fair and justice-oriented assessment literacy in the context of ambitious teaching. We think it will be useful for teachers who want to work together to develop assessment literacy competencies in the interests of better learning for their students, for administrators who are crafting and implementing a vision of assessment literacy with their colleagues, and for those whose role is to support teachers in becoming assessment literate across their careers, such as teacher educators, professional learning providers, and teacher leaders.

We would be delighted to learn that this book was being used stimulate thinking among teachers, leaders, and preservice providers about how to create an assessment literate teacher workforce. We hope that whatever your role in education, you will find value in our book.

CHAPTER 1

Fair and Justice-Oriented Assessment Practices

The maxim "the only thing constant in life is change" applies to all aspects of society—including education.[1] Three symbiotic components of the educational process—teaching, learning and assessment—shift over time in response to a range of different factors, including demographic changes, labor market needs, and new information from the learning sciences about how people learn.[2] In this chapter, our purpose is threefold: (1) to consider how these factors, when taken together, provide the imperative for fair and justice-oriented assessment; (2) to discuss the forms of fair and justice-oriented assessment that ensue; and (3) to lay the groundwork for assessment literacy that later chapters will address in depth.

First, we will establish how education came to the imperative for fair and justice-oriented assessment. Then we will discuss what constitutes fair and justice-oriented assessment practices and why these practices need to be privileged in the assessment landscape. In this regard, we will introduce the concept of teachers' sociocultural consciousness and explain its importance as foundational to fair and justice-oriented assessment use. Finally, we will offer some examples of fair and justice-oriented assessment practices that embrace the goals for learning discussed in the chapter.

THE IMPERATIVE FOR FAIR AND JUSTICE-ORIENTED ASSESSMENT PRACTICES

Changes in educational goals and provision are catalyzed by several factors, three main ones of which we briefly discuss here: (1) demographic changes, (2) labor market needs, and (3) advances in the learning sciences.

Demographic changes

According to the National Center for Education Statistics (NCES), of the 49.6 million students enrolled in public elementary and secondary schools in the United States in fall 2022,

- 22.1 million were White;
- 14.4 million were Hispanic;
- 7.4 million were Black;
- 2.7 million were Asian;
- 2.3 million were of two or more races;
- 449,000 were American Indian/Alaska Native; and
- 182,000 were Pacific Islander.

Public school enrollment increased between fall 2012 and fall 2022 among students who were

- Hispanic (from 11.4 million to 14.1 million);
- Asian (from 2.3 million to 2.7 million); and
- of two or more races (1.2 million to 2.3 million).

Public school enrollment decreased between fall 2012 and fall 2022 among students who were

- White (from 25.4 million to 22.1 million);
- Black (from 7.8 million to 7.4 million); and
- American Indian/Alaska Native (from 534,000 to 449,000).

Between fall 2021 and fall 2031, the percentage of students who are Hispanic is projected to continue increasing, from 28 to 30 percent. In addition, the percentages of students who are Asian or of two or more races are projected to increase, each from 5 to 6 percent, respectively.[3] Also noteworthy is that the percentage of public school students in the US who were classified as English learners was higher in fall 2020 (10.3 percent, or 5.0 million students) than in fall 2010 (9.2 percent, or 4.5 million) students.[4] It is clear from the NCES reports that an already diverse US student population is becoming increasingly diverse, ethnically, racially, and linguistically.

Adding to this diversity among the student population, from 2022 to 2023 the number of students who received special education and/or related services under the Individuals with Disabilities Education Act was 7.5 million, or the equivalent of 15 percent of all public school students. Among students receiving special education and/or related services, the most common category of disability was a specific learning disability (32 percent).[5]

Labor market needs

A recent report from the World Economic Forum (WEF) described the current labor market as the "fourth industrial revolution" and called for new models of productivity, which would create massive changes in the skills required to contribute to the economy. The report notes that "many of today's school children will work in new job types that do not yet exist, most of which are likely to have an increased premium on both digital and social-emotional skills," and laments that "education systems in developed and developing economies alike still rely heavily on passive forms of learning focused on direct instruction and memorization, rather than interactive methods that promote the critical and individual thinking needed in today's innovation-driven economy."[6]

The WEF report echoes similar calls from the Organisation for Economic Co-operation and Development (OECD) regarding the broad competencies students need to have for success in school and life and for the economic benefit of the societies to which they belong:

- critical, creative, analytical, and metacognitive thinking;
- complex problem solving skills and collaboration;
- digital literacy;
- social and emotional skills such as empathy, self-awareness, respect for others, and the ability to communicate; and
- the ability to learn to learn in school and beyond through life.

Advances in the learning sciences

Knowledge in the area of human development and learning has grown at a rapid pace over the past two decades, and with it an emerging consensus about the implications of this research for equity.[7] In response to this research, Na'ilah Suad Nasir, educational researcher and president of the Spencer Foundation, and coauthors propose four key principles to foster deep learning and equity: (1) learning is rooted in evolutionary, biological, and neurological systems; (2) learning is integrated with other developmental processes whereby the whole child (emotion, identity, cognition) must be taken into account; (3) learning is shaped in culturally organized practice across people's lives; and (4) learning is experienced as embodied and coordinated through social interaction.[8] We may add that assessment design and intention should not be immune from these principles.

When we consider the significant disparities in educational outcomes by race, ethnicity, economic status, and disability that persist in the United States, these factors take on increased salience. The imperative is for all students, not just a select few, to have access to educational experiences that are grounded in key principles to foster deep learning and equity and that result in their achievement of broad competencies referenced above. And in order to support students' development of these broad competencies, we need effective assessment practices that are fair and justice-oriented.

ASSESSMENT PRACTICES TO DATE

For several decades standardized assessments using mainly multiple-choice items have dominated assessment practices in the United States. By definition, these assessments are administered to students during some common time period of necessarily limited duration, and are intended to serve a monitoring purpose for educational systems. However, assessing whether students have learned particular ambitious instructional goals requires us to look at specific, often complex and extended performances, which can take more time than standardized testing, especially the large-scale annual tests that most students are required to take.[9]

As distinguished assessment scholar Lorrie Shepard points out, by the mid-1980s research evidence had called for instructional changes that would engage students in more meaningful and challenging learning than they generally experienced.[10] At the same time, portfolios, performance assessments, and other open-ended tasks were developed to more fully capture learning goals that require students to produce evidence of their thinking, rather than merely selecting a correct answer. However, with the increasing use of high-stakes accountability testing and its pervasive influence on instruction and assessment, the move to such assessment formats was derailed. Of particular significance to this derailment was the federal policy, The No Child Left Behind Act, signed into law in 2002.

The No Child Left Behind (NCLB) Act

NCLB was a policy whose goal was to reduce persistent achievement gaps among groups of students. Under NCLB, eligibility for most federal funds was dependent on each state submitting an accountability plan. States were required to establish curricular standards, assess students on those standards, and make the assessment data public. NCLB required every school to be on a path to have 100 percent of students meeting "proficiency" standards in a short time, with attendant consequences for schools that did not make adequate yearly progress. There is evidence that NCLB had some positive benefits for special populations.[11] For example, one study found that students with disabilities who attended schools that were identified as "consistently accountable" were more likely to experience highly effective practices such as appropriately challenging reading and mathematics programs, increased instructional time and support, and greater access to assistive technology.[12] However, other research also documented ways in which district administrators often blamed the assessment performance of students with disabilities as the only factor keeping their schools from achieving annual yearly progress. A focus on preparation for these assessments led to teachers spending more time remediating content that was likely to be targeted on the standardized assessments at the expense of other instructional priorities.[13]

When Congress reauthorized the law as the Every Student Succeeds Act (ESSA) of 2015, the consequences were removed, but the standards, assessment, and reporting requirements remained. Research shows that, at best, these accountability regimes had modest positive impacts on assessment scores while generating some perverse consequences, such as teaching to the test, focusing instruction on students near the proficiency thresholds, and diverting attention from untested subjects and grades.[14]

Before the beginning of the twenty-first century, many national organizations issued reports calling for "world class standards" and more challenging curricula, in response to the perception that US students were not keeping up academically with many of their international peers.[15] Around 2010, new and ostensibly higher-level content standards for mathematics, English language arts (ELA), and science were introduced by most states to replace the array of existing individual state standards that were being tested under NCLB. The College and Career Ready Standards (CCRS)[16] were intended to raise student achievement and ensure that all students could graduate from high school with the knowledge and skills necessary to succeed in college, career, and life.

Two federally funded consortia of states, the Smarter Balanced Assessment Consortium (SBAC) and the Partnership for Assessment of Readiness for College and Careers (PARCC) were formed to create "next-generation" assessments aligned to Common Core State Standards, which would be administered annually in grades 3 through 8 and once in high school.[17]

Both consortia had the goal of creating assessments that focused on higher-order thinking and the application of knowledge, using constructed response items or performance tasks. These assessment types were to be a significant departure from the traditional forms, such as multiple-choice questions centered on recall, that had been a cornerstone of the US educational system for decades.[18] However, even with the best of intentions, there were many challenges: the initial assessments were seen as much more difficult than previous assessments, took significantly longer for students to complete, and were costlier than ones that were more reliant on multiple-choice items; there was also political backlash about too much federal involvement in local education. The consequence of these concerns is that some states left the consortia and developed their own accountability assessments. PARCC began with twenty-four states but now no longer exists, although their assessment item banks have been incorporated into a few state assessments. SBAC started with thirty-one state members, and now twelve states and one affiliate jurisdiction use the SBAC assessments, the largest of which is California.[19]

In two separate studies, panels of State and National Teachers of the Year and Finalists for State Teacher of the Year examined previous mathematics and English language arts state assessments from six states and the two consortia assessments that replaced them.[20] Both studies used Norman Webb's Depth of Knowledge (DOK) framework to examine the cognitive complexity of the items. The DOK framework has four levels that describe the increase in cognitive complexity or thinking that are required by a question or task: Level 1: recall and reproduction; Level 2: skills and concepts; Level 3: strategic thinking; and Level 4: extended thinking. In the ELA assessments, they found there was a shift from largely Level 1 and 2 items on the former state assessments to predominantly Level 2 and 3 items on the consortia assessments, representing a positive increase in cognitive complexity and an increased requirement for students to apply their conceptual understanding to assessments. However, the former state mathematics assessments and the consortia mathematics assessments were mostly Level 1 and Level 2 items, with only a slight increase in cognitive complexity. For mathematics, at least, the aspirations of "next-generation" assessments have largely been unmet.

According to leading assessment expert Scott Marion, the impact of NCLB and ESSA accountability policies has rippled through the assessment system and changed the nature of district and classroom assessment systems; teachers create instructional activities and classroom summative assessments that mimic the types of test items on the annual test, and district leaders overemphasize interim tests as part of students' test preparation. Assessment initiatives to improve instruction and student learning, such as student portfolios and proficiency-based graduation requirements, have been squeezed out in an effort to raise end-of-the-year test scores.[21]

This brief background on the factors spurring educational changes and on the undoubtedly unintended consequences of accountability assessments brings us to the need for fair and justice-oriented assessment practices in support of all students. We need to equip teachers and school and district leaders with assessment literacy competencies to mitigate the potentially negative impact of assessment on student learning, referenced earlier. Fair and justice-oriented assessment practices do not stand alone and cannot be regarded as a panacea to fix all inequities in the educational system. As we will emphasize throughout this book, these assessment practices are intimately connected with teaching, learning and curriculum, each one acting in concert with the others. Teaching a diverse student population requires a core, but flexible curriculum that can be adapted to reflect local circumstances. It also requires teachers to employ a wide range of pedagogical strategies, using sophisticated reasoning based on evidence of student learning to decide which ones to activate for which students. In other words, teachers respond to the variability among students rather than merely implementing uniform techniques or routines.[22] In the next section, we present what constitutes fair and justice-oriented assessment practices that form the basis for developing assessment literacy competencies among teachers.

FAIR AND JUSTICE-ORIENTED ASSESSMENT PRACTICES

As we noted in the preface, in the interests of equity, we propose that students should experience fair and justice-oriented assessment practices. By *fair* we mean that all students have the right to be advantaged by assessment use regardless of any racial, social, economic, cultural or linguistic factors.[23] We use the term *justice-oriented* to mean assessment that promotes different ways of knowing and seeks to leverage and sustain learners' cultural practices and knowledge.[24] A primary concern for assessment literacy is how assessment use can be fair and justice-oriented so that it supports high quality outcomes for all students.

In this section, we lay out the elements that contribute to assessment quality and the synergistic actions that teachers take in assessment use in the interests of fair and justice-oriented assessment. Before turning to specific fair and justice-oriented assessment practices, we believe it is essential to first address teachers' sociocultural consciousness. Chapter 7 addresses specific ways in which teachers can develop sociocultural consciousness, but we begin our discussion of fair and justice-oriented assessment practices by considering what the term *sociocultural consciousness* means and why it is so significant to equitable assessment.

Sociocultural consciousness

The student population in the United States is becoming increasingly diverse, while the teaching profession remains predominantly White (approximately eighty percent), including in schools where the majority of students are not White.[25] As a result, many teachers are likely to be teaching students that have backgrounds, cultures, and lived experiences that differ from their own in substantive ways. Teachers' sociocultural consciousness permeates and influences all aspects of their assessment use. To engage in fair and justice-oriented assessment practices, teachers need to expand their sociocultural consciousness by understanding that "one's worldview is not universal but is profoundly shaped by one's life experiences, as mediated by a variety of factors, chief among them race/ethnicity, social class and gender."[26] Part of this process entails teachers recognizing the ways in which privilege and power operate in society in general, and within school systems in particular, and striving to ensure that their efforts do not contribute to inequity with respect to teaching, learning, and assessment.

For teachers, developing a sociocultural consciousness includes analyzing attributes of their own culture, becoming aware of the values-based and lifestyle components of culture and the interrelationships of language and culture, and considering how their own culture, and the variety of ways in which they personally experience privilege or lack of privilege, may influence their work with students.[27] For instance, do teachers unconsciously favor students whose cultural background or ways of speaking are similar to their own? Do teachers have high expectations for some students and not for others?

It is important that teachers learn about the lives and experiences of groups of people who have different life experiences from them, particularly with respect to the students they teach. By learning about other groups, teachers can appreciate the differences between their own experiences and perspectives and those of others and become sensitive to how others view the world.[28] A high school teacher reflects on how she has developed her own sociocultural consciousness:

> I've been fortunate to have real conversations with students about their experiences. I've taken the opportunity to learn about different cultures, traditions, systemic barriers and privileges, learning differences, et cetera while finding ways to honor each student's talents and funds of knowledge [resources students bring to learning from their families, community, culture, background and interests[29]]. This in turn helped me talk with colleagues about student and teacher perspectives. I've approached conversations with compassion and tried to understand other's perspectives and experiences. Yet, I am also willing to call out discriminatory practices and beliefs. It's not always easy and it's important.[30]

Sociocultural consciousness further entails teachers developing an affirming attitude toward students who differ from them and acknowledging "the existence and validity of a plurality of ways of thinking, talking, behaving, and learning."[31] With an affirming attitude toward students and their backgrounds, teachers take an additive approach by including content or concepts, themes, and perspectives from diverse cultures in the curriculum without changing its basic structure.[32] Assessment aligned to the curriculum will also then reflect an additive approach to assessing the students' learning; assessments have more salience for students when they reflect their interests, cultures, and ways of knowing.

An affirming attitude also shapes teachers' expectations of students: they believe that all students are capable of achieving high levels of learning, they engage them in rigorous learning experiences, and in supportive ways hold them accountable for meeting the expectations.[33] Teachers' assessment practices will be reflective of these expectations.

In addition, having an affirming attitude impacts teachers' ability to make asset-based interpretations of assessment evidence. An asset-based interpretation focuses on the meaning of what students are communicating in their responses to determine what they understand and do not *yet* understand. It also offers helpful information about what is next to guide decisions about pedagogical action intended to advance the learning of each student.[34]

With this background on sociocultural consciousness, now let us turn to considering fair and justice-oriented assessment practices in detail. Table 1.1 summarizes the assessment quality elements and related teacher actions. The far left column identifies the components of quality assessment: learning goals, assessment evidence, and asset-based and future-oriented interpretations and actions, all of which operate in synchrony. The column to the far right of table 1.1 delineates the symbiotic actions that teachers need to take to support fair and justice-oriented assessment practices.

For most of its history of use, assessment has been primarily focused on the cognitive domain—for instance, reading comprehension in ELA and computation and problem solving in mathematics. However, to be consistent with advances in the learning sciences, assessment should reflect cultural, socio-emotional dimensions of learning and development in tandem with the cognitive domain that has traditionally been given prominence.[35] Table 1.1 shows these dimensions in relation to the individual assessment components. In practice the cognitive, socio-emotional, and cultural dimensions of learning and development are integrated. We separate them here for the purpose of considering what each entails and to tease out the related competencies needed for assessment literacy in later chapters.

Figure 1.1 shows the intersection of the three dimensions of learning—cognitive, socio-emotional, and cultural—with the three components of assessment quality included in table 1.1—learning goals, evidence, and interpretation/action.

TABLE 1.1 Fair and justice-oriented assessment practices

<table>
<tr><th colspan="3">Assessment quality components</th><th>Fair and justice-oriented teacher actions</th></tr>
<tr><td rowspan="3">Learning Goals</td><td>Cognitive</td><td>• Are meaningful and challenging
• Are informed by a progression/ trajectory of learning
• Reflect distinct ways of knowing/ reasoning specific to a discipline and how students come to learn these distinct ways</td><td>• Make clear the expectation that all students will develop high-level thinking, reasoning, and problem-solving skills
• Take responsibility for students achieving high expectations
• Use an equity-oriented curriculum</td></tr>
<tr><td>Cultural</td><td>• Are informed by students' culture, language, lived experiences, and interests</td><td>• Elevate and legitimate the linguistic, cultural, and substantive practices of students</td></tr>
<tr><td>Socio- Emotional</td><td>• Are motivating to students
• Are perceived by students as worthwhile</td><td>• Disrupt pattern of student agnostic goals</td></tr>
<tr><td rowspan="3">Assessment Evidence</td><td>Cognitive</td><td>• Tasks are aligned with learning/ assessment goals
• Tasks offer multiple ways to display knowledge and understanding</td><td rowspan="3">• Provide access for all students to show what they know and can do using any assistive technology as needed
• Ensure assessment content is recognizable and relevant to students
• Support students to view assessment as having genuine worth and utility for their learning</td></tr>
<tr><td>Cultural</td><td>• Tasks reflect students' lived experiences
• Tasks integrate students' funds of knowledge</td></tr>
<tr><td>Socio-Emotional</td><td>• The purpose of the assessment is clear to students
• The task is perceived as worthwhile and relevant by students</td></tr>
<tr><td rowspan="2">Interpretation</td><td>Cognitive</td><td>• Assessment evidence supports asset-based interpretations of what students are able to do
• Assessment reporting and/or feedback assists students to understand their own learning status</td><td rowspan="2">• Aware of what shapes their teacher positioning and how it might impact interpretation and action</td></tr>
<tr><td>Cultural</td><td>• Consideration of results is done in a way that reduces or minimizes factors that might impact performance</td></tr>
</table>

(continued)

TABLE 1.1 *continued*

Assessment quality components			*Fair and justice-oriented teacher actions*
Interpretation	Socio-Emotional	• Consideration of student attitudes to and interest in assessment content • Assessment reporting and/or feedback supports students' feelings of self-efficacy	• Holistic interpretation of evidence
Action	Cognitive	• Action is tailored to the edge of students' learning • Next steps use students' ideas as productive starting points	• Mediate everyday forms of knowing and academic content • Position students as competent • Sustain student learning within the context of their language, literacies, and cultural ways of being • Engender a sense of belonging
	Cultural	• Next steps include cultural/ funds of knowledge in future learning activities	
	Socio-Emotional	• Next steps support students playing an active role in responding to evidence of their own learning	

FIGURE 1.1 Assessment quality components intersected with dimensions of learning

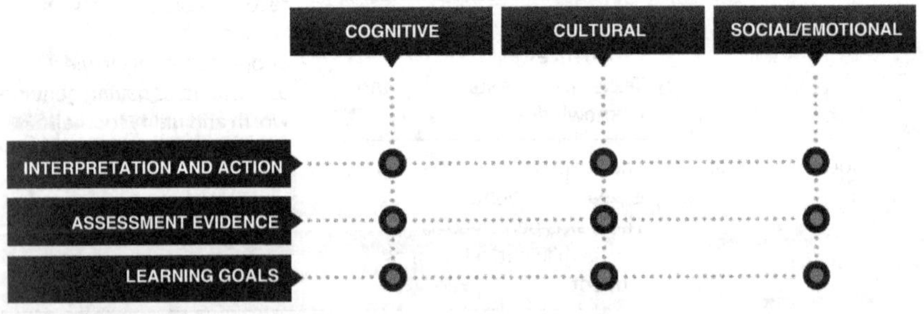

Let us now consider each of the factors in table 1.1.

Learning goals

Learning goals, the foundation for both instruction and assessment, are derived from academic learning standards and curriculum content. The cognitive dimension of instruction and assessment requires that learning goals are meaningful and challenging for all students.[36] Goals are situated within a progression of learning so that they build on students' prior knowledge and connect to future learning.[37] Learning goals are also informed by the distinct ways of knowing and reasoning specific to a discipline and by how students learn these distinct ways of knowing.[38] For example, a disciplinary-based goal for historical writing might be that students are learning to make interpretations based on evidence to develop an argument about another place and time, just as historians do.[39] When teachers set goals with these cognitive features for instruction and assessment they are clearly signaling that they have high expectations for all students, they believe that all students will develop high-level thinking, reasoning, and problem-solving skills, and they take responsibility for ensuring that all students will achieve the expectations.

Teachers are also advantaged when they have access to an equity-oriented curriculum, which provides the backbone for instruction and assessment. To be equity oriented, a curriculum should be (1) structured around a progression of learning to support conceptual organization, and lead students through increasingly sophisticated levels of knowledge and skills; (2) rooted in contemporary understanding of learning—for instance, using apprentice-style approaches to disciplinary learning (discussed in chapter 2); (3) designed to offer multiple pathways for learning; and (4) amenable to adaptation so as to be reflective of and relevant to the diversity of perspectives, histories, and cultures of the students. A proscribed curriculum that maintains the invisibility of many students and that does not permit any adaptations, while maintaining the structure, is not likely to be designated equity oriented.

Learning goals from an equity-oriented curriculum can be tailored to make connections to local circumstances and students' lived experiences and funds of knowledge. For example, many Indigenous people view themselves and the natural world as part of an extended ecological family that shares ancestry and origins. They regard life in any environment as viable only when humans view nature as family and they believe that Indigenous people are affected by and in turn affect the life around them.[40] In response to this view, a science learning goal for a class of predominantly Indigenous students might be an investigation of these driving questions: How are our homelands and waters being impacted by climate change and ocean acidification?, What should we do?, and What are our responsibilities?[41] Learning goals that integrate the cultural dimension also embrace the socio-emotional dimension. Consequently, students perceive the goal as worthwhile and relevant, which in turn impacts their motivation.[42] When teachers integrate the cultural and socio-emotional dimension into learning goals, they are elevating and legitimating the students' linguistic, cultural, and substantive practices, and disrupting patterns of student-agnostic goals.

Assessment evidence

A one-size-fits-all approach to assessment will not permit all students to show what they know. Therefore, assessment tasks or situations should offer multiple entry points and modalities in which knowledge and reasoning can be displayed.[43] Evidence of learning comes from planned tasks or situations that are fully aligned with learning goals embodying the cognitive and cultural dimensions of learning, and that prompt students to say, do or create something that shows the status of their learning.[44] For example, students could be asked for a written response, a pictorial representation, a diagram, or be invited to give an answer to a question during a class discussion. If the assessment content is not aligned to the learning goal, students may be assessed on concepts they have not yet learned, and teachers and students may receive misleading or distorted information about where student learning stands in relation to the goal. When the learning goal embodies the cognitive and cultural dimensions, the assessment task, aligned to the goal, will reflect students' funds of knowledge and lived experiences. For example, in English language arts a task to assess written arguments to support claims with clear reasons and relevant evidence could be designed to give students a choice of topics that address the range of cultural backgrounds, lived experiences, and interests represented among the student body. Similarly, an assessment focused on students' ability to identify both explicit and implicit ideas from textual evidence could offer students a choice of texts. When students are given opportunities to be involved with topics of interest to them, they are more likely to engage in learning than when topics have little relevance to their lives.[45] A further benefit is that providing students with choice among prompts has a positive impact on both student perception of competence and outcomes.[46]

Providing multiple entry points to students is not unique to ELA. For example, a mathematics assessment designed to reveal students' current understanding of multiplication and division asks sixth-grade students, in preparation for extending their understandings of multiplication and division to divide fractions by fractions, to: (1) explain how to respond to a given problem (which could be tailored to match students' interests, cultural background, language facility and so on) in words and draw a diagram to show this; (2) show a calculation to solve the problem; and (3) make up problems of their own to match two different given calculations. This assessment gives students the chance to show what they know using different modalities, as well as providing the teacher with insights into their current levels of understanding and any difficulties they encountered.[47]

When these features of assessment quality are present—alignment with learning goals, tasks that reflect students' backgrounds and offer multiple entry points and modalities—fair and justice-oriented teacher actions encompass providing access for all students to display the current status of their high-level thinking, reasoning and problem-solving skills, and ensuring that the assessment content is recognizable and relevant to students. From a socio-emotional perspective, teachers support students to have a positive view of assessment by understanding the purpose of the assessment (i.e., what the evidence will be used for) and how their learning can be advanced and deepened through the assessment use.

Interpretation of evidence

As discussed earlier, teachers use the analysis of the evidence in relation to the goals to develop an asset-based explanation or interpretation of the assessment evidence (qualitative and quantitative) that focuses on what students can do in order to build appropriately on that knowledge and skill base in the future. Teachers interpret evidence in a holistic way, taking account of the interrelationship of cognitive, cultural, and socio-emotional perspectives to develop an explanation of what the evidence indicates about student performance relative to the learning goals. Integrating the three perspectives factors in who students are and what they bring to the assessment context that can shape their performance. In this way, a more fair and justice-oriented interpretation is yielded than when focusing exclusively on the cognitive that has traditionally dominated assessment practices.

From a cognitive perspective, teachers engage in evidentiary reasoning, informed by their understanding of what meeting the assessment goal entails, to determine what students can do so that future learning can be scaffolded based on their strengths.[48] Teachers also support students' metacognitive strategies to help them understand their present state of learning, offering feedback that helps students constructively understand where their learning stands in relation to the desired goal and suggestions or hints for them to consider to make progress. When teachers have a well-developed sociocultural consciousness they are more apt to guard against providing feedback that is differentially filtered through a negative view of students' social class, ethnicity, cultural or language background, or disability. It also contributes to teachers' ability to interpret student responses by being aware of not privileging students' linguistic and cultural patterns and practices that are more familiar to them.[49] Particularly in the case of assessments that are external to the classroom, such as district assessments, interpretation should account for factors that might impact student performance. Such factors include cultural mismatch with assessment content or students' perception of content as irrelevant or linguistic confusion in accessing meaning of content. An example of cultural mismatch is using only Western figures for assessing minoritized students understanding of the genre of biography; an example of linguistic confusion is when students do not understand differences among terms such as *synthesize*, *analyze*, *evaluate*, and *discuss*.[50] Contrasting results on these external assessments with student responses to more locally created classroom assessment can provide a more complete view of students.

Interpretation from a socio-emotional perspective is also shaped by teachers' knowledge of students' attitudes to, and interest in, the assessment task content and their knowledge of the students' sense of self-efficacy with regard to the discipline.[51] Students with a strong sense of self-efficacy believe they are capable of performing well on academic tasks and are more willing to persist in the face of difficulty.[52] Students' interpretation of their assessment outcomes is a key component that determines self-efficacy—they may feel that they will do well on a mathematics assessment but not very well on a science one.[53]

An augmented picture of students' assessment performance based on teachers' deep knowledge of their students provides important contextual insights that optimizes a fair and justice-oriented interpretation of assessment evidence.

ACTION

Taking action is a crucial step in assessment use, since the purpose of classroom assessment is to guide decisions to advance student learning. Teachers' action based on interpretation from a cognitive perspective is matched to the "edge" of student learning and is designed to extend and deepen students' thinking and skills by supporting them to take manageable next steps.[54] Such action can take varied forms, such as providing additional scaffolding, sharing ideas and approaches from other students, introducing a new learning activity, using representations, asking questions or prompting student thinking, offering direct instruction, or giving feedback to guide revision and reflection that sensitively takes account of students' feelings of self-efficacy in the discipline.[55] When students are able to accomplish their next steps in learning, they are positioned as competent individuals who can continue to make progress.

Teachers also use diverse student ideas and experiences revealed in the evidence as productive starting points for mediating between everyday forms of knowing and those accepted and used within specific content areas.[56] For example, second-grade students were learning about adaptation to answer the question "Why do animals live where they live?" To elicit their initial ideas, the teacher invited the students to discuss in small groups: "Which is the odd one out in bird, cat, fish, and elephant?" When asked for their responses, most students said the elephant (because they reasoned that elephants could not be pets). Although this response was based on their lived experiences and was not what the teacher anticipated, she built on the students' idea by asking them to think about how various features of the elephant, cat and bird helped those creatures survive in their environments, setting up for the observation of characteristics of fish, the only creature that lived in water.[57]

Action from a cultural perspective requires that "pedagogies be more than responsive of or relevant to the cultural experiences and practices of young people—it requires that they support young people in sustaining the cultural and linguistic competence of their communities while simultaneously offering access to dominant cultural competence."[58] For example, in English language arts, strengthening students' understanding of symbolic meanings in literature can be accomplished by reading rap lyrics and other texts that the students are familiar with, and then supporting them to use their insights from this experience to examine more formal canonical texts.[59] In mathematics, cognitively demanding tasks that are the next steps for students based on assessment evidence can be modified to make them more culturally relevant. The structure of the task can be maintained while reflecting contexts that are familiar to the students and their communities. For instance, if a teacher wanted to revise a hexagon pattern task focused on angles and lines of symmetry, they could connect it to patterns in local architecture and design that are familiar to the students, or to those from architecture and design in different parts of the world that would resonate with the students' cultural heritage.[60] The students' own cultural heritage would be affirmed, and those students who did not share the same background could be introduced to and taught to value and appreciate the culture of their peers.[61]

Teachers' action based on interpretation that integrates the socio-emotional dimension of assessment supports students to regard assessment as a means for learning and improvement through their own efforts. Students are not simply recipients of teachers' pedagogical actions, but can take an active stance to responding to evidence of learning as a result of teacher and peer feedback or of their own self-assessment. Such action can include making decisions about how to use feedback (or not to use it, since feedback is not a mandate), or about whether to adapt their learning strategies or modify or change their learning goal. When students take their own action, they are developing skills related to self-regulation, which are increasingly regarded as necessary for life-long learning.[62] Self-regulated students are more persistent, resourceful, and confident, an advantage for them in both school and work.[63]

When teachers integrate cognitive, cultural, and socio-emotional perspectives in all their assessment practices, they are establishing a safe environment for students that engenders a sense of belonging. Students see their lives and communities connected to teaching, learning, and assessment and they develop an agentive stance to learning, leading to a growth mindset that values hard work and persistence to achieve the high expectations that have been set for them.

EXAMPLES OF FAIR AND JUSTICE-ORIENTED ASSESSMENT

In the final section of this chapter, we present three examples of fair and justice-oriented assessment and discuss why they can be regarded as such.

Example one: Scaffolded assessment task that allows for multiple response modalities

The first example is an assessment task (figure 1.2) from fifth-grade science that is anchored in the phenomenon of smell traveling from the kitchen to the nose and engages students in the practices of developing models and constructing explanations.[64] To respond to the task, students need to understand a disciplinary core idea related to the particle nature of gas. Figure 1.2 shows an English learner student's model and explanation of the phenomenon.

Why example one represents fair and justice-oriented assessment practice

First, this task includes a scaffold related to the practice of developing models. Students are reminded that a model of a system "should include both components

FIGURE 1.2 Science assessment

You are in the school cafeteria, and you smell food coming from the kitchen.

a. Develop a model of how the smell of food travels from the kitchen to your nose. Your model should include both *components* and their *interactions*.

b. Based on your model, explain in words (1) how the smell of food travels from the kitchen to your nose and (2) why you cannot see the smell. [Response in box shows what the student wrote]

You can smell the food because the smell is of gas partical and it goes and hits off each other to travel. smell is there but it's to small to see.

Source: Loren Llosa, S. E. Grapin, and A. Haas, *Integrating Science and Language for All Students with a Focus on English Language Learners: Science and Language Assessment Shifts* (Brief and Webinar prepared for the New York State Education Department, 2020).

and their interactions." This scaffold, which is removed over the course of the year as students become more proficient with developing models, provides support for all students to show what they know.

Second, in this task, the student responds using both visual and linguistic modalities. The student uses dots and arrows to show how gas particles travel from the kitchen to the nose. Then, they explain in words, based on their model, how the smell of food travels and why they cannot see the smell. While important for all students, using multiple modalities is especially beneficial for English learners who have sophisticated science ideas but are still developing the language to communicate those ideas in English.

Third, to respond to this task, students can draw from everyday and specialized registers. In this response, the student uses the everyday expression "hits off each other" to describe how gas particles move freely. The student also refers to a singular gas particle ("a gas partical"[65]), although the visual model shows multiple gas particles traveling across the room. The use of two registers keeps the focus on the meaning of what students are communicating.

As a result of the scaffolds, the linguistic and visual modalities, and the ability to use two different registers in their responses, all students, including English learners, can provide evidence of their understanding of an important disciplinary idea at whatever level of sophistication they are able to accomplish.

Example two: Connecting historical events to current struggles for racial equality

The second example shown in figure 1.3 is a history assessment that gauges whether middle school students can identify the historical event or development depicted in a photograph from the past and evaluate the historical significance of the development.[66]

Why example two represents fair and justice-oriented assessment practice

The topic of the assessment, the March on Washington for Jobs and Freedom, brought people together from all over the United States. African American students will see people who look like them depicted in the image, and having studied the March all students will know that people of different races and backgrounds were also present, making the topic relevant for a broad swath of students. Relevance is also achieved by the connections students can make about the March with current struggles for racial equality and for many people to expand economic and educational opportunities. The assessment task invites students to behave like historians by engaging in reasoning from a primary source.

The assessment task offers constructed response items, which provides access for all students to demonstrate their knowledge and reasoning abilities, and encourages the expression of diverse perspectives. The task also includes a scaffold about the criteria for determining if an event is historically significant so that students have guide posts for considering their responses, maximizing the potential for them to reveal their historical understanding. Based on their score, students can use the rubric to understand what they need to do to improve, a practice that

FIGURE 1.3 History assessment

Directions: Answer the following question using the photograph, the source information, and your knowledge of history.

<u>**Source information**</u>
Date: August 28, 1963 **Location:** Washington, D.C.

Question 1: What historical event does the image depict?

An event is historically significant if it:

- was important or influential at the time it occurred,
- had lasting effects on people and/or society,
- was a moment of change or transition in history, or
- was representative of broader trends or changes in society.

Question 2: Why is the event depicted historically significant?

The assessment task has an accompanying rubric for scoring the student responses.

Rubric

To answer this question correctly, students must identify the event depicted in a historical photograph and clearly explain why the event is historically significant. For the first question, successful students will identify this as a photo of the March on Washington for Jobs and Freedom in 1963. For Question 2, successful students might elaborate on one or more of the following:

- The protest garnered significant national and international attention, putting pressure on Congress and the Kennedy Administration to pass significant civil rights legislation. This pressure ultimately influenced the passage of the Civil Rights Act of 1964.

- It was one of the largest political demonstrations in United States history, with about a quarter of a million protestors gathered in Washington, D.C.

FIGURE 1.3 (continued)

- Speeches from civil rights leaders like Martin Luther King Jr., Roy Wilkins, John Lewis, and A. Philip Randolph were distributed widely and their words had a lasting impact on the Civil Rights Movement. King's "I Have a Dream" speech was broadcast on television and is considered one of the most influential public addresses in United States history.

Level	Description
Proficient	**Question 1**: Student clearly and specifically identifies the event depicted in the photograph. **Question 2**: Student clearly and specifically explains why the event is historically significant.
Emergent	**Question 1**: Student provides correct information related to the event but does not clearly identify the significant event. **Question 2**: Student correctly elaborates on the event but does not clearly explain why the event is historically significant.
Basic	**Question 1**: Student does not correctly identify the event. **Question 2**: Student does not provide a correct or relevant explanation for why the event is historically significant.

Source: Printed with permission from Joel Breakstone, Executive Director of Digital Inquiry Group.

can be combined with peer feedback, or using peers as sounding boards to decide how to improve a response.

Example three: Teacher questioning that meets students where they are

The final example centers on assessment in the form of teacher dialogue with third-grade students during the course of a mathematics lesson.[67] The students are working on a problem that requires them to apply their knowledge of multiplication and addition. They are seated in groups of three discussing "what the problem is asking them to do" and how they might go about solving it. The teacher moves from group to group, engaging in interactions with them. When joining one group, she listens in for a while and then asks them: "Can anyone inform me of what you are working on? Can you tell me a little bit more about what you are doing as a group?" One of the students responds:[68]

ROBERTO: Well we kind of think it's multiplication cuz you could tell here . . . well, it says *Ricardo had 135 US stamps* and then we read the next sentence: He has *three times as many foreign stamps as US stamps*. So then right when it says has three times as many, we might think that's multiplication. Cuz you know how in division, it says in each, mostly in division it says in each, and mostly in multiplication it says times.

Acknowledging that the student has begun to identify some information he thinks will help solve the problem, the teacher then asks, "Now what is the question—what is it that they want you to solve?" A second student in the group joins the conversation while the others listen:

IMHOTEP: They are asking us to solve how many do we have altogether. Like all of 'em . . . three times as many as 135 . . . and that would be like adding 135, 135, 135. But since we're working on multiplication and division we have to do it the opposite way. It means dividing to find out the answer . . . to get three times as many as 135.

Recognizing that neither of the students is completely clear about what the problem is asking them to do, the teacher then asks Imhotep to reread the problem aloud. At the end of the reading, the teacher repeats the last line of the question: "so how many stamps did he have altogether?" Roberto immediately responds; "well there's actually two things—there's 'altogether' and one other, 'how much does it equal.'" The teacher responds: "So the word 'altogether' informs you of what?" Stephanie replies "they're asking us how much does it equal."

The teacher then says:

Well it started off as multiplication when listening to Roberto and you felt that this was a really multiplication problem. But when Imhotep reread the question, it seemed that it was an addition problem.

Stephanie follows up this statement by saying that she thinks it is also a multiplication problem. Then the teacher asks: Do you think it might be both?" Stephanie replies that she does, and the teacher responds: "Do you think that's what they're asking you to do? Are those the next steps? So maybe multiplication and addition? I'm going to leave that one that one up to you." Imhotep then says:

I have an idea. Why don't we . . . first we do the problem there's multiplication. Then the next problem . . . we do it again, but this time addition. And the last one, we could do it as division . . . So if we have it all the same, we have the answer.

The teacher responds:

> Well, I'm going to leave that up to you as a group . . . and I want you to really think . . . what would be your next step? Would you start with multiplication and then add? And if that's the case, what would you be multiplying and what would you be adding? OK? [Students nod]. Go ahead and continue.

Why example three represents fair and justice-oriented assessment practice

In the course of these exchanges with her students, the teacher embedded questions in the ongoing flow of the conversations that are focused on the instructional tasks the students are engaged in. From the opening moves of the conversation, the teacher adopted a collaborative stance with the students, one that encourages the students to become partners and share the *knowledge authority* with their teacher. From the conversation's opening the teacher pursues a particular objective through questioning: the students' understanding of the problem and of the relationship between multiplication and addition. The exchange can be characterized as an assessment conversation in which the teacher takes immediate action in the context of a discussion to nudge student thinking forward.

She first invites the students to participate in response to her question, "Can anyone inform me of what you are working on? Can you tell me a little bit more about what you are doing as a group?" It's important to note that although the teacher has listened to the students' discussion, she does not immediately target a particular point with a question, but instead offers the students an open-ended opportunity to explain their thinking in relation to the problem. The nature of the question provides the students with multiple entry points to reveal their thinking.

At no point in the conversation does the teacher foreclose the students' thinking but rather moves the conversation forward with her questions and statements. Neither does she tell the students if they are correct or incorrect. Instead, she responds to the evidence she obtains in her interaction by nudging the students' thinking so that they are clearer about the problem and have begun to make connections between addition and multiplication. Students are positioned as competent collaborators in the conversation and their agentic stance is maintained throughout. In her final response to Imhotep's idea, the teacher asks questions to help bridge students from where they are in their thinking to taking steps to solving the problem.

Across three different assessment formats we can see many of the components of fair and justice-oriented assessment. These components can be designed into any task, for any grade level, and in all subject areas. If they are absent, then the assessment task loses its potential to provide teachers and learners with the information they need to make decisions that will benefit all students regardless of race, ethnicity, socio-economic status, language background, or disability.

A FINAL THOUGHT

In this chapter, we have considered the need for fair and justice-oriented assessment practices and the components that contribute to assessment quality. We have also noted that assessment practices are synergistic with teacher and learning. In this vein, we end the chapter with a quote from a recent report, *Reimagining Balanced Assessment Systems*, published by the National Academy of Education. We propose all assessment designers and users consider this question: "To what degree and in what ways does this assessment—its content and practices—support or hinder rich and equitable classroom learning environments?"[69] We should expect no less from assessment than to support equitable classroom learning environments.

SUMMARY: KEY TAKEAWAYS

- Three main catalysts for educational change are (1) demographic changes, (2) labor market needs, and (3) advances in the learning sciences.
- All students need to have access to educational experiences that foster deep learning and equity and that result in their achievement of broad competencies for success in today's world.
- The impact of accountability policies has rippled through the assessment system and changed the nature of district and classroom assessment systems in ways that do not always benefit ongoing student learning.
- In the interests of equity, we propose that students should experience fair and justice-oriented assessment practices.
- To engage in fair and justice-oriented assessment practices, teachers need to expand their sociocultural consciousness.
- To be consistent with advances in the learning sciences, assessment should reflect cultural and socio-emotional dimensions of learning, and development in tandem with the cognitive domain.

- In practice, three components of assessment quality—learning goals, evidence, and interpretation/action—intersect with cognitive, cultural, and socio-emotional dimensions of learning.
- The components of fair and justice-oriented assessment can be designed into any task, for any grade level, and in all subject areas, and provide the teachers and learners with the information they need to make decisions that will benefit all students regardless of race, ethnicity, socio-economic status, language background, or disability.

CHAPTER 2

Ambitious Teaching

All young people deserve an education that can ignite excitement and enthusiasm about learning and inspire confidence in a future that is full of possibilities. Yet all too often, students are offered "a desk-bound, test- and compliance-driven experience that leaves them passive, uninspired and flat-out bored."[1] It is axiomatic that this kind of school experience is a mismatch with contemporary understanding about how people learn. Students need invitations to thinking from teaching that is informed by an up-to-date understanding about learning so that they can develop deep disciplinary knowledge and engage their full selves in learning, cognitively, socially, emotionally, and culturally.[2] This chapter describes what such teaching, commonly referred to as *ambitious teaching*, entails, and discusses why it is both foundational to and reciprocal with fair and justice-oriented assessment teacher actions.[3] We begin with a description of the principles and practices of ambitious teaching and provide brief examples of classroom practice related to six key elements. Next is an extended example of ambitious teaching taken directly from a middle school science classroom. Finally, we consider the interrelationship among ambitious teaching, assessment practices, and fair and justice-oriented teacher actions discussed in the previous chapter.

AMBITIOUS TEACHING

A consensus report published by the National Academies of Sciences, Engineering, and Medicine (NASEM) synthesized recent research from a range of fields of study on how people learn.[4] From the report's synthesis, five conclusions emerged that impact classroom practice, and which are embodied in ambitious teaching:

Conclusion 1: there is a complex interplay among a learner's prior knowledge, experiences, motivations, interests, language, and cognitive skills; educators' own experiences and cultural influences; and the cultural, social, cognitive, and emotional characteristics of the learning environment. This conclusion speaks to the reciprocal relationship among the students with their home, community and lived experiences, the teachers' own cultural and experiential influences, and the classroom environment's characteristics. In practice, it means that teachers who are modeling ambitious teaching practices will take account of students' prior knowledge from school and from their home cultures, including their home language, when establishing learning goals and when creating learning experiences that tap into students' interests and motivate them to want to learn. Teachers cultivate an awareness of what shapes their teacher positioning, which was discussed in chapter 1. The classroom ought to be a place where students are valued for who they are and what they bring to school. It must be an emotionally safe place where students develop relationships of trust and respect, and where all students share responsibility for their own and each other's learning.

Conclusion 2: Learners need to be involved in directing their own learning through targeted feedback that enables the development of metacognitive skills, challenges that are well matched to the learners' current capacities, and support in setting and pursuing meaningful goals. This conclusion first makes clear that students are not passive recipients of learning but rather active agents who can be self-directing as a result of receiving and using constructive feedback that engages their thinking, and of developing metacognitive skills—the ability to monitor their progress toward goals and make adjustments to learning strategies or existing goals. Second, it spells out that students need to participate in rigorous tasks and activities, matched to the edge of their current learning, that will challenge their thinking in new and interesting ways on the way to meeting demanding learning goals. From this conclusion we can also understand that students need to receive the right amount of scaffolding to support their participation in learning and assist their progress to achieve their goals.

Conclusion 3: It is necessary to adopt an asset-based model in which curricula and instruction connect academic content to the learning students experience outside of school. An asset-based model of teaching was discussed in chapter 1, particularly in relation to teachers' awareness of what shapes their teacher positioning. It bears repeating here that an asset-based approach to teaching means that students' cultures and backgrounds are regarded as assets—not deficits—that can be leveraged for learning, making connections between what students already know from their experience to the academic content. It also necessitates that teachers have high expectations for all students. Adopting an asset-based approach to assessment requires that teachers interpret assessment information through the lens of what students *can* do in deciding on next steps to advance learning.

Conclusion 4: Teachers must teach the language and practices specific to particular disciplines in order to help students develop deep understanding in the discipline. When applying this conclusion to practice, teachers apprentice students to a discipline, a process through which students build an understanding of disciplinary concepts, principles, practices, representational forms, and language conventions.[5] For example, when students are apprenticed to the discipline of science, they behave a scientist would, asking questions, developing and using models, and planning and carrying out investigations.[6] Discourse-based instructional strategies—for example, planning tasks and activities that require students to collaborate and discuss their ideas, help students listen to each other. When they listen to each other carefully, they can build on each other's thinking and develop deeper discipline-based knowledge and skills.[7]

Conclusion 5: Assessment is a critical tool for advancing and monitoring students' learning in school. It is noteworthy that this conclusion is included in a report that focuses on how people learn, signaling its importance to the process of learning. Throughout the book's chapters, we will address assessment use and assessment literacy in the context of optimizing student learning.

In the next section, we tease apart the NASEM conclusions into six key elements of ambitious teaching, with examples of practice of each one: (1) providing challenging learning goals for all students; (2) apprenticing students to a discipline; (3) engaging students in rich, multimodal tasks with multiple entry points: (4) using discourse-based instruction; (4) attending to who students are; (5) supporting student metacognition; and 6) establishing a supportive, safe environment.

PROVIDING CHALLENGING GOALS FOR ALL STUDENTS

Ambitious teaching centers on challenging learning goals for all students, matched to the current edge of students' learning, and on each student's engagement in meaningful learning opportunities, grounded in the expectation that all students can develop deep knowledge, conceptual understanding, and analytic practices in the discipline.

A classroom example of challenging learning goals for all students

This example is taken from an inclusive third-grade classroom in which 35 percent of the students have a recognized disability under the Individuals with Disabilities Education Act and over 50 percent of the students receive free or reduced lunch.[8] In second grade, the students focused on opinion writing, providing reasons for their opinions or arguments based on their own experiences—for instance, in response to the prompt "Do cats or dogs make better pets and why?" In their current science unit, the students had been investigating animal habitats and had developed the understanding that a habitat is made up of sufficient space, food, water, and shelter and could differ in the specifics of each depending on the animal. They were now going to learn about scientific argumentation, or, as the teacher put it, "the structure of a science argument," using evidence from multimedia resources to support their opinion (claim) about a specific habitat. The teacher invited them to begin thinking about scientific argumentation by reading an exemplar in pairs and identifying what they thought made the text a science argument in contrast to writing their own opinions based on their experiences. As they discussed in pairs, the teacher monitored their conversations, asked questions to extend their thinking, and if needed, acted as a scribe to record a student's ideas. Once they had completed their paired discussions, the teacher led a whole-class discussion about what they had identified as the criteria for a quality science argument, and why, using several strategies to ensure equitable participation. For example, based on her observations of the paired discussions, if a student had only one or two ideas to share, which were likely to be shared by others, she invited that student to contribute early on in the class discussion. If particular students seemed reluctant to participate, she intentionally asked them questions such as, "What do you think about what [student name] shared?" or "What might you add to what [student name] shared?" or "What might you agree or disagree with that has been shared so far?"

Once everyone contributed an idea, she engaged the class in a quick brainstorm to list the criteria and then invited the students to return to their partner discussion to think about which were the most important criteria for science argumentation. Following this activity, the teacher brought the class together again and asked each pair to share the criteria that they thought were essential for a science argument and why, ultimately leading the class to a consensus set of criteria to guide their writing.

All students participated in a rigorous learning experience that led them to understand and internalize criteria for writing a science argument. No distinction of learning goal was made for the students with disabilities who were offered support by the teacher to participate and achieve the goal.

APPRENTICING STUDENTS TO A DISCIPLINE

Ambitious teaching apprentices students to a discipline (e.g., mathematics, science social studies, English language arts) through which they learn the models of thought, the practices, and the language of the discipline as a means to achieving deep learning and transfer. For instance, when apprenticed to the discipline of mathematics, students develop conceptual understanding of mathematical concepts, operations and relations; they formulate, represent and solve mathematical problems; and they engage in logical thought, reflecting on, explaining, and justifying mathematical arguments.[9] As apprentices to the discipline of history, they engage in a process of investigation, and they learn about the interpretive nature of history and that it is an evidentiary form of knowledge.[10]

A classroom example of apprenticing students to a discipline[11]

In a lesson focused on answering the central historical question, "How did Frederick Douglass view Abraham Lincoln?," secondary school students built on their prior knowledge of the American abolitionist movement, the Civil War, and emancipation by examining a timeline of events from August 1863, when Douglass told Lincoln he had stopped recruiting African American men to enlist in the Union army because Black soldiers were receiving unequal treatment, to December 1865, when Lincoln was assassinated. Their task was to read the timeline with this question in mind: "How did the relationship between Douglass and Lincoln change from June 1864 to June 1865, and why?" The teacher then elicited students' initial ideas about the nature of the change and the possible reasons for it. She would return to these ideas throughout the lesson as they were modified as a result of reading and discussing primary source documents. Next, the teacher told the students that in the lesson (two class periods) they were going to read three documents by Frederick Douglass to investigate how he viewed Abraham Lincoln, and to do this they would source, contextualize, and corroborate the documents. The teacher reminded them that historians make claims based upon evidence found in historical documents, and that when they gather evidence they evaluate the reliability of different historical sources and corroborate, or compare, information across multiple sources and try to contextualize them.

The teacher explained that in this class period the first document the students would be reading was a letter that Frederick Douglass wrote in 1864 to an English journalist who had donated clothes to recently emancipated people in need. Before the students read the letter, the teacher read it aloud and modeled how to think about its sourcing and context. The students were then invited to read the letter in pairs and to consider how the context in which the letter was written might have influenced its content. They were given a graphic organizer to respond to questions about the source and context, which they would subsequently add to when reading Douglass's eulogy for Lincoln and the speech he gave at the dedication of the Freedmen's Memorial to Abraham Lincoln in Washington, DC.

The lesson engaged students in thinking like a historian and in experiencing history as a process of investigating questions and constructing interpretations of historical events from reading primary and secondary sources.

ENGAGING STUDENTS IN RICH, MULTIMODAL TASKS WITH MULTIPLE ENTRY POINTS

Throughout their apprenticeship into a disciplinary way of thinking, ambitious teaching engages students in rich, authentic tasks and activities that tap into their interests and motivations. The tasks and activities have the right level of challenge with appropriate scaffolding—the linguistic or conceptual tools to bridge the gap between present and intended understanding.[12] The extent of scaffolding should fit the Goldilocks principle, permitting students to engage in productive struggle without leading to frustration.[13] Learning tasks and activities offer multiple entry points and modalities so that students can develop understanding in different ways and their learning is not constrained by a one-size-fits-all pathway.[14]

A classroom example of engaging students in a multimodal task with multiple entry points

In preparation for reading the Greek myth about Phaeton, a class of middle school students, many of whom were English learners, were invited to work in pairs and analyze an image of the Rubens painting *The Fall of Phaeton*, now in the National Gallery of Art in Washington, DC, to draw some inferences from pictorial evidence of what the myth, which bears Phaeton's name, might be about.[15] The students were also given an image of a draft Rubens made on wood before he worked on the full painting so that they could see more clearly the main details in the pictorial composition. No prior knowledge about the myth or about the artist was required to participate in the activity and the students could use their own linguistic resources (English or Spanish) to respond.

The students were asked to spend three minutes collaboratively describing and analyzing what they saw in the sketch and the painting. They had questions to guide their analysis, such as, Where does the scene appear to take place?, Who seems to be the main character?, What appears to be happening?, and What may be going on? The teacher told the students that there were no correct or incorrect responses, and what counted was their own interpretation based on the pictorial evidence they saw. The students were encouraged to identify the evidence they were using the draw their inferences as they responded to the questions.

The open-ended nature of this task enabled all students' access and allowed them to use their own language repertoire to draw inferences from the images at whatever level of sophistication they were able to accomplish. The students were using a different modality from text in preparation for reading the myth to support their comprehension of the narrative.

USING DISCOURSE-BASED INSTRUCTION

Ambitious teaching reflects the perspective that learning is social and that interaction is fundamental to cognitive development.[16] Consequently, ambitious teaching is discourse based and promotes interactions that enable students to think in different ways.[17] Through this thinking-centered orientation, students are encouraged to express their ideas, build off each other's thinking, ask and answer questions, and challenge ideas to make sense of academic content.

A classroom example of using discourse-based instruction[18]

In the excerpted assessment example of classroom discourse below, which was transcribed from a one-hour long videotaped lesson, we can see how the teacher, Gabriela Cárdenas, engages in discourse with her students as they work to understand odd and even numbers.[19] The students, some of whom are English learners, are in a combined first- and second-grade classroom and come from a wide range of socioeconomic backgrounds.

The excerpt briefly illustrates how student discourse supports participants to develop mathematical ideas. The discussion stems from a warm-up activity for the lesson when the teacher asked the students to think about possible patterns that can be made up of eight beads. The teacher asks, "How could you organize those beads?"

NINA: Well that's two and then . . . well you have to add them up all together, because eight is an equal number and so you can do . . . but you can do this with a lot of numbers, but one thing it has is where maybe you have two groups and you can't do that with a seven because all the groups want the same amount. So you can't give three to one group and four to the other group, cuz that wouldn't be fair. So you add, so it would have to add up to be four and four.

MS. C: So Sandra is saying that the number eight is an equal number. And that it's an equal number whereas seven is not. Hmmm. Tomas, what do you think?

TOMAS: Of course, because, say you would count by twos like that, because you see it's an equal number, because four plus four is eight.

MS. C: Okay.

TOMAS: And just like Sandra said, seven is made with three and four.

MS. C: So you're saying Tomas you agree that eight is an equal number.

TOMAS: Yes.

MS. C: Equal in the sense that if we take that number and partition it into two groups, we can end up with four and four?

TOMAS: Yes. And these are the equal numbers, like if I counted by twos. Two, four, six, eight. Those are all equal numbers.

MS. C: All equal numbers? Does everyone agree?

Not all students agreed and the discussion continued for a few minutes longer, ultimately leading students to define an even number as "a number made up of two of the same whole numbers." Ms. Cárdenas chose not to confirm Sandra's contribution as correct but instead supported the students to contribute their ideas, making their thinking public as they made sense of the concept through the discourse opportunity. We will return to the discourse practices of this classroom in more detail in chapter 3.

ATTENDING TO WHO STUDENTS ARE

As is reflected in the NASEM conclusions, research has pointed to the importance of attending to students' own cultural contexts in teaching and learning. Zaretta Hammond, an expert on culturally responsive teaching, explains that "*culture*—how one makes meaning of the world based on shared beliefs, norms, cosmology, and so forth—*is the software to the brain's hardware* [italics in the original]."[20]

While teachers have always known about the importance of planning learning based on prior knowledge acquired in school, ambitious teaching entails understanding students deeply and leveraging their prior knowledge from their homes and communities to make sense of academic content. Cultural mental models, understandings, and experiences create cognitive *hooks* or reference points that help to organize schema into a knowledge network that facilitates individuals' understanding of how things work.[21]

As noted earlier, ambitious teaching adopts an asset-based approach to learning, which in the context of attending to students' own cultures and lived experiences embraces culturally sustaining pedagogy. This means that teachers support young people in sustaining the cultural and linguistic competence of their communities, while simultaneously offering access to dominant cultural competence.[22]

A classroom example of attending to who students are[23]

This example is taken from a class in a virtual high school, which has a very ethnically diverse student body, including African American, Arab American, Hispanic, mixed race, and White students, most of them coming from low-income homes. The lesson was part of a unit focused on the English language arts standard: Analyze a particular point of view or cultural experience reflected in a work of literature from outside the United States, drawing on a wide reading of world literature.

To teach this standard, the teacher chose the novel *A House on Mango Street*, by Sandra Cisneros, for several reasons. She thought it had a strong cultural element, and the content was relevant and age appropriate for her students; the chapters were also structured as vignettes, offering her the opportunity to ask students to read and analyze these short, very descriptive pieces together during a class period. She found her choice paid off in terms of students' engagement with the text, particularly for those students who typically found reading to be a "waste of time."

To begin the lesson, the students, many of whom initially believed they did not possess unique cultural experiences, were asked to individually write to the prompt: If someone stumbled upon your current social media account, what might they see? What would they learn about you? They then reviewed a Funds of Knowledge inventory to identify any categories from their cultural background that they might have omitted, such as family traditions and values, household chores, and family outings.[24] Next, they shared their responses with a partner in virtual breakout rooms, using a protocol to promote equitable participation during the discussion: Equal time for each partner, no interruption, confidentiality, no criticism, undivided attention.[25] Finally, the teacher brought the students back together as a whole group and led a discussion to help them understand the characteristics that create their own identities and culture.

During subsequent class periods, the students read and analyzed Cisneros's text, making connections between what they had learned about their own and their peers' cultural backgrounds and the messages Cisneros was conveying in the vignettes. The students' culminating projects were to: (1) write four vignettes in Cisneros's style to showcase the profound aspects of their unique lives; and (2) choose one aspect of their culture to research and discuss.

The teacher began the lesson with a cognitive hook for reading the novel, and engaged in culturally sustaining pedagogy through connecting the students' own experiences with Cisneros's writing, inviting them to create vignettes about their own culture in Cisneros's style, and research an aspect of their own culture to deepen their understanding of their cultural background.

SUPPORTING STUDENTS' METACOGNITION

Ambitious teaching supports students to develop metacognition, their ability to think about their own thinking. Metacognition is part of the broader construct of self-regulation, which refers to students' ability to manage their own learning productively by monitoring their progress and self-directing their actions toward achieving goals. In the process, students develop a sense of agency, which in turn fosters motivation.[26]

Targeted feedback from teachers in relation to learning goals is an instructional strategy that can assist students in developing metacognition. Feedback should engage students' thinking about their progress and about how they can take action to close the gap between their present state and the intended learning. Student agency is preserved when they are able to make decisions about if and how to use the feedback, including the need to revise goals or set new ones.

Students' metacognitive capacities and agency are also enhanced through self-assessment, an important facet of classroom assessment, in which students generate their own internal feedback through reflecting on their learning status in relation to specific learning goals.[27] They determine how well they are moving forward to meet the goal and take action to advance their own learning.

A classroom example of supporting students' metacognition[28]

Racially and ethnically diverse twelfth-grade students in a biotech and engineering class were engaged in project-based learning and design thinking—a nonlinear process that teams use to redefine problems and creative innovative solutions to prototype and test—to respond to a driving question: How do we make Payton, a second grader, happy and independent in her classroom? (Payton has significant visual and physical impairments and uses an iPad and document camera to gain access to the curriculum and activities of the classroom). The students developed initial design prototypes of tools for Payton to use based on what they already knew about her. After visiting Payton in her classroom when she tried out their designs, the student teams reflected on their prototypes, using sticky notes to record their thinking in response these questions:

- What might be working well with your initial design?
- What might you have done differently now that you've seen Payton using it?
- What did you notice about her environment that might impact your design?
- What might be a "radical" idea for your second iteration?

When the teams had completed their self-assessment, they were invited to share their ideas with the whole class and their teacher and their peers provided constructive feedback. After the feedback session, students returned to their teams to consider their own reflections and the feedback they had received, organizing and categorizing their ideas recorded on the sticky notes along with the related feedback. From this review, they decided on how they would improve their designs to better meet Payton's needs. They repeated this self-assessment and feedback process when they had completed their second iteration.

The teacher had created a community where self-reflection and feedback are a normal part of business. She also provided questions to structure their self-assessment and feedback, and codeveloped classroom norms to support public presentation and feedback sessions. Students who are active agents in learning regard each other as resources for supporting their learning.

ESTABLISHING A SUPPORTIVE, SAFE LEARNING ENVIRONMENT

The NASEM conclusions described at the beginning of the chapter specifically reference the learning environment, signaling the importance of cultural, and socio-emotional factors to student learning. Specifically, the NASEM report concludes that "motivation to learn is fostered for learners of all ages when they perceive the school or learning environment is a place where they 'belong' and when the environment promotes their sense of agency and purpose."[29]

In practice, ambitious teaching attends to the environment by establishing a collective orientation, which is characterized by high expectations for all students; positive, trusting relationships with the teacher and among peers; and teachers and students sharing responsibility for learning. Establishing clear norms and routines provides the structure in which a collective orientation can be achieved. Ambitious teaching also promotes students' feelings of affirmation and belonging by using their lived experiences to make learning more relevant for them and to build knowledge and understanding.

Several preceding classroom examples have implicitly referenced a safe, supportive learning environment—for example, the third-grade inclusive class where all students worked together on challenging goals, the second-grade mathematics discussion where students built on each other's ideas, the virtual high school where the students' own culture was leveraged for learning in English language arts, and the biotech and engineering class where the students provided each other with constructive feedback. None of these examples of teaching and learning would have been possible if students had not felt safe to share their ideas with the teacher and with each other. It is likely that in these classrooms some of the norms established for a collective orientation were: give each other the time and space to talk, actively listen to each other, think carefully about what you hear, give others time to think, respect alternative viewpoints, and respond positively and constructively to others' ideas.

A noteworthy point about the learning environment is the model of relationships that teachers have with their students. For instance, teachers express caring about their students by projecting warmth and promoting feelings of trust between them and their students, by communicating their expectations of students' abilities, and by challenging their students to grow when they communicate high expectations for students' performance.[30] These features of teachers' relationships with their students not only enhance students' feelings of safety and connectedness in the classroom, they also provide models of how students can relate to each other in supportive ways.

In the next section, we illustrate many of the elements reference above related to ambitious teaching with an extended description of a lesson from science teacher, Dr. Wendy Johnson, whose campus has one of the most diverse student populations in her state.

AN EXTENDED EXAMPLE OF AMBITIOUS TEACHING

Ambitious teaching in science focuses on students making sense of phenomena by engaging in three dimensional learning: science core ideas, practices, and crosscutting concepts. The lesson described below is taken from a unit of study for ninth-grade students that combines physical science and life science performance expectations from the Next Generation Science Standards (NGSS).[31] The science teachers in her school decided to combine biology and physics into a single freshman course for two reasons: they wanted students to develop a firm foundation of matter and energy (physical science) that they could build upon throughout high school; and they knew that life science examples are more familiar to students because of their own lived experiences. Dr. Johnson began planning for the unit by bundling three physical science and life science performance expectations from the NGSS:

- **HS-PS1–7:** Use mathematical representations to support the claim that atoms, and therefore mass, are conserved during a chemical reaction.

- **HS-LS1–6:** Construct and revise an explanation based on evidence for how carbon, hydrogen, and oxygen from sugar molecules may combine with other elements to form amino acids and/or other large carbon-based molecules.
- **HS-LS1–7:** Use a model to illustrate that cellular respiration is a chemical process whereby the bonds of food molecules and oxygen molecules are broken and the bonds in new compounds are formed, resulting in a net transfer of energy.

NGSS Performance Expectations are "bundled" into groups that can be used to explain a phenomenon. However, these standards are complex and too large to be assessed on smaller classroom assessments. Therefore, Dr. Johnson broke the three performance expectations into what she refers to as "five learning standards" that would build on one another over the course of the unit. Each standard represents about five class periods of learning.

1. Use the particle model of matter to explain observations.
2. Identify atoms and molecules and use them to track changes during chemical reactions and changes in the mass of objects.
3. Use nutrition labels to support claims about the types of molecules and amount of energy in different foods.
4. Use models and evidence to explain what happens to atoms and energy when organic molecules burn.
5. Use models and evidence to explain how animals use atoms and energy from food to grow and move.

The standards encompass the science core ideas that atoms make up all matter, chemical reactions rearrange matter, and that living things get their matter and energy by rearranging atoms from food. Students engage in the NGSS practices of Developing and Using Models and Constructing Explanations and apply the crosscutting concepts Energy and Matter and Systems and System Models throughout the unit. Dr. Johnson used the learning progression from the Carbon TIME Project that she had contributed to as a graduate student to inform the order of the standards.[32]

The driving question for the unit that she posed to the students was their goal for investigation and also tied the standards together: "What happens to the fat you 'burn off' during exercise?" Dr. Johnson chose this question because she knew that it would be intriguing to her students, and yet also accessible since they have all experienced exercise in physical education classes or as members of various sports teams. To stimulate students' interest, Dr. Johnson began the first class period of the unit by inviting them to watch a video of a discussion about the concerns surrounding a contestant on the reality show *The Biggest Loser*, in which contestants routinely lost significant proportions (as much as 60 percent) of their body weight. Her students discussed the concerns about losing too much weight too quickly that the video had prompted. The phenomenon, therefore, connected to students' own lives in connection with a healthy diet and regular exercise, while also drawing them into the social controversy around weight loss obsession and the potential for fat-shaming created by this reality show.

After their discussion, the students were invited to generate their initial ideas about the question "What happens to the fat you 'burn off' during exercise?" by completing an "Expressing Ideas and Questions" handout that Dr. Johnson had prepared. Her intention was to not only help her gain insights into what students already knew and did not know at the start of the unit. Equally important, as Dr. Johnson notes, was "for students to know what they know and do not know at the beginning of the lesson so that they can recognize how their ideas change over the course of the unit." The questions included "How does a person lose body weight?," "Where does the fat go?," and "What questions do you have about how exercise makes a person lose weight?" Dr. Johnson further probed the students' thinking and stimulated discussion with questions such as "Why do people breathe faster and deeper when they exercise?," "Where does the air go and what happens to it inside the person's body?," and "How is it related to losing weight?" Students shared many different ideas and she helped them to recognize that they did not understand how breathing and burning fat are connected.

Dr. Johnson then used a probe, modeled after Paige Keeley's probes in *Uncovering Student Ideas in Science*, which asked students to choose a response that best matched their own ideas about what happens to the fat that you burn off during exercise.[33] Students were invited to vote anonymously for the ideas that they agreed with. They could vote for more than one idea and their choices were:

1. The fat turns into energy
2. Atoms from the fat breathed out

3. The fat burns up and disappears
4. The fat turns into heat
5. The fat turns into sweat

Using Post-it notes to record their response, most of the students voted for number 1, about half for number 5, and one student voted for number 2, the correct answer (although number 5 is not completely wrong). Dr. Johnson found that tallying students' anonymous votes and publicly displaying the results was important because otherwise over the course of the unit students would begin to believe that they "always knew" the correct answer. The record of students' initial ideas and questions on the driving question board, and the results of their vote on the probe became important evidence of how their ideas were shifting.

Dr. Johnson then led a class discussion, prompted by their responses to the probe, during which students shared how they breathe faster and deeper when they exercise. However, they were not able to explain why. Dr. Johnson used this discussion to convince students that they needed to learn more about air before they could explain how it is related to burning fat. Over the next two class periods, students learned about the particle nature of air. Dr Johnson began the first period by telling the students that a syringe has a lot in common with our lungs and that they were going to work in small groups to investigate how air moves in and out of a syringe.

They began, in Dr. Johnson's words, "by playing with the syringes." During this time, Dr. Johnson moved around the class, interacting with students, while they made comments such as "the air is getting sucked in" and "it pulled in air and pulled it out." She stressed that the students were to make observations, not to offer explanations, and used examples like asking students to describe what they felt on their face if they put the syringe up close and moved the plunger back and forth. One student commented "I can feel this little wind."

After their exploration, Dr. Johnson provided students with a chart to record (figure 2.1) their observations, reminding them again that as scientists they were observing and not explaining at this point.

To ensure that all students, including the English learners in the class, could participate in discussions of the observations for which they needed no prior science knowledge, they were encouraged to use their own linguistic resources. When one student said, "it's really hard to push" another English learner student was

FIGURE 2.1 Chart for recording observations

Scenario	Observations
With the stopper off, pull the plunger back.	
With the stopper off, push the plunger into the syringe	
With the stopper off, pull the plunger back	
Put the stopper on and push the plunger back into the syringe	

confused and said, "but it's not hard like a table." The first student clarified what he meant by *hard* in this context.

The students then created a consensus model to represent the syringe with the stopper pulled back with the cap off (full of air—mass is greater than when there is no air) and the cap on (no air—mass is lower; this creates a vacuum that makes the plunger snap back into place when you let go). It was important to come to a class consensus about how to the represent air particles in their models so that all could use the same conventions moving forward. For instance, while the students were discussing their model as a group, Dr. Johnson drew an example on the board saying, "I see that most people drew circles here. Can you tell me what that means?" Then she would make sure everyone agreed on how to show the air particles and what it indicated.

In the next two class periods, the students examined a sheep's heart and lungs and read a short text about the anatomy involved in breathing. Initially, the students thought the lungs were hollow like a balloon and that somehow the lungs change the air and then push it back when a person exhales. Through their observations and discussion, students came to the realization that lungs are more like a sponge, and that when a person inhales, air fills the microscopic spaces of the lungs that are covered in blood vessels and allows for gas exchange with the bloodstream. Dr. Johnson also created a model of the lungs using a balloon inside a bell jar. The balloon was connected to the air outside the jar through a straw. When she pulled down on the plastic sheet across the bottom of the jar, air rushed into the balloon through the straw. From this demonstration and follow-up discussion students learned that air is not "sucked into the lungs" as they had expected, but rather moves from a higher pressure (outside the body) toward a lower pressure (inside the body) when the diaphragm moves downward. Dr. Johnson then invited the students to apply what they had learned to draw a model of the bell jar demonstration that included air particles, similar to the models they had made previously to explain their observations of the syringe. The students shared and discussed their models, making adjustments to their own as a result of discussing them with their peers and Dr. Johnson.

In week's final class period, Dr. Johnson asked the students to complete an individual checkpoint assessment she had created to provide information to her and to them about what they had learned during the course of the week related to the first standard. Dr. Johnson refers to the checkpoint assessments as "Game Day," when the students apply the core ideas and practices they learned throughout the week to explain a new phenomenon (see chapter 3 for more about checkpoint assessments).

It is important to note that the first lesson (which spanned five class periods, and was focused on the particles making up air and how they behave) lays the groundwork for further learning about air in order to lead the students to be able to answer the first driving question "What happens to the fat you 'burn off' during exercise?" This first lesson, as in all subsequent lessons, is a "manageable chunk" so that students can keep track of how their learning is developing and is conceptually connected. The following week, in the "next manageable chunk," Dr. Johnson built on the what the students had learned so far about air particles by concentrating on the specific molecules in air and how atoms are rearranged in chemical reactions to make new molecules.

WHAT WE CAN LEARN FROM THE EXAMPLE OF AMBITIOUS TEACHING

In this example of practice from Dr. Johnson, we see how the elements of ambitious teaching are put into practice in one classroom. She apprenticed students to the discipline of science by guiding them through an investigation to answer a question about a phenomenon that is familiar to them. She accessed students' prior knowledge, connected school learning to outside school activities and experiences, engaged the students in challenging learning, enabled student learning through self-assessment, metacognitive thinking, and feedback, and assisted all students to gain access to disciplinary ways of understanding the topic.

Dr. Johnson used the first class period in this carefully developed sequence of learning activities to create initial curiosity on the part of the students with a driving question that connected to their personal experiences either in regular school physical education classes or from participation on sports teams. Through the use of the opening video she also connected to the learning to a broader cultural discussion on the dangers of extreme weight loss. She created a learning environment in which collaboration, respectful disagreements, and recognition of the assets that each student brings to the learning are the norm as the group worked toward consensus. A student who displayed confusion over word meaning was not teased by his peers but rather was provided with clarification to enable him to continue to follow and contribute to the discussion.

The learning experiences are tightly aligned with meaningful goals and are structured in a way that illustrates how Dr. Johnson anticipated and met students' questions and areas of confusion. Students move between generating their own ideas, to working and talking in small groups, to sharing ideas with the whole class for broader feedback and consensus building. This discourse-rich classroom provides students for whom English is not their first language multiple occasions to listen to others talk, and to contribute and express ideas as they are able, whether verbally, in writing, or with diagrams. The small group discussions, in particular, provide students a sense of safety to try out and refine ideas before participating in discussions with the larger class. By making student thinking visible to the whole class (through anonymized voting on potential explanations), Dr. Johnson supports students' metacognitive thinking as they reflect on what they first thought compared to what they finally understand.

The lesson, which represents high expectations for students as they learn connections between physical and life sciences through crosscutting ideas, is rich in academic discourse that students learn to use as they develop disciplinary ways of thinking. For instance, we see this in how students are reminded to first fully observe a phenomenon before trying to explain it, and also in the opportunities to refine their models as a representation of updated ideas that came from listening to explanations from their peers and discussing their models. While Dr. Johnson orchestrates student learning with a carefully designed sequence of experiences, this is a not a class dominated by the teacher declaring knowledge for students to write down in lab books, but one in which students construct and hone their own understanding over time.

The final conclusion from the NASEM study refers to the importance of assessment use for monitoring and advancing learning. We saw some uses of assessment use by Dr. Johnson—for example, students voting for the idea that best matched their own, and the range of questions she asked while students were engaged in their activities and discussions. In the final section of this chapter, we consider how the fair and justice-oriented teacher actions discussed in chapter 1 accrue when assessment practices are integrated with ambitious teaching.

INTERRELATIONSHIP AMONG AMBITIOUS TEACHING INTEGRATED ASSESSMENT PRACTICES AND FAIR AND JUSTICE-ORIENTED TEACHER ACTIONS

Figure 2.2 shows the interrelationship among ambitious teaching, assessment practices, and fair and justice-oriented teacher actions. The left column of

FIGURE 2.2 Interrelationship between ambitious teaching, assessment practices, and fair and justice-oriented teacher actions

Ambitious Teaching ↔ **Fair and Justice-Oriented Teacher Actions** ↔ **Assessment**

Ambitious Teaching

- Focuses on rigorous, challenging goals to enable deep disciplinary learning
- Engages students in rich, authentic learning tasks/activities that center on powerful disciplinary ideas and practices
- Makes use of what resources students bring with them to the classroom (interests, aspirations, language, knowledge from homes and communities)
- Engages students in learning tasks/activities that offer multiple entry points and modalities
- Sustains student learning within the context of their language, literacies, and cultural ways of being
- Offers a supportive and collectively-oriented classroom environment in which learning develops in response to others' insights questions and feedback

Fair and Justice-Oriented Teacher Actions

- Awareness of what shapes their teacher positioning and how it might impact interpretation and action
- Elevates and legitimates the linguistic, cultural and substantive practices of students
- Mediates everyday forms of knowing and those used within specific content areas
- Makes expectation clear that all students will develop high-level thinking, reasoning and problem solving skills
- Uses an equity-oriented curriculum
- Provides access for all students to show what they know and can do
- Ensures assessment content is recognizable and relevant to students
- Promotes an agentic stance to assessment
- Engenders a sense of belonging
- Positions students as competent

Assessment

- Teachers and students have a shared understanding of learning goals and assessment criteria
- Student are assessed on what they are learning/ have been learning
- Makes knowledge and thinking visible through a variety of means that are contextualized to students
- Informs asset-based interpretations of evidence
- Provides useful information for taking instructional action to enhance learning
- Includes self- and peer assessment

figure 2.2 summarizes the key points related to ambitious teaching that have been discussed previously. The right column references important assessment practices, particularly in connection with classroom assessment. The middle column describes the fair and justice-oriented teacher actions that are made possible when these assessment practices are integrated with ambitious teaching.

In order to truly take into account students' cultural context, educators must examine how their own experiences and cultural influences shape who they are and their positioning as teachers relative to their students. Being sensitized to their own social and cultural identities can help teachers develop *self-other openness.*[34] With this openness teachers can both be aware of and set aside any personal attitudes and values, particularly with respect to those students who may be very different from themselves, which might militate against their adoption of an asset-based approach to teaching.[35] Ambitious teaching engages students in asset-based goals, learning tasks, and activities that value and reflect perspectives of the students' personal and community contexts. The tasks and activities utilize multiple modalities for making sense of content. From an assessment perspective, these learning tasks, including discourse, make knowledge and thinking visible through a variety of means that are contextualized to students and provide evidence to inform next steps in learning for both teachers and students.

Ambitious teaching with integrated assessment is enabled when teachers have access to and use a strong, coherent, standards-aligned and equity-oriented curriculum that provides the necessary backbone for both teaching and assessment. Rigorous learning goals, the foundation for both ambitious teaching and assessment, are derived from equity-oriented curriculum content (see chapter 1) and tailored to address the "complex interplay among learners' prior knowledge, experiences, motivations, interests, and language and cognitive skills."[36] Teachers and students have a shared understanding of these learning goals (what is to be learned in a lesson or unit) and the criteria for meeting the goal (what they will be able to either say, do, make or write).[37] The fair and justice-oriented teacher actions for this teaching-assessment integration are that there is an expectation that all students, regardless of background, will develop high-level thinking, reasoning, and problem-solving skills.

Because students are assessed on the specific knowledge and skills they have been taught, the questions and expectations are more recognizable and relevant to them than other assessment tasks (e.g., external interim or state summative assessments) that may not reflect contemporaneous goals.[38] Also, because the tasks make use of the resources that they bring to school from their lived experiences, linguistic, cultural, and substantive practices of students are elevated and legitimated and have the payoff of helping them develop a sense of belonging in the classroom. Moreover, students' access to academic content is mediated through what is familiar to them. As a result of this familiarity, students can convey what they know and can do more equitably than in student-background-agnostic situations. Integrating teaching, learning, and assessment in ways that honor students' cultural and linguistic resources contributes to more fair and justice-oriented classroom assessment.

The evidence yielded from these tasks and activities supports asset-based interpretations, which entail a shift from a binary categorization, often framed in classrooms as "got it" or "didn't get it," to a more fine-grained view that identifies what students understand and what is not *yet* understood. From this evidence, teachers and students are able to determine the next steps that are challenging, yet manageable, and can move learning forward. As a result, students are positioned as competent to learn what comes next, and are not overwhelmed by a list of all that is not known, which can be the case when learning and assessment are not framed around fair and justice-oriented teacher actions.[39]

Student self-assessment

Classroom assessment is not only concerned with teachers' use of assessment evidence, but also with students' self-assessment, a process through which they make determinations about how their learning is progressing relative to specific goals, and then take steps to advance their own learning. As noted earlier, self-assessment and self-regulation are complementary processes that can lead to improvements in achievement and autonomy.[40] Teachers who are oriented to supporting students' self-assessment provide clear learning goals and criteria for achieving them; instruction in, and assistance with, self-assessment; and opportunities to revise work, adapt learning strategies, or modify learning goals. While formative assessment is a primary context for self-assessment, summative assessment information should also be used by students in collaboration with their teachers to reflect on their achievement and to set future goals.

Using similar structures needed for successful self-assessment, peer assessment gives students the chance to receive feedback from their classmates. In general terms, students develop greater levels of accountability to monitor their own progress toward the learning goals as a result of peer feedback.[41] Students also benefit from being the provider of feedback.[42] Taking this role helps students develop internal standards for quality work and supports their capacity to make better judgments of their own work.[43]

From the perspective of fair and justice-oriented teacher actions, self- and peer assessment promote an agentic stance to assessment. Students are not regarded as mere recipients of assessment information but rather as competent individuals who are trusted to actively participate in the assessment process, making judgments about their own and their peers' progress with suggestions for next steps.

A FINAL THOUGHT

In this chapter we have aimed to describe what constitutes ambitious teaching based on conclusions drawn from a recent report on how people learn, to provide examples of their application to classroom practice, and to discuss the interrelationship among ambitious teaching, integrated assessment, and fair and justice-oriented teacher actions. We conclude the chapter with a request for readers. Ambitious teaching is not a binary construct. It is not a case of teaching ambitiously or not teaching ambitiously, but rather that each teacher is somewhere along a continuum of expertise. In this regard, we encourage readers, whether individual teachers or a grade-level or department team, to pause here and take some time to reflect together on ambitious teaching in relation to their own practice, using questions such as: To what extent do lessons reflect all elements of ambitious teaching?, What elements are not well represented?, What are the current strengths that can be built on?, and What would it look like to move on one or more elements toward more ambitious teaching? From these kinds of reflections, a continuum of expertise may emerge, and teachers can share evidence of where they think they are on the continuum and discuss how to move forward.

We also request that those readers who are responsible for supporting teachers—district and school administrators—reflect on to what degree they are assisting their colleagues to implement ambitious teaching practices and what they might need to do to strengthen the professional support they offer.

We strongly encourage readers to take the time for this reflection because the rest of the book will continue to draw on this vision of ambitious teaching and assessment practices that are integrated with it.

SUMMARY: KEY TAKEAWAYS

- Ambitious teaching is informed by up-to-date understanding of how people learn.
- Key elements of ambitious teaching are:
  - providing challenging learning experiences for all students;
  - apprenticing students to the discipline;
  - engaging students in rich, multimodal tasks and activities with multiple entry points;
  - using discourse-based instruction;
  - attending to who students are and what they bring to the classroom from their homes and communities as resources for learning;
  - supporting students' metacognitive thinking; and
  - establishing a safe learning environment.
- Ambitious teaching goes a long way toward laying the groundwork for fair and justice-oriented teacher actions.
- There is an interaction among ambitious teaching, assessment practices, and fair and justice-oriented outcomes for all students.

CHAPTER 3

Classroom Assessment Types and Uses

Depending on what teachers want to know about student learning and when they want to know it, they can make use of different forms of assessment to provide the information they are seeking, allowing them to make decisions about their instruction and evaluate the effectiveness of their teaching. For instance, they might want to know the current status of student understanding relative to a concept they are teaching at a particular point in a lesson, or how well the students understand that concept at the end of a period of learning such as the end of a unit. Education leaders at the school and district level and state- and federal-level policymakers also need access to assessment information about student achievement for making resource allocation decisions or helping them to monitor long-term educational trends. In the introductory chapter of the recent volume, *Reimagining Balanced Assessment Systems*, published by the National Academy of Education, the editors argue that no single assessment can serve the full range of uses and users of assessments, but all assessments should "support, directly or indirectly, the teaching and learning that occurs in the classroom" and "must be compatible, though different in grain size or specificity."[1]

Classroom teachers will be concerned primarily with the instructional utility of assessment. In this regard, assessment experts Carla Evans and Scott Marion in their book *Understanding Instructionally Useful Assessment* contend that "an instructionally useful assessment provides insights that can positively influence the interactions among the teacher, student, and the content about student learning strengths and needs relative to specific learning targets that are the focus of current, immediately past, or near future instruction."[2] They caution that not all assessments are instructionally useful, a misconception, in their view, that is exacerbated by "commercial interim assessment marketing materials and misinformed educational leaders who continue to talk about how teachers should use data from standardized assessments to inform instruction."[3] Routinely, standardized, commercially produced assessments are treated as the most accurate and meaningful indicator of a student's achievement. However, results from these assessments fall short of being useful for teachers or supporting the ambitious teaching practices discussed in chapter 2. This is because in the reports of results, primarily intended as status updates for students, the reporting categories are coarse given the relatively short length of the assessment. Furthermore, the information is quantitative rather than being in the form of qualitative insights into what students can already do.[4]

Instruction happens minute-by-minute and day-by-day, but standardized assessments results are too distal from contemporaneous learning goals, and are unlikely to reflect anything related to students' funds of knowledge (resources students bring to learning from their families, community, culture, background and interests[5]) to be of direct value to teachers' daily practice. Moreover, the generality of the information provided from many assessments, which may only be loosely connected to local curricula, and from state annual achievement assessments, which by design broadly survey the breadth of state content standards, has little value for teachers' ongoing classroom work.[6] This is not to say that teachers cannot find some utility from state achievement assessments—for example, to reflect on their own teaching or to identify the strengths and needs of new classes of students at the beginning of a school year (for additional discussion on this topic, see chapter 8). Such assessments may also have a signaling function in that they communicate what item types and tasks teachers should include in their classroom assessment repertoire, provided that they do not run counter to the goals of ambitious teaching.[7] However, these uses should not be confused with instructional utility.

External standardized assessments are best used at the state, district, and school levels by administrators and policymakers for purposes such as monitoring medium- and long-term educational trends, evaluating program/curricula quality, and helping to identify resource and professional learning needs. To use a traffic analogy, these assessments need to stay in their designated lane and not transgress into an instructional utility lane in which they have no place.

According to Scott Marion and colleagues, a question that designers and users of assessment need to ask is "To what degree and in what ways does this assessment—its content and practices—support or hinder rich and equitable classroom learning environments?"[8]

In this chapter, we consider the assessment types that teachers have available to them. First, to provide context for our consideration of assessment, we discuss a conception of convergent and divergent assessment, proposed by researchers Harry Torrance and John Pryor.[9] Then, drawing from this conceptualization, we outline a framework of assessment types, their purpose, methods, and information, and provide examples of how these assessment types can work in practice to support student learning. We also analyze each example in terms of how it reflects the fair and justice-oriented dimensions of assessment outlined in chapters 1 and 2.

A FRAMEWORK FOR CONSIDERING ASSESSMENT APPROACHES

Typically, as noted in the Preface, assessment types are categorized as either summative or formative. Formative assessment is used to guide ongoing teaching and learning decisions. Summative applications of assessment are concerned with evaluating what has been learned to date, for example, at the end of a unit, a course or a program. For the purpose of this chapter, we chose not to use these two categories and instead draw from Torrance and Pryor's research on classroom practice in which they identified two conceptually distinct approaches to assessment use: *convergent* and *divergent*.[10] We believe that Torrance and Pryor's conception of assessment shifts the discussion from a definitional one about what formative assessment is and what summative assessment is and what the relationship between them should be, and allows for a clearer focus on their purposes and uses. Rather than adopting a dichotomous approach, Torrance and Pryor emphasize the importance of managing the balance between convergent and divergent assessment and action within an agenda of learning for all students to ensure that they make progress in ways that build on their knowledge and competence within the discipline.[11]

In their conceptualization, convergent assessment aims to find out *if* the student knows, understands or can do a predetermined thing. Its characteristics can include an analysis of the interaction between the student and the curriculum from the point of view of the curriculum (i.e., what curriculum learning outcomes the student has met), a focus on contrasting errors with correct responses, judgmental or quantitative evaluation, the intention to teach what is next in the curriculum, and a view of assessment as accomplished by the teacher. Divergent assessment emphasizes finding out *what* the students know, understand, or can do in order to tailor instructional responses to where students are in their learning. It is characterized by a number of factors, including an analysis of interaction between the student and the curriculum from the student's point of view (i.e., what is the current status of student thinking in relation to curricular goals), by the insights it yields into students' current understanding, by prompting metacognition, by the intention to teach in the students' zone of proximal development, which necessitates flexible planning, and by reflecting a view of assessment as accomplished jointly by teacher and student.[12]

Torrance and Pryor suggest that teachers not adopt one assessment approach over the other, but rather be aware of the possibilities inherent in both, and "how they match with, and might be developed in the context of, their own classroom situation."[13] They stress that teachers have to balance the individual, divergent, and creative thoughts of the students generated in the dynamic context of the group with the need to structure learning experiences and pursue the essentially convergent requirements of the curriculum or standards. Teachers make decisions about which approach to adopt based on a consideration of what is to be assessed, when, and why. While there may be clear-cut occasions for using a particular approach—for instance, when wanting to know if students have met the learning goals of a unit or course of study, or when wanting insights into how students are processing an idea while engaged in a learning task—the assessment approaches may not be as categorical as Torrance and Pryor's conceptualization might suggest; the edges between the two may be more blurred. In this vein, it is useful to think of the two approaches in a *dynamic interplay* that involves, often in the same lesson, planned actions by teachers (convergent responses), as well as actions that are contingent on what students say and do (divergent responses).

Within Torrance and Pryor's original conceptualization, students are primarily recipients of assessments in the convergent perspective, whereas in the divergent view they are participants as both an initiator and a recipient. In our adaptation of their conceptualization, we recognize that there is more scope in divergent assessment for student involvement—for example, through the development of metacognitive skills and the ongoing use of feedback—but we advocate for student agency in convergent assessment as well. For instance, in line with the goals of fair and justice-oriented outcomes discussed in chapter 1, students may be given a choice in response modes to a problem or task as well as being able to choose a problem or context that better reflects their culture and identity from a selection that still incorporates the requirements of the curriculum and standards.[14] One example of student choice is when high school students who were investigating environmental justice (i.e., the fair treatment of people of all races, cultures, incomes and educational levels with respect to the development of enforcement of environmental laws and policies) were invited at the end of the unit to consider how their own value system compared with others they had encountered in their investigation and to choose how they would present their response. This assessment approach allowed students to draw both from the content they had learned about and from their own culture and lived experiences, as well as to select a preferred response mode.[15]

While feedback to students from their teacher, peers, and their own self-assessment is a feature of divergent assessment, students can and should also receive feedback on any convergent assessment—for instance, through discussions with teachers about where they were successful in their learning, and any plans for improvement before moving on to what is next in the curriculum.

The next section focuses on divergent assessment in the classroom, with examples of this approach.

Divergent assessment

Table 3.1 shows the divergent assessment framework, the purpose and method of the assessment approaches, and the information they provide for teachers and students. All the assessment methods in a divergent approach, except possibly those that are curriculum-embedded and might be required by the school, are under the control of teachers and their students, or the "learning and teaching persons," an arrangement favored by the authors of an influential Gordon Commission report.[16]

Assessment practices that occur in the context of ambitious teaching, discussed in chapter 2, have the potential to provide important sources of evidence that both teachers and students can use to advance all students' learning toward rigorous goals. The three examples below illustrate how teachers use divergent approaches

TABLE 3.1 Divergent classroom assessment framework

Divergent assessment	*Purpose*	*Method*	*Information*
Prior to studying a new topic	Determine what students already know, understand and can do	Open-ended questions	What students already know, understand, or can do related to the topic Anticipated ideas
Designed into ongoing teaching and learning	Inform ongoing teaching and learning Critically reflect on teaching	What students say, do, make or write as they are engaged in learning tasks Discourse Open-ended questioning Analysis of student work Student self-/peer assessment Metacognitive monitoring relative to goals	Insights into current learning status relative to lesson-sized goals Emerging or partially formed understanding Difficulties or misconceptions
Curriculum-embedded assessments	Determine progress Give direction to proximate instructional planning Critically reflect on teaching	Designed into curricular materials Student self-assessment	Insights into current learning status relative to curricular goals—what students know and what they still need to learn Difficulties or misconceptions

outlined in table 3.1 in the context of ambitious teaching: (1) prior to studying a new topic; (2) in assessment designed into ongoing teaching and learning; and (3) in curriculum-embedded assessments.

PRIOR TO STUDYING A NEW TOPIC

The first example related to table 3.1 comes from a science unit for ninth-graders that was described in chapter 2. Recall that the driving question for the unit was "What happens to the fat you 'burn off' during exercise?" To ascertain what her students already knew, understood and could do, the teacher, Dr. Wendy Johnson, began the first class period of the unit by asking students to complete a handout,

"Expressing Ideas & Questions," that she had prepared to elicit their understanding of what happens to fat that you "burn off" during exercise. The items in the handout were:

> The main thing you see the contestants doing on the *Biggest Loser* was exercising. When exercising, a person breathes faster, their heart beats faster, and their body temperature increases. Why do you think these things happen during exercise? How are they related to losing weight?
>
> Contestants on the *Biggest Loser* work with diet coaches and have chefs prepare their meals. Why do you think that there is so much focus on food? Why do we need food? What happens to the food inside a person's body?
>
> After the show ended, Rachel gained 20 pounds. Today she weighs about 125 pounds and considers this her "ideal" body weight. She says that maintaining this body weight is just as much work as it was to lose 155 pounds on the show. How did she gain back 20 pounds? What do you think she means when she says that it is difficult to maintain her new weight?
>
> How does a person lose body weight? Where does the fat go? Draw and label arrows to show your ideas about what materials might be moving into, out of, or through a person as they eat, exercise, and lose weight.
>
> What questions do you have about how food makes a person gain weight?
>
> What questions do you have about how exercise makes a person lose weight?

From the students' responses to the questions and in a discussion stimulated by her further probing questions (see chapter 2), Dr. Johnson was able to ascertain, as she anticipated, that the students did not realize that burning fat through exercise is connected to breathing. She was able to plan a productive starting point for their investigation: learning about the particle nature of air.

What We Can Learn from the Prior to Studying a New Topic Example: Students engaged in rigorous discussion about their own ideas and were positioned as competent. The task was relevant to students, and they could use everyday language and their knowledge from their personal and school experiences to make sense of phenomena. The task provided access for all students to show what they knew and could do.

DESIGNED INTO ONGOING TEACHING AND LEARNING

Ambitious teaching places emphasis on student discourse either with each other or with the teacher, which provides opportunities to reveal students' thinking as they interact to make sense of ideas. The excerpted assessment example of classroom discourse below is from Gabriela Cárdenas's class, introduced in chapter 2. Recall that the students, some of whom are English learners, are in a combined first- and second-grade classroom and come from a wide range of socioeconomic backgrounds. Ms. Cárdenas engages in discourse with her students as they work to understand odd and even numbers.[17] Prior to this class period, the students had been learning to "decompose" and "compose" two- and three- digit numbers.

At the beginning of the class period, Ms. Cárdenas introduced an activity to "just warm up our brains to start thinking numbers, to start thinking patterns." From the stimulus of eight beads, four of one color, four of another, Ms. Cárdenas first invited the students to think about different ways in which they could group the beads to make patterns for a necklace. Students shared ideas with an elbow partner about the different patterns they could make. After listening in on a few pairs' discussions, she brought all the students back together as a whole group to talk about the different patterns, and whether they were the same or not. In the course of describing how two patterns were the same, a student made a claim about an "equal" number, and it is at this point that the excerpt begins (note that some of the exchanges between students were not included for brevity, but that all students' comments are verbatim).

NINA: Well that's two and then . . . well you have to add them up all together, because eight is an equal number and so you can do . . . but you can do this with a lot of numbers, but one thing it has is where maybe you have two groups and you can't do that with a seven because all the groups want the same amount. So you can't give three to one group and four to the other group, cuz that wouldn't fair. So you add, so it would have to add up to be four and four.

MS. C: So Nina's saying that the number eight is an equal number. Huh? And that it's an equal number whereas seven is not. Hmmm. Ruby? [Ruby's hand is raised]

RUBY: Of course, because, say you would count by twos like that, because you see it's an equal number, because four plus four is eight. And just like Nina said, seven is made with three and four.

JARED: I'm in disagreement. I think every number is an even number, because if you take a five for example, you can split it into two and two, but then you take the extra one and you split it in half.

NICO: When you split a one into halves, it's called 0.5, 0.5. So if you put one half in one box, and the other half in another box, so it would be 2.5 in total both.

MS. C: So I would be taking that one, and splitting that one in half, that what you're saying is that I would then put a 0.5, 0.5, which in another words, represents half.

NICO: 2.5 and 2.5 in total.

MS. C: So one would be 2.5 and here I would have 2.5. So were we able to split five equally?

NINA: I don't agree.

MS. C: Nina.

NINA: Because I feel like this is not exactly, how do I say this, it is a number, but in some senses it's not. Because like, ah, how do I say this?

JARED: Points are basically . . . they're basically numbers, but they're numbers within other numbers.

MS. C: So a fraction of a number?

JARED: Yes. A fraction.

MS. C: Now I heard someone use the word whole. Was that you Camillo?

CAMILLO: Yeah.

MS. C: So tell me a little bit more. Because they're talking about a fraction of a number and if we were able to take that five and split that five equally . . . 2.5 and 2.5, that's equally, but . . .

CAMILLO: A whole number's just a regular number. Not 2.3 or anything.

MS. C: So 2.5 would not be a whole number?

CAMILLO: No.

MS. C: But it would be equal amounts. Now we said that eight was an equal number, but seven was not, right? But now there's another word, and Camillo mentioned the word whole, saying yes, it's equal amounts, but it's not a whole number. So Nina, I think, yes eight can be broken up into equal parts. Can seven? Well five was, right? But Camillo, you said, or Camillo, Matteo, you said that eight is an even number. What's even? Go ahead.

MATTEO: It's a number made up of two of the same whole numbers.

MS. C: Okay. So if I have eight and we're saying eight . . . would eight be even?

MATTEO: Yes, because four and four are the same number and they're both whole numbers.

MS. C: So you're saying that even numbers, when we partition them or break them apart, if I can do it evenly, equally, like four and four, then that would be an even number.

MATTEO: But they have to be whole numbers.

After letting this conversation develop for several more minutes, Ms. Cárdenas then drew on it to discuss the day's learning goal, which was focused on dividing two- and three-digit numbers into equal shares.

What We Can Learn from the Designed into Ongoing Teaching and Learning Example: Students engaged in rigorous discussion with the teacher's expectation that they were capable of it. Their ideas were regarded as valuable, legitimate, and generative for discussion. For instance, Ms. Cárdenas did not foreclose the discussion by treating Nina's response as convergent assessment by saying, "No, you mean 8 is an *even* number." In a convergent assessment context, the teacher might have noted that Nina did not appear to understand the terms odd and even and then moved on to the main part of the lesson. Instead, Ms. Cárdenas chose a divergent approach, where she was interested in better understanding the current thinking of both Nina and other students.

The discussion allowed for different students to present their ideas based on their previous mathematical knowledge and interests. Students had varying levels of familiarity with some mathematical terms, but even when they did not know specific vocabulary, they were able to describe their thinking. Ms. Cárdenas supported them to see themselves as competent mathematicians who are able to challenge each other's ideas. In the process, Ms. Cárdenas learned about her students' mathematical understandings, and their capacity to reason and argue. She also had evidence from this discussion of her students' ability to participate meaningfully in a discussion by listening to each other and building on other student's ideas, using phrases like "And just like Nina said" and "I'm in disagreement."

By encouraging the discussion and bringing certain ideas to the fore, such as when she had Camillo share his thinking about the word *whole*, Ms. Cárdenas was able to orchestrate a mathematically rich discussion that gave her insights into which students had more sophisticated ideas, and which also helped develop some students' vocabulary and understanding. None of this would have happened had she corrected Nina's original comment and moved on.

At the end of the next mathematics class period, Ms. Cárdenas may have chosen to adopt a convergent approach by asking questions intended to give her insights into whether an individual student or a group of students understood the concept of even numbers and could name it, for instance, by asking "Can you tell me what an even number is?" In the event that students did not provide an accurate response, she could then use a divergent approach to probe their thinking further, such as "Can you tell me why you think that?" In this way, she is moving between convergent and divergent approaches determined by what it is she wants to know about her students' learning.

CURRICULUM-EMBEDDED ASSESSMENT

As we saw in chapter 2, ambitious teaching practices in science focus on students making sense of phenomena by engaging in three dimensional learning: science core ideas, practices, and crosscutting concepts. Figure 3.1 shows an example of curriculum-embedded assessment that fifth-grade students complete during a physical science unit focused on the phenomenon of garbage.[18] All the assessment tasks in the unit were designed to align to the New York State P-12 Science Learning Standards.

The task blends a science and engineering practice, a disciplinary core idea, and a crosscutting concept. Students use the crosscutting concept "Patterns" to interpret the data in the tables in order to generate evidence for the argument, which they then write. Students also engage in argument from evidence, one of the science and engineering practices, and they use their understanding of the disciplinary core idea that materials are identified by their properties as the reasoning that links their evidence to their claim. The task also includes scaffolds related to the practice of engaging in argument from evidence: Students are reminded that an argument "should include a claim, evidence, and reasoning." They are also provided two boxes, one for the claim and one for the evidence and reasoning. Finally, students are provided "hints" as reminders of what counts as a claim, evidence, and reasoning in a science argument.[19]

While more convergent in nature than the prior example of classroom discourse, this assessment invites students' own ideas and, therefore, can provide

FIGURE 3.1 Curriculum-embedded assessment

Rafael is carrying out an investigation to find out what happens to his garbage over time. He puts a piece of a soda can and a piece of an orange into a bottle with water and soil and leaves the bottle open for two weeks. He records his observations at the beginning of the investigate and then again after two weeks.

Material: Soda can

	Color	Texture	Smell	Reflectivity
Beginning	red	smooth	none	shiny
After 2 weeks	red	smooth	none	shiny

Material: Orange

	Color	Texture	Smell	Reflectivity
Beginning	orange	smooth	fruity	shiny
After 2 weeks	brown	fuzzy	bad-smelling	dull

Based on these observations, **has the Orange changed after two weeks?** Write an argument based on evidence to answer this question. Your argument should include a claim, evidence, and reasoning.

a. Claim (Hint: Answer the question)

b. Evidence and Reasoning (Hint: Support your answer using evidence from the tables)

Source: Llosa et al., "Integrating Science and Language."

teachers with insights about what students know and can do and what they still might need to learn with respect to data interpretation, claims, and evidence, and with this degree of scaffolding.

Below is an English learner's response, as the student wrote it.

Claim:

Yes the orange did change after two weeks

Evidence and Reasoning:

The orange properties change thats how I now that after 2 weeks it change.

Some of the properties that change is the color before it was orange and now its brown and the texture before was smooth and now its fuzzy.

The student uses the specialized term *properties* and is precise in comparing the properties of the orange at the beginning of the investigation with the properties after two weeks. The student provides evidence for and reasoning about the changes, supporting their answer from the table. With less-than-perfect English, the student is able to express accurate science ideas. The teacher has evidence that she can use to build on the student's current understanding as they progress through the curriculum, potentially removing the scaffolds in future assessment tasks related to argument.

What We Can Learn from the Curriculum-Embedded Example: The task has relevance for students because it is anchored in local phenomena that draw on students' everyday experiences. The assessment focuses on high-level thinking and reasoning, and legitimates the linguistic practices of the students by inviting them to use whatever language resources they have. As Professor Lorena Llosa, one of the assessment developers, explains, the main point of the assessment is "to highlight the importance of 'hearing' the science in students' responses instead of focusing on linguistic accuracy because that has implications for the type of feedback or subsequent instruction that the teacher would provide. A teacher who prioritizes linguistic accuracy would focus on the grammatical inaccuracies in the response. A teacher who focuses on 'what' the student says and not 'how' they say it would provide very different feedback."[20] The design of the assessment task, in effect, shapes the teachers' positioning and its impact on the teacher's interptation and action. In this case, the teacher might say: "Good job articulating a clear claim and providing evidence from the table to support your claim that the orange changed (because the properties changed)." This feedback is asset based and not only positions the student as competent but also legitimates the linguistic resources that the student brings to the task. In future instruction, this student's teacher can provide multiple opportunities to develop more sophisticated language.

SELF- AND PEER ASSESSMENT

Earlier in the chapter, we noted that students' own self- and peer assessment are features of divergent assessment, making students equal stakeholders in assessment with their teachers. Self-assessment involves students thinking about the quality of their learning, judging the degree to which it reflects explicitly stated goals or criteria, and making adjustments accordingly.[21] In peer assessment, students assess the status of an individual peer's learning—or their classmates' learning as a group—against the same criteria they use to reflect on their own learning, and then they provide feedback to their peer. These two student aspects of divergent assessment do not happen without teaching and continued support from teachers.

With regard to eliciting students' initial ideas at the beginning of the science unit, Dr. Johnson notes that "it is important for students to know what they know and do not know at the beginning of the lesson so that they can recognize how their ideas change over the course of the unit." She emphasizes that "divergent assessment is important not only for the teacher to understand student thinking, but also for students to understand their own ideas and identify gaps in their knowledge. When students formulate their own questions about a topic it motivates their learning and scaffolds the metacognition necessary for deep learning."

Although we do not see either self- or peer assessment occurring in the excerpt from Ms. Cárdenas's lesson, she routinely provides opportunities for students to engage in both practices. For instance, the students have *peer assessment buddies* with whom they share their mathematical problem-solving strategies and solutions and obtain feedback using a three-part structure: What has your peer done well? What clarifying question do you have? What is a suggestion for improvement? In her regular assessment conferences with students, Ms. Cárdenas always begins by asking her students to reflect on how well they think they are meeting the learning goal, and why. Their response is the starting point for an extended conversation about their learning.

In the curriculum-embedded example, students could be invited to engage in self-assessment by responding to questions such as "Do you think your responses show a good understanding of what you have been learning about? Why? Why not?," or "Are there things from this unit that you feel you need to learn more about to deepen your understanding? What are they and why do you want to learn more about them?" In addition to supporting students to assess their own learning progress, their responses will likely provide their teachers with important insights for future action.

The extended example of self-assessment below comes from an eleventh-grade English language arts class in a school with a majority Hispanic, and a significant African American student population. All the students in the school take Advanced Placement (AP) English language in grade 11 and AP English literature in grade 12.

Joe Nelson had noticed that when his students were invited to use any kind of a rubric for self-assessment and to set a goal for future work, they would all choose something from the column describing the highest level of performance, regardless of their starting point. Mr. Nelson wanted his students to learn how to accurately assess their current learning status and to set realistic goals, continually refining those goals as they developed in their ability to self-assess and as they made progress with their skills.[22]

In the class period prior to the one described here, the learning goal was to deepen the students' understanding about the relationship between rhetorical choices and tone to establish a purpose in writing. The students read the first and second foreword from Stephen King's *On Writing*, and identified specific rhetoric that conveys the tone. Then, in small groups, they discussed the effect of the tone on the purpose of the memoir.

In this class period, the learning goal read "I am learning to assess group performance and set goals that deepen my learning during discussions." To support this goal, Mr. Nelson introduced a student participation discourse continuum which had four levels: beginning, developing, progressing, and extending. An example of a descriptor at the beginning level is "Students do not, or rarely, build on one another's ideas, making the discussion a series of disconnected ideas." And at the extending level: "Students frequently build on one another's ideas, provide feedback, support various perspectives and make connections to advance ideas. The discussion is well connected and flows easily."

At the beginning of the class period, students worked in the same small groups as the day before to talk about what they noticed about the discourse continuum. Then the whole group came together to share their ideas. Next, each small group worked together to assess their group's discourse about rhetoric and tone from the previous lesson. The teacher went around during this time to ask the students to describe the evidence from their previous conversation used to determine their current discourse level on the continuum.

After determining which level they had reached the previous day, the small groups looked at the next level to the right on the continuum and read through the description. They decided on one of the actions from the adjacent rubric level that they would consciously focus on in their next discussion and recorded it on paper and posted it on the wall. This would be referred back to in the next class period's discussion. After the initial introduction, this process of assessment became a regular feature of student self-assessment and goal setting after every discussion in which the students participated. When reflecting about the use of the continuum for self-assessment, one student noted: "The higher we are [on the continuum], the better the class is." Another student added: "It's always an accomplishment because we started off "beginning" and we're like at 'progressing' and we really want to get to 'extending.' I feel like we made progress today—it felt really great—a lot of people talked in our class."

What We Can Learn from the Self- and Peer Assessment Example: Students engaged in rigorous discussion about their own performance in discourse; they were assumed to be capable of it. All students were able to participate in the discussion about their performance with the teacher supporting the students by asking for evidence for their decisions. Through this structure of using the discourse continuum, the students were positioned as competent and were able to take ownership of their learning, determining for themselves what their next steps would be to achieving the discourse goals. The self-assessment process also engendered a sense of belonging and success among the students.

CONVERGENT ASSESSMENT

Table 3.2 shows the framework for convergent assessments that are available for classroom teachers' use, the possible methods of assessment, and the information they yield. Generally, the assessments in this table are under the purview of individual teachers, or are developed through collaboration among groups of teachers.

The three examples below illustrate how teachers use convergent approaches outlined in table 3.2 in the context of ambitious teaching: (1) during a lesson; (2) at the end of a lesson (one or more class periods), a series of lessons or unit(s); and (3) at the end of a course, semester or year.

DURING A LESSON: HINGE-POINT QUESTION

Teachers might ask convergent questions to find out whether students have understood an idea at an important stage of the lesson. Assessment expert Dylan Wiliam has referred to such questions as *hinge-point* because they are used to check understanding of a concept and get a response from every student in order to make a decision about moving on in the lesson or going back to revisit a concept.[23]

One of the principles of hinge-point questions that Wiliam notes is to design questions that elicit the correct response for the right reason.[24] Wiliam provides

TABLE 3.2 Convergent classroom assessment framework

Category	*Purpose*	*Method*	*Information*
During a lesson	Inform immediate or near immediate teaching and learning	Teacher questioning Hinge-point question Student task Discussion	Whether students know, understand or can do something in particular
At the end of a lesson (one or more class periods), a series of lessons or unit(s)	Elicit information about curriculum learning outcomes Take stock of learning Inform planning and mid-term curricular/ instructional planning Assign grades Critically reflect on teaching/learning	Student work products from specifically designed activities Performances (e.g., portfolio, culminating projects), with associated rubric(s) Unit assessments, or assessments that cover larger chunks of the curriculum designed/ selected by teacher(s) Assessments embedded in/provided with curricular materials Student self-assessment	Cumulative record of learning (portfolio) Point-in-time record of student achievement relative to medium-term goals Insights into what students know, understand and can do Student strengths and needs
At the end of course, semester or year	Evaluate achievement Inform curricular/ pedagogical planning Assign grades Critically reflect on teaching/learning	Student work products and performances (e.g., portfolio, culminating projects), with associated rubric(s) Assessments that embody curricular outcomes/standards teacher(s) designed/ selected by teacher(s) Assessment provided with curricular materials Student evaluative reflection with teachers	Cumulative record of learning (portfolio) Point-in-time record of student achievement relative to outcomes/ standards Student strengths and needs

this example of a question about measurement in science as an illustration of how to do this:

1. Two or three measurements are always enough.
2. She should take five measurements.
3. If she is accurate, she only needs to measure once.

4. She should go on taking measurements until she knows how much they vary.
5. She should go on taking measurements until she gets two or more the same.

Number 4 is the only single correct response to this question. Students who do not understand the main point are highly unlikely to get the correct answer because the incorrect responses are sufficiently plausible to be attractive to students with incomplete understandings.

While this task is designed as convergent assessment and is intended to be a quick and efficient way to gauge a class's understanding, a teacher could turn it into a divergent opportunity by displaying the percentage of responses for each question and asking those who responded differently from number 4 why they had responded that way, or by asking the class as a whole why their peers might have chosen specific answers. The nature of the information from the two approaches would be different and lead to different instructional pathways.

What We Can Learn from the Hinge-Point Question Example: Higher-order thinking is being promoted. The assessment content is recognizable to students. Students can be aware that the teacher designed learning experiences that respond to their learning needs are identified from the hinge-point question, which sends a message that the teacher believes all students are capable learners.

AT THE END OF A LESSON, A SERIES OF LESSONS, OR UNIT(S)

In this example, we return to Dr. Johnson's ninth-grade science lesson described in chapter 2. Recall that the lesson focuses on developing students' understanding of the connection between breathing and burning fat. After a series of instructional activities that she was also able to use as formative assessment opportunities, at the end of the week Dr. Johnson asked the students to complete an individual checkpoint assessment, which she referred to as "Game Day," where the students apply the core ideas and practices they learned throughout the week to explain a new phenomenon. The end-of-the-week checkpoint is shown in figure 3.2.

This assessment task converges on the learning that the Dr. Johnson is intending. It can provide her and her students with information about their understanding of how air is related to losing fat while exercising after the first lesson

FIGURE 3.2 End-of-the-week checkpoint

Watch the video of a person using an air pump to blow up an inflatable paddleboard. https://tinyurl.com/paddleboardpump

The video explains that it will get more difficult to use the air pump as you add more air to the paddleboard and what you can do so you don't get too tired.

It takes about 10 minutes to fully inflate the paddleboard. After 5 minutes of pumping, the paddleboard will look fully inflated, but it will be squishy if you try to stand on it in the water.

After pumping for 5 minutes, the man put the squishy paddleboard on a scale and saw that I weighed 21.5 pounds. Then he continued pumping for 5 more minutes until the board was very firm and he weighed the paddleboard again.

1. Make a model to show what is happening inside the paddleboard that you can't see.

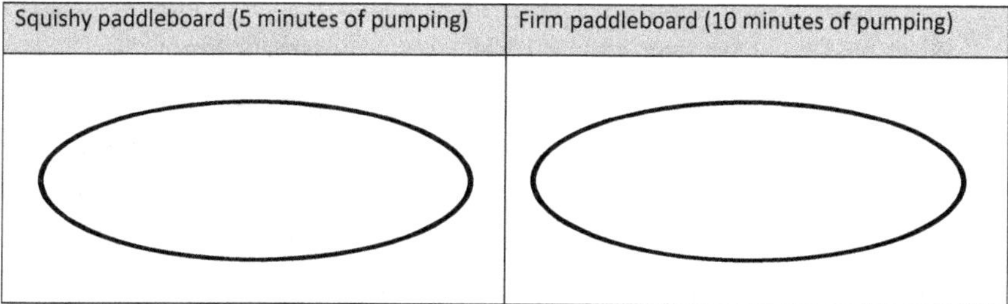

Squishy paddleboard (5 minutes of pumping)	Firm paddleboard (10 minutes of pumping)

2. Explain what happened to the weight of the board as the man added more air by completing the statement:
   The squishy paddleboard weighed 21.5 pounds. After pumping for 5 more minutes the paddleboard weighed------------------(Choose one: the same, more, less) because--
   (Explain why)

3. Use your model to explain why the paddleboard felt squishy after 5 minutes of pumping and firm after 10 minutes of pumping.

4. Use your model to explain why it becomes more and more difficult to add more air to the paddleboard as you use the pump to inflate it. What is happening inside the paddleboard that makes it harder to add more air?

of the unit in which the students have learned that air is made up of tiny particles and that it has mass. Dr. Johnson uses this assessment task for summative purposes to assign a grade. However, it is also used formatively to help her plan her next lessons and because the students use her feedback on the assessment for retake opportunities in the future.

Dr. Johnson comments on her use of the assessment approaches:

> The Expressing Ideas & Questions tool is an example of a fully divergent assessment. The syringe instructional activity [see chapter 2] was somewhere in between divergent and convergent in that I wanted to hear students' ideas and reasoning, but by the end of the activity we had to agree on how to represent what we learned about air in the final model that explains why it is so hard to pull back the plunger when the cap is on the syringe.
>
> I view the lesson (week) as a continuum that moves progressively from divergent to convergent. I started with questions that were very open-ended (about air and breathing related to exercise) and allowed for very divergent thinking. Then throughout the week the lesson and assessments become more and more convergent until I give the checkpoint assessment (the paddle board) on Friday.

What We Can Learn from the End-of-Lesson Assessment Example: The students are assessed on what they have been learning—the first "manageable chunk" in their investigation. Dr. Johnson has not waited unil the end of the unit to assess what students have learned about air, its composition, and its mass. She wants students to be aware of what they know so far rather than waiting until the end of the unit to assess their understanding. The task addresses rigorous goals for all students, and shows to students that their teacher expects that they will all develop high-level thinking and reasoning skills. It bridges everyday forms of knowing and those used in the discipline. Students are invited to use whatever linguistic resources they have to complete the task.

AT THE END OF A COURSE, SEMESTER, OR YEAR

Teachers by grade band, department, or at the school level may elect to use a common approach for assessment learning at the end of a long period (e.g., unit, semester, or year). To that end, they may jointly develop

- end-of-unit, end-of-semester, or end-of-year assessments, or
- create the criteria and requirements for student portfolios (representative selections of student work over a specified period), along with the criteria for assessing the portfolios.

One example of such a portfolio comes from a group of middle school teachers whose students are predominantly English learners. The teachers decided that the student portfolios at the end of a course on myths and legends from ancient culture should meet these criteria:

- Include a selection of items that are representative of curricular outcomes and of what the student(s) knows and can do.
- Include selections that show students' command of multimodally communicating knowledge and expertise to others.
- Help students develop a positive self-concept as learners.
- Include student self-assessments/evaluative reflections.
- Support the assessment, evaluation, and communication of student learning.

An item that students were required to include in the portfolio was a narrative of one of the Greek myths they had read and discussed during the course. They were asked to tell the story of the myth to someone else, and they could either audio record or write it using the criteria below:

- Get your audience's attention and use "hooks" to get people to listen to you intently.
- Structure the narrative into recognizable components.
- Describe what complication emerged and how it was solved or how things developed.
- Invite your listener/reader to consider what may have happened if characters had acted differently.
- Close with some sort of a generalization or moral.[25]

Teachers reviewed the portfolio item (as they did with each one that students were required to include) and provided improvement-oriented feedback related to the criteria. The students were then able to use the feedback to revise their narratives and respond to these questions:

- How was your initial narrative different from your final one?
- What have you learned about narratives?

Student reflection tasks as a culminating portfolio entry can be used to structure student-led parent-teacher conferences, as well as providing students with an opportunity to reflect on their own learning progress. A grade can be awarded to students' final version of their narratives, using a rubric that is based on the specific criteria given to students so that there are no surprises. Collaborative grading of student essays by the group of teachers who administered the same essay or task to students can support fairer grading practices.[26] One strategy is to ensure that all the teachers have a common understanding for each level of the rubric before using it. Another strategy is for each teacher to select a small number of essays that they believe represent each level of performance on the rubric and exchange with another teacher to score. Disagreements should then be discussed and resolved, and the rubric clarified if needed. A third strategy is for teachers to score the essays from a different class, and to score them without seeing student names so that personal biases are less likely to impact scoring.

What We Can Learn from the End-of-Course Assessment Example: The assessment focused on a rigorous goal and provided opportunities for all students to show what they know, using whatever linguistic resources they had. The students were positioned as competent to use the feedback for improvement and to reflect on their own learning.

GRADES

Grading is a particularly impactful use of assessment information. In common with many researchers, we think that grades should be assigned based on convergent assessment results after a more or less extended period of learning, rather on an acculumation of formative assessment information while students are still in the process of learning.[27] However, because it has been a ubiquitous feature of classroom assessment in the US for over a century, and because to this day grades are regarded as indicators of student performance in schools, grading warrants special consideration in the discussion of classroom assessment.[28]

Famously, Paul Dressel observed that a grade was "an inadequate report of an inaccurate judgement by a biased and variable judge of the extent to which a student has attained an undefined level of mastery of an unknown proportion of an indefinite material."[29] While this observation may be a harsh critique of grading, nonetheless, it encapsulates much of the criticism leveled at teachers' grading practices. For instance, there is great variability in the grades teachers assign to students, due to differences in grading criteria, or lack of criteria; differences in teachers' standards and in their leniency or severity related to grading, and inconsistencies in their views of the purposes of grading; and the inclusion of nonachievement factors such as effort, participation, and attention in a student's grade.[30] With respect to the latter, collapsing all this varied information about a student into a single grade renders the grade meaningless.[31]

Dressler's comment might lead one to think that all attempts at grading should be abandoned (and there are some who have that perspective).[32] However, there are actions that can be taken to improve the meaning and utility of grades for both students and teachers. Fundamentally, grades should be derived solely from what students know and can do, rather than on behavioral factors such as participation. In addition, grades should be based on assessment results or on clear criteria for assigned work, and not on any other extraneous aspects.[33]

As noted earlier, science teacher Dr. Johnson requires her students to complete a checkpoint assessment during the final class period for the week's lesson. The grades she assigns for the week are based solely on the results of this assessment (learning tasks are not graded) and reflect only what students know and can do. She uses a five-point scale for scoring the assessment "because it 'translates' to a 100-point scale seamlessly": 5—mastery (5/5 = 100 percent), 4—adequate or satisfactory (4/5 = 80 percent), 3—minimally meets standard (3/5 = 60 percent) 2—not yet met (2/5 = 40 percent), 1—no evidence (1/5 = 20 percent). Students can use their scores to identify where they need more practice or support. Dr. Johnson builds in retake opportunities on previous standards into later assessments, so students have the chance to update their scores from prior assessments. The final unit assessment reassesses all of the standards for the unit so that students have many opportunities to show what they know.

What We Can Learn from the Classroom Checkpoint Assessment for Assigning Grades: The teacher creates challenging and stimulating learning opportunities and the students are only assessed and graded on what they know and can do, and are given multiple opportunities to demonstrate their learning. No extraneous factors are included. It is noteworthy that when teachers include factors such as noncompletion or lateness of homework in a grade, they may be creating bias due to circumstances beyond students' control—for example, lack of parental help for English learners, or after-school employment to support their families.[34] A telling finding from grading expert Joe Feldman is that when teachers omitted homework and judgments about behavior and effort from their grades, the difference in grades between White and non-White students lessened considerably.[35] Permitting retakes related to the standard in later assessments sends the message that learning important ideas is a cumulative process, and invites an orientation to learning rather than to performance.

To this point, we have focused on classroom assessment that are, in the main, within the purview of teachers. In the next section, the focus is on assessments that are external to the classroom.

EXTERNAL ASSESSMENTS

The convergent assessments shown in table 3.3 are typically externally mandated by a school's or district's administration. They range from diagnostic and progress-

TABLE 3.3 Convergent assessment, external to the classroom

Category	*Purpose*	*Method*	*Information*
When a student is not responding to a specific curricular/ instructional intervention (not for all students and used infrequently)	Identify possible causes for lack of progress	Standardized diagnostic assessments (e.g., math and reading) Standardized diagnostic assessment (not administered by teachers, e.g., psychological batteries, speech and language assessments; results provided to teachers with guidance on teacher action)	Insights into student learning challenges Insights into students' psychological functioning Insights into students' communicative abilities
At regular, frequent intervals (e.g., weekly/biweekly)	Monitor student progress over time Identify students who are not making adequate progress Critically reflect on teaching/learning	Progress monitoring: curriculum-based assessments	Student strengths and needs Progress in response to intervention
Externally-mandated assessment (Mainly for administrators and policy makers' use, but can also be used by teachers for critical reflection on teaching)	Accountability Monitor trends Evaluate programs Inform systemic planning Critically reflect on teaching/learning	District standardized assessments State standardized assessments	Student achievement of benchmarks and standards Student strengths and needs

monitoring assessments to district standardized assessments to end-of-the-year state standardized assessments.

Diagnostic and progress-monitoring assessment

An example of an assessment that is used for diagnostic and progress monitoring purposes on important reading skills is the Dynamic Indicators of Basic Early Literacy Skills (DIBELS).[36] They are designed to be short (one minute) measures that can be used to regularly detect risk and monitor the development of early literacy and early reading skills in kindergarten through eighth grade. The measures have been thoroughly researched and have been demonstrated to be a valid and reliable indicator of early literacy development.[37] They are not intended to be in-depth or comprehensive measures of reading, but rather "are designed to help teachers figure out how the children are doing with some skills that support their reading progress."[38] For example, if the assessment reveals that a student is reading words accurately, but slowly, the teacher can provide extra practice rereading stories and passages to improve their reading rate or fluency. Teachers who use DIBELS for progress monitoring might require students to complete one or two of the individual DIBELS tests as often as once a week in order to assess how students are responding to additional help to support foundational reading skills.

Statewide assessment

With respect to statewide assessment, it bears returning to the cautions that Evans and Marion expressed about what it takes for assessment information to be instructionally useful for teachers. In their view, the features that characterize instructionally useful assessments are coherence with local curriculum rather than broad coherence with state standards, item types—selected versus constructed response, the grain size (and thus actionability) of the information, the nature of the feedback (scores versus qualitative insights), and the timing of the results. They argue persuasively that annual accountability assessments or assessments that students take two or three times per year are unlikely to be closely aligned to a local curriculum, use rich tasks that provide detailed insights into student thinking, or provide results at a level of detail and in a time frame that is truly actionable from an instructional perspective. They maintain that the inability of large-scale summative assessments to directly inform next steps in teaching and learning should not be viewed as a design flaw of those assessments, but rather that those assessments have a different audience, one that is not classroom teachers. It is important for state leaders to clarify that these accountability assessments provide information primarily for state, district, and school leaders about student performance at various levels of aggregation.

The Oregon Department of Education (ODE) is a trailblazer with respect to assessment use, and ODE's recently released guidance, *The Right Assessment for the Right Purpose*, is clear about the purpose and use of assessments for educators across the state. The ODE clarifies the appropriate use of statewide assessments:

> Results are useful for guiding state policy decisions and making systems-level decisions at the state-, district-, and school-levels. Districts include state assessment results in improvement planning to assist with systems questions, such as efficacy of new district curriculum, new professional development plans, and allocation of resources etc.

The guidance also states:

> Because instruction and learning experiences are based on state standards—and formative assessment practices are integrated into instruction—formative assessment enables educators and students to co-pilot learning so that they are partners in both *building* knowledge and skills and *demonstrating* knowledge and skills. By measuring specific state standards, the interim, classroom summative, and performance tasks let educators know whether, after a period of instruction, students are able to demonstrate the knowledge and skills they were taught. This information should be used for reflection by both educator in terms of instruction and by the student in terms of effort and engagement.[39]

The convergent and divergent nature of assessment is clear from these quotes, in terms of confirming what knowledge and skills have been achieved versus assessment practices that support "co-piloting" of learning as it is emerging.

It is noteworthy that the guidance does not try to make an argument for how Oregon's statewide assessment results could be used to inform instruction, but rather it is clear about the kinds of evaluation questions the data can answer.

A FINAL THOUGHT

In this chapter we have discussed the array of assessment types and approaches for teacher use in support of ambitious teaching and fair and justice-oriented assessment practices. Each assessment has the goal of improving teachers' teaching and students' learning. When teachers critically reflect on the information that any of the assessments in the above tables provide, they can usefully think about the effectiveness of their teaching. When they interpret assessment results they have guidance about what action to take to advance their students' learning. In this vein, we end the chapter with a quote from Jan McArthur, who encourages us to see the "joy" in assessment use.

> Assessment represents an important moment in the life of a teacher in two ways. First, it can signify a moment of student achievement, which should be a joyous event when we see some of the outcomes of our students' learning. Second, it can signify the necessity for care and commitment, which should be joyful in its own way: this is the moment where we see what our student does not understand, and therefore how we can continue to help them.[40]

SUMMARY: KEY TAKEAWAYS

- Teachers need instructionally useful assessment information, but not all assessments provide such information.
- Divergent assessment enables students and teachers to explore *what* students know, understand, or can do.
- Convergent assessment focuses on uncovering if students know, understand, or can do a specific outcome.
- While divergent and convergent assessment serve different roles, in practice, teachers can navigate between the two within an agenda of learning for all students.
- Student grades should be a reflection of what students know and can do and not include other factors such as compliance for work completion, effort, or participation.
- Assessment use should support amibitious teaching and promote fair and justice-oriented outcomes.

CHAPTER 4

Supporting Teacher Professional Learning

Jennifer Gonzalez, hoping to be certified as an accomplished teacher, wrote about her experience of the National Board for Professional Teaching Standards (NBPTS) assessment process: "These [National Board] standards scared me. The more I read, the more I thought, *I don't do that. I don't do that. Not that either. Who* does *all that?*" In a panic about the seeming impossibility of the challenge she was facing, she reached out to a mentor. Below is an excerpt from what she wrote about that conversation.[1]

JENNIFER: These standards. There's just so much! They're impossible! I hardly do any of these things!

MENTOR: (*pause*) . . . So start.

JENNIFER: . . .

MENTOR: Start doing some of them. No one does all those things all the time. It's an ideal. Something we should all be trying to do. If you haven't been doing them yet, now's the time to start.

> That advice helped more than she knew. I took a breath, stepped away for a day or two, then looked through the standards again and picked a few areas I could work on. Instead of turning my anxiety on the standards themselves, dismissing them as unrealistic, I began to recognize their value.

Jennifer, who eventually did become National Board Certified, was initially overwhelmed by the process and the scope of what the NBPTS were describing. Jennifer's story about her initial reaction may not be dissimilar to some readers who have read the first three chapters of this book. Chapter 2, which focused on ambitious teaching, may have described some practices that make you think "who does all that?" Or maybe reading about convergent and divergent assessment in chapter 3 has left you wondering if undertaking these assessment practices successfully is really possible. Jennifer was reflective on her own practice, and motivated to change as she drew on her support network. She was able to use the NBPTS as an external reference point to help her identify areas of practice to begin to improve, and she did not try to change everything at once. As we will discover in this chapter, motivation to change; a support network in the form of a coach, a mentor, or a grade-level team; an injection of expertise; and a willingness to try new ways of working by focusing on and deliberately practicing one thing at a time are all critical components of improvement. And incremental change is very possible, taking it just one step at a time.

In this chapter we will describe a broad framework to think about how to support teacher learning, along with sharing some concrete examples. We begin by reflecting on some markers of assessment literacy expertise displayed in the examples already presented in the earlier chapters, and then examine how the research literature on teacher professional learning can be employed to encourage the development of this kind of assessment expertise.

ASSESSMENT LITERACY EXPERTISE

What do we mean by fair and justice-oriented assessment literacy expertise? Table 1.1 provides a detailed breakdown of the components of assessment literacy. It should be clear that expertise is not just about knowing about types of assessment, but also the ability to implement a wide range of assessment practices, and to adjust them to the content, students, and context of the learning. In summary, expertise in assessment literacy is an educator who routinely

- designs or selects assessment tasks and prompts that reflect meaningful learning goals, are informed by students' culture, language, and lived experiences, are coherent with ambitious teaching, are accessible to students, and provide multiple ways for students to reveal what they know, understand, and can do;
- engages students meaningfully in the assessment process; and

- analyzes, interprets, and uses a wide variety of assessment information and supporting data, such as student interviews or classroom learning walks, to make asset-based decisions that inform next instructional steps and student learning.

Chapter 1 included three examples of assessment tasks that together illustrated aspects of fair and justice-oriented assessment and the ways in which assessment knowledge, skills, and dispositions are expertly deployed by these teachers: a fifth-grade science task that allowed students to reveal emerging ideas about the particle nature of gas in multiple ways, a middle school history task that required students to engage in historical analysis of a primary source, and a discussion with a combined class of second- and third-grade students to assist their developing understanding of the relationship between addition and multiplication.

All three of these teachers used open-ended tasks and prompts to gain insight into students' thinking. They recognized that the current status of student thinking could be revealed through what they wrote, drew, or said. The teachers used deep pedagogical content knowledge to select or develop tasks that addressed knowledge and skills described in their content standards so that their instruction was aligned to standards, but not taught in a decontextualized way that focused on one isolated standard at a time. This deep knowledge base was also required when teachers examined student work or listened to their discussions to make interpretations about what students know (divergent assessment) rather than just confirming that they do or do not understand the topic at hand (convergent assessment), as described in chapter 3. The chapter 1 mathematics discussion about the multiplication task illustrated the nuanced way in which the teacher entered into the conversation to help students clarify their understanding of the task rather than telling them what the problem was asking them to do or how to solve it. This example illustrates how one marker of teaching expertise—the ability to take up cues from students—plays out specifically in relation to assessment literacy. Another marker of expertise is being able to closely monitor learning and provide feedback to students. Had these tasks been multiple-choice questions, these teachers could have been limited to commenting on the correctness of an answer choice, and perhaps probing student thinking about their selection of the distractor options.

None of the teachers who provided examples of their assessment practices would claim to have been assessment experts when they graduated from their preservice programs. Rather, they developed these skills over time, in collaboration with their peers and with the support of administrators. A broad body of literature documents the development of expertise, across diverse groups of people with particular skill sets, from champion chess players to London taxi drivers to emergency medical technicians. Noted researchers such as David Berliner have applied this general body of work to teachers to identify what expert teaching looks like. Differentiating experience from expertise, Berliner commented, "the acquisition of experience does not automatically denote expertise."[2] In the same way that there is no quick route to expertise in teaching, there is no shortcut to becoming assessment literate. The seeds of assessment literacy should be sown in teachers' preservice experiences and continue to grow as teachers progress through their careers. Our aim in this book is to offer suggestions of how teachers can be involved in continued professional learning in their workplace settings, and receive support to develop their knowledge and skills toward increased expertise in fair and justice-oriented assessment literacy over the course of their careers.

In the next section we explore the concept of expertise in teaching, and approaches for supporting the development of professional competencies.

Markers of expertise

While research shows an overall relationship between years of experience and impact on student learning, some studies suggest that the greatest amount of growth occurs during teachers' early years of practice.[3] Other research has shown that improvement can continue over twenty years of teaching, and more general research on the development of expertise in any domain suggests that it can take around ten years of "deliberate practice" to achieve high levels of mastery.[4] One study of teachers applying for certification from the NBPTS used a set of features of teaching expertise to explore potential differences between those who were and were not successful in their application.[5] In this study, before certification decisions were known, all the candidates' materials were examined for evidence of these features. Ultimately, the group of teachers who were awarded the National Board Certification outperformed the group who were not certified on each of these markers, with significant differences for eleven of the thirteen features listed below:

- a better use of knowledge;
- extensive pedagogical content knowledge, including deep representations of subject matter knowledge;
- better problem-solving strategies;
- better adaptation and modification of goals for diverse learners, better skills for improvisation;
- better decision making;
- more challenging objectives;
- better classroom climate;
- better perception of classroom events;
- better ability to read the cues from students;
- greater sensitivity to context;
- better monitoring of learning and providing feedback to students;
- more frequent testing of hypotheses;
- greater respect for students; and
- display of more passion for teaching.[6]

In chapter 1, we noted three symbiotic components of the educational process: teaching, learning, and assessment. Expertise in teaching is therefore inextricably linked to expertise in assessment literacy to promote student learning. In table 1.1 and again in figure 2.2 we presented a set of fair and justice-oriented assessment-related teacher actions. These actions align well with the features of teaching expertise highlighted above in the study with the National Board Certified teachers. Expertise in assessment literacy draws on competencies such as hypothesis testing, improvisation, problem-solving, decision-making, and teachers being attentive to the details of their subject matter, their students, and their classroom climate.

We have seen these competencies in action in the classroom examples of practice provided already. In the high school science example in chapters 2 and 3, we observed how Dr. Wendy Johnson tests her hypothesis about what specific background knowledge and understandings a class of students brings to a new unit through her initial driving question assessment. In chapter 3, Gabriela Cárdenas illustrated what improvisation can look like as she responded to her students' thinking during a discussion of equal and even numbers. Her deviation from her lesson plan showed how she listened to her students' comments closely, respecting their emerging efforts to engage in mathematical argumentation to generate a discussion that was beneficial to the entire class. Problem-solving and decision-making go hand in hand, as illustrated by the mathematics small group dialogue about a task requiring students to apply their knowledge of multiplication and addition that the teacher joined in chapter 1. In real time, she needed to make sense of what the students understood and were still struggling with, and then decide how to advance their thinking without taking away their autonomy.

These assessment literacy competencies are necessary so that teachers can adapt instruction and assessment to meet specific student needs, elevate students' ways of knowing and doing, notice and meet the needs of all students in a classroom, and be reflective on how their own personal experiences impact classroom practice.

In this vein, the Canadian researcher Christopher DeLuca and his colleagues have proposed that teachers' assessment literacy skills need to be situational and flexible, in recognition of the fact that teachers will have to adapt their assessment practices at both a macro and micro scale to respond to the needs of their students.[7] At a macro level, a teacher might modify an assessment to allow for multiple means of representation of student ideas, whether giving students choice in how they elect to present evidence or allowing students to respond in whatever language that enables them to most clearly reveal their understanding. At a micro level, a teacher may need to respond in the moment—for example, during a discussion to adjust the next question they ask, or by identifying a need to bring the whole class or a small group of students together to clarify some misunderstanding, based on observations of how students are responding to a task.

Some of these features of expertise—such as better perception of classroom events, better ability to read the cues from students, better decision making, and extensive pedagogical content knowledge—relate directly to assessment as *classroom noticing*, an essential component of classroom assessment.[8] Expert teachers are able to observe patterns in student responses and identify which ones will be most productive as a focal point for the class as a whole, making judgments about when to have a student share an advanced strategy or idea to push all the students' thinking, or when to look at a response that is likely to represent a common student misunderstanding or partial understanding. They are also able to examine errors in student work to identify the approach a student took, and then use that current understanding of student thinking to scaffold their next learning step.

Other features of expertise point to the subtleties in practice that teachers develop to create a classroom climate that is conducive to assessment. These expert teacher actions require that teachers have developed automaticity over certain aspects of their teaching practice, in order to free up cognitive space to attend to the classroom nuances. Novice teachers often struggle with routines such as starting and ending lessons, maintaining a collaborative classroom climate when learning is challenging, and having smooth transitions between lesson activities. These activities require so much of their attention that they are unable to engage in impromptu thinking or reflection as the lesson is unfolding. As a result, they are less likely to deviate from a lesson plan, even when student comments might suggest a change to the plan would allow them to capitalize on a "teachable moment."[9] This is illustrated by Dr. Johnson's frequent use of driving questions to open new units as a way of ascertaining the prior knowledge that students have about the new topic. The students are familiar with this routine and understand that revealing misunderstandings or partial conceptual understandings is not something that will be penalized but will help the teacher plan next steps. Because of this familiarity, Dr. Johnson is able to closely attend to what students say and write rather than wasting cognitive resources redirecting students.

Moving from novice to expert

In terms of developing expertise, the renowned researcher Robert Glaser identified three stages of teacher learning: (1) externally supported; (2) transitional; and (3) self-regulatory.[10] The novice or externally supported stage is typically considered the preservice time period. At this stage, candidate teachers receive a significant amount of external support from program faculty and cooperating teachers. These supporters are generally responsible for structuring the learning environment and deciding on the most crucial areas of knowledge and skill that beginners need. The transitional stage can occur, in part, in the course of a beginning teacher's induction period, during which time the teacher is expected to engage in more independent self-monitoring and self-reflection, while also being provided with supports, such as a school-based mentor or a district-provided coach. As teachers gain more experience and independence, they will move to the self-regulatory phase when they take much more control over their own in-service learning, while still drawing on the support of peers and possibly external experts.[11]

These stages of development reflect an apprenticeship model for learning in a community of practice—a group of people who share a common set of practices, procedures, and standards used to achieve a particular goal.[12] With regard to the development of assessment literacy knowledge and skills, professional learning communities provide a context within which learning can be advanced, enacted, reflected on, and revised.[13] We explore professional learning communities more extensively later in the chapter, but for now we note that newcomers to the community are helped to develop a set of knowledge and skills so that they shift over time from *legitimate peripheral participants* to full members of the community.[14] The specific size and composition of a community of practice to build assessment literacy competencies can vary. For example, it could be made up of a grade-level group of elementary school teachers, or high school language teachers, or be a cross-disciplinary group in middle schools. Over the course of a teacher's career, as described by the Glaser stages of learning, different people will influence a teacher's move from being a peripheral practitioner, not yet fluent in the teaching, learning, and assessment skills of an experienced teacher, to a self-directed expert learner who is likely, in turn, to be supporting the apprenticeship of other novice teachers.

SUPPORTING THE DEVELOPMENT OF PROFESSIONAL EXPERTISE

Experience does not assume expertise; expert teachers are developed, not born. For these reasons, teachers need to engage in professional learning that specifically focuses on developing assessment literacy competencies consonant with the stage of their career. The content of such professional learning experiences must be clearly geared to the requisite knowledge and skills for assessment literacy, while simultaneously applying the general principles identified from the professional learning literature.

In the following section, we discuss several approaches that can be adopted for teacher learning in assessment literacy. We begin with recommendations from a meta-analysis of studies on effective professional learning and examine how school-based professional learning communities are one way to enact the recommendations. We then explore three different approaches of developing teachers' assessment literacy skills: (1) framing assessment literacy learning through challenges and dilemmas; (2) assessment audits that engender teacher ownership and agency; and (3) peer observation to embed changes into practice. We include practical examples of each one.

Recommendations from a meta-analysis of studies on effective professional learning

While there have been multiple studies by experts such as Linda Darling-Hammond related to features of effective professional learning, they often draw on teacher self-reports about the impact or value of that learning.[15] Until recently, there have not been any validated explanatory accounts of what differentiates more from less effective professional learning. A group of researchers, led by Sam Sims, recently undertook a meta-analysis of 104 randomized controlled trials, and found qualified empirical support for their theory of effective professional learning.[16] These researchers' theory of the critical components of effective professional learning is broadly consistent with previous studies. However, their meta-analysis gives a firmer foundation on which to build professional learning activities. They proposed that, to be effective in bringing sustained improvements to teaching and therefore positive impacts on student learning, professional learning needs to

1. provide insight about teaching and learning;
2. motivate teachers to make changes to their practice;
3. provide techniques for putting these insights to work; and
4. enable teachers to embed change in practice.[17]

These four components provide a roadmap for the design of professional learning, particularly as the research findings suggest that professional learning programs are more effective when they attend to all four of these components. Below, we explore how the researchers further identified mechanisms to implement each of these four components, drawing on cognitive and behavior science and on domains outside of teaching, and we provide some illustrative examples.

Professional insight about teaching and learning

The purpose of professional learning is to support teachers in refining, modifying, or potentially making significant changes to their teaching practice. Understanding teachers' starting points is an important aspect of introducing new learning. To enable teachers to develop insights about a specific aspect of teaching and learning, the new learning should both revisit or connect to existing teacher knowledge, and engage teachers in a way that manages the cognitive load so that they are not presented with an overwhelming number of ideas that do not seem connected. The cognitive load may vary by teacher, since more experienced teachers will have greater capacity to handle more complex situations, which points to the need for differentiated teacher learning experiences. Learning about assessment will often require input from an external source such as shared readings or videos, outside experts, school or district coaches, or expert teachers.

An example of using an external source to promote assessment literacy comes from two teacher leaders, Larrissa Peru and Kasie Betten. We noted in chapter 1 that grading is particularly impactful use of assessment information and is often characterized by randomness and bias. In an effort to move their colleagues to fair and justice-oriented grading practices, Ms. Peru and Ms. Betten engaged them in book study about effective grading to provide new insights on best practices.[18] Before launching into reading the book, they asked teachers to complete a *web of belief* to help them identify experiences, values, or beliefs relevant to grading practices, which they used to shaped future discussions. They also later helped teachers identify which of the ideas particularly came into conflict with their existing ideas and beliefs. An important lesson here for other professional learning contexts is that Ms. Peru and Ms. Betten realized that if their colleagues were not provided with a chance to confront challenges to their current thinking, it would be too easy for them to dismiss new thinking about how they assigned grades.

Elsewhere, we have proposed a critical feature of effective professional learning is to encourage teachers' ownership and agency related to changing practices.[19] In this particular example, we see how Ms. Peru and Ms. Betten created the opportunity for teachers' ownership and agency in their professional learning experience. Rather than just telling the teachers what the book recommended, or how they should change their grading practices, they involved teachers in an explicit reflection opportunity, which laid the groundwork for their willingness to adopt new practices.

Motivation to make changes to practice

The researchers proposed three mechanisms through which to motivate change: (1) presenting evidence for change either from compelling sources and credible research about the impact of changing practice, or from testimonials from other respected teachers about how changes affected their teaching or students; (2) engaging teachers in specific goal setting to help teachers become more invested in their learning; and (3) reinforcing the importance of the focal teaching practice that teachers are being asked to attend to.

With respect to compelling arguments to motivate teacher change, Dylan Wiliam proposes a moral argument based on "the demonstrable empirical fact that when teachers do their job better, their students are healthier, live longer, and contribute more to society. With such an imperative, even the best teachers have a moral duty to improve."[20] A second argument, a pragmatic one, is that "while preparation for the world of work is just one of the aims of education, it is perhaps the one where the demands are changing most rapidly," and teachers must change their practices in order to keep up with the accelerating changes in the world of work.[21] While these arguments may be abstract, they can be coupled with research evidence about the impact of classroom assessment practices on a variety of student outcomes, including engagement, motivation, and achievement.[22] The Michigan Assessment Consortium (MAC) provides an example of sensitivity to such arguments and research. The MAC is a professional association of educators who believe quality education depends on accurate, balanced, and meaningful assessment. To prepare all students for success, the MAC's work has focused on promoting research-based practices, such as ambitious teaching undergirded by equitable approaches to assessment that both advance and verify learning. In this regard, the MAC assumes the moral argument in its support for teacher learning, providing pathways for both novice and advanced learners, so that all teachers can continue to improve their craft.

While results from well-designed research studies will be compelling for some teachers, others will dismiss those results because they were from a similar type of school or "weren't with students like mine." For those teachers, it is much harder to dismiss proof of the impact of student learning when the compelling source is a teacher in the same school. When teachers are centered on a particular change in assessment practices—for instance, better reflecting students lived experiences in learning goals, or making asset-based interpretations of evidence—profitable professional learning opportunities can occur when peers share successes and the benefits to their students as well as what they did to make the improvements.

In one school district, the school leadership team deepened teachers' motivation to participate in professional learning with an alternate method. They asked teachers directly to identify the goals of professional learning for the next school year. They surveyed the mathematics teachers about areas in which they were interested in advancing their knowledge and skills. One common request was to help them improve their multitiered systems of support (MTSS) implementation, particularly for Tier 1, which covers the high-quality instruction that all students receive. The school leadership team brought in outside experts to focus specifically on formative assessment for Tier 1 students, and the connection between meeting the Tier 1 needs in MTSS and the use of coherent formative assessment practices. Providing a forum for teachers to interact with input from other sources of expertise is another powerful mechanism for professional learning, particularly when it occurs over an extended period so that deeper learning can take place.[23] The school leadership also made explicit connections between the teacher survey responses and the year-long learning opportunities so that teachers would be motivated by recognizing that their requests were being honored and supported.

Techniques for putting these insights to work

The third component of effective professional learning is the provision of concrete techniques for putting the insights into practice, addressing the "knowing-doing" gap. The researchers identified five support mechanisms for this purpose: instruction, practical social support, modeling, rehearsal, and feedback. In doing so, they highlighted the importance of providing teachers with practical ideas for how to put their new learning into practice. Guidance can be offered from other, more experienced colleagues, who have already adopted the specific practice and can talk about what worked well for them, difficulties they experienced, and ways they addressed those problems. It can also take the form of explicit modeling of what it looks like in practice through direct observations of other teachers in the same school, or video examples, or detailed written descriptions of practice. Rehearsal refers to structured opportunities outside of the classroom that allow for practicing the new learning and can go hand in hand with modeling; teachers participating in professional learning might first observe a lead person model the instructional or assessment approach, and then practice it with their colleagues before trying it in the classroom with students.

Feedback, the final support mechanism, helps teachers reflect on their rehearsals before transferring new learning to the classroom. This process of modeling, rehearsal, and feedback may be more frequently used in preservice education before beginning teachers have access to classrooms and students, but many aspects of classroom assessment such as providing feedback to students, asking probing questions to provoke deeper thinking, or using learning progressions to interpret student work can be practiced with colleagues to develop fluency.[24]

These five support mechanisms can be thought of as components of *deliberate practice*, which entails specific and sustained efforts to do something that a person cannot do well.[25] The characteristics of deliberate practice (in any area, not specifically teaching) are (1) a motivated subject who is attending to task at hand and willing to exert effort to improve; (2) a scaffolded task that takes into account the prior learning of the subject; (3) the opportunity for brief instruction to support performance of the task; (4) the provision of informative feedback to the subject about his or her performance; and (5) the opportunity to repeatedly engage in similar tasks over time.[26]

An example of addressing the "knowing-doing" gap comes from Dylan Wiliam and his formative assessment work with groups of teachers in New Jersey.[27] He always provided concrete examples of practice and encouraged deliberate practice. Wiliam routinely began his introductory professional learning sessions with what he called "five key strategies" that he considered nonnegotiable and essential features of formative assessment. However, because these strategies can sound abstract and implementation may not initially be obvious, he also included many specific techniques for each of the five strategies. He presented these as starter ideas that teachers could then modify, refine, or otherwise make locally relevant. The only stipulation was that the revised technique still adhered to the principle behind the key strategy on which it was based. He encouraged teachers to meet regularly to share their experiences and modifications and for the group to act in some ways as a testing body, asking "What's formative about that?" to help ensure that new variations of techniques still were aligned with the intended focus on the five strategies for formative assessment. Encouraging teachers to meet regularly to discuss their experiences also overlaps with the idea of supporting ownership and teacher agency as a key professional learning tactic.

Processes to embed change in practice

The final component of effective professional learning addresses a recognized phenomenon: that teachers may begin to apply new ideas and practices but then revert to established habits rather than continue the new ones. From their meta-analysis,

Sam Sims and his colleagues identified four mechanisms that can help teachers embed new techniques into their long-term practices. These mechanisms include continued rehearsals in a realistic classroom context, action planning in which a teacher commits to when and how a new technique will be embedded in a future lesson, and making connections to classroom prompts or cues to help a teacher remember the specific conditions when they will implement a new technique. Finally, teachers should be encouraged to self-monitor or self-assess how the new practice is working and what modifications might be needed.

An example of how action planning, as part of the work of being in a community of practice, supports commitment to change comes from a year-long case study of a group of high school teachers focused on formative assessment. Each time the participating teachers met, they documented in writing how they were planning to try new techniques, or revise others after having talked about their initial implementation and received feedback from their group.[28] In an interview, one teacher described the benefits of this process:

> I think specifically what was helpful was the ridiculous [action planning] forms. I thought that was the dumbest thing, *but* I'm sitting with my friends and on the form I write down what I am going to do next month. Well, it turns out to be a sort of "I'm telling my friends I'm going to do this" and I really actually did it and it was because of that. It was because I wrote it down and I had it in my little packet and that idea of making improvements and sort of informally, which is much more powerful than formally, committing to doing it. I was surprised at how strong an incentive that was to do actually do something different, so I was happy with that, that idea of writing down what you are going to do and then because when they come by the next month you better take out that piece of paper and say "did I do that" and even if you didn't do it, you *knew* that you made a commitment to do and that's a—you weren't going to write me up, nobody was going to do anything terrible to me—but just the idea of sitting in a group, working out something, and making a commitment, even something as informal, I was impressed about how that actually made me do stuff.

The cycle of action planning, reporting on progress at the next meeting together, and then creating a new action plan for the next month kept formative assessment practice at the forefront for this group of teachers, helping to translate interesting ideas from a professional learning setting to embedded in ongoing classroom practice.

Although the researchers described four components of effective professional learning, they are not entirely distinct. For example, goal setting, action planning, and self-monitoring are closely related concepts that operate together and can variously play a motivating role, support putting insights to work, and ultimately embed them in practice. Peers play an important role across multiple mechanisms by providing implementation advice, allowing peers to observe them in practice for the purpose of modeling or in order to receive feedback on a new practice, as we describe in more detail in the Peer Observation section below.

School-embedded professional learning communities

Applying the concept of apprenticing into a specific community of experts, schools have been moving to regular time blocks of time for teachers in the same department or grade-level team to learn together.[29] These professional learning communities can take the form of short weekly blocks of time, longer monthly blocks, or more irregularly scheduled time periods, such as an occasional early closure for students so that teachers can meet for the afternoon.

The term *professional learning community* was most recognizably coined by Rick DuFour and Robert Eaker in 1998 to refer to a specific approach for collective inquiry into student learning that included a significant amount of time examining and learning from common assessments and developing systematic interventions.[30] The term now more broadly refers to a forum for participants to come together and deepen their knowledge and expertise by interacting on an ongoing basis.

A learning community could have been the forum for jointly creating the criteria that the middle school teachers established for selecting items for student portfolios described in chapter 3. Teachers could use the dedicated learning time to first develop their own collective understanding of the nature, purpose, and structure of the portfolio assessment. The group could then collaboratively plan how they would communicate the purpose and structure to their students. Finally, after students had completed their portfolios, the teachers could review student work to reflect on the evidence of learning, the implications for next instructional steps, and any refinements they would make to the process in the future.

One way to structure a portfolio review could be for every teacher to select three portfolios that represent differing levels of knowledge and skills. The teachers could then spend time in a round-robin review of portfolios before using a revised version of the criteria presented in chapter 3 to support the reflection process. Student interviews about their perceptions of the portfolio process could also be included in the review. Questions to guide the teachers' review could include:

- To what extent are the curriculum outcomes reflected across the portfolios?
- What is the evidence of each student's strengths and weaknesses from their portfolio? What are the instructional implications for different students?
- How do students see themselves as learners? How can we continue to build students' perceptions of themselves as agentic learners?
- How do our evaluations align with student self-reflections of their portfolios?
- How can we help students become more self-aware of their own strengths and areas for growth?
- How can we communicate our evaluations about student learning to them?
- What would we do similarly or differently next year for this unit? How might we use portfolios as part of the assessment process for future units for these students?

This example focuses on portfolio assessment, but a similar process can apply to any of the forms of convergent and divergent assessment discussed in chapter 3.

Professional learning communities can foster teacher agency by giving participants the time and space to be intentional about and responsible for the management of their learning. They can learn with and from their peers in the specific context of the curricula that they use and their student community.[31] As Nick Smith commented about teacher learning communities at his school, "the power of collaboration and peer learning cannot be overstated. Teachers appreciate the chance to exchange ideas within their departments and across grade levels, enriching their practices and fostering a supporting professional learning community."[32]

Focusing on challenges and dilemmas

Another way to consider learning about assessment literacy is through the lens of challenges and dilemmas. For example, during a recent professional learning webinar with teachers and school and district leaders, the topic of grading came up.[33] A teacher shared the following comment in the chat: "We have a lot of testing because of the amount of points the teachers are required to meet each 9 weeks. Then all the progress monitoring required."

The requirement to grade so many pieces of work every nine weeks was clearly a source of frustration to this teacher, and something that she felt was getting in the way of her ability to make greater use of formative assessment practices. She expressed her desire to know more about what other districts did, asking, "How many points do different districts require each quarter?" Because she was thinking about a very district-specific requirement, her question was pragmatic, but missed the opportunity to more broadly consider how her district was approaching grading.

This teacher's grading question is relevant to a survey that Christopher DeLuca conducted with teachers about assessment challenges that they faced. He worked with them to reframe those challenges as dilemmas through collaborative reflection on how a specific challenge connects to, aligns, or misaligns with broader assessment and teaching beliefs, theories, policies and norms.[34] Dilemmas offer the option of trying out different approaches to find a resolution, and commonly fall into one of four nested categories: conceptual, pedagogical, cultural, and political.[35] In the context of assessment literacy, a conceptual dilemma is related to the underlying knowledge aspect of assessment literacy that a teacher requires, while a pedagogical dilemma is related to the ways in which a teacher might put that assessment knowledge into practice. A cultural dilemma moves the focus from beyond the teacher to one that involves other participants in the assessment process, including students, parents and caregivers, or other colleagues. The political dilemma is the most far-reaching, and can provide opportunities to explore questions that relate to the broader community of those involved in assessment, particularly those making policy decisions. Situating a specific challenge in one of these dilemma categories can prompt strategies or solutions that could be experimented with.

Applying this dilemma framework to reconsidering the teacher's grading challenge, we can see that each of the dilemmas could open up different lines of inquiry and suggest different next steps:

Conceptual dilemma: how do we think differently about formative and summative assessment as they relate to grading?

Pedagogical dilemma: how do we incorporate formative assessment practices into our units of instruction while also ensuring that we generate summative assessment information at the end of every marking period for grading purposes?

Cultural dilemma: how do we change school culture and parent attitudes toward grading and the different purposes of assessment?

Political dilemma: how do we understand the underlying concerns of district leadership and the problems they are trying to address by mandating the number of graded pieces of work every nine weeks?

Had the teacher been helped to reframe her question into one or more of these dilemmas, it could have resulted in a much longer inquiry into grading, with different approaches and collaborators involved. This dilemma could have motivated the teacher to engage in an inquiry that was personally meaningful to her in a collaborative manner, since a solution would require input and buy-in from many others. Additional learning resources to inform her inquiry might have included focusing on deepening her own knowledge base about formative and summative assessment, thinking with peers about how to apply that knowledge base to specific units of instruction, preparing to engage in broader discussions with students and families about grading, and having conversations with school and district leadership to understand their perspectives on grading and working collaboratively with them to bring the practices more in line with best grading practices.

USING ASSESSMENT AUDITS TO DEVELOP OWNERSHIP AND AGENCY

Ownership and agency are significant elements of professional learning and can be enhanced when professional learning is treated as an inquiry process—for instance, when teachers bring their problems of practice to a professional learning community for exploration, reflection, and feedback. There are times when school and district leadership might identify areas of professional learning for which they have evidence of a systemwide need. In this event, the leadership should maintain an inquiry stance that supports teachers acting as problem-solvers rather than recipients of expert knowledge.[36]

An example of an inquiry in response to teachers' feeling overwhelmed by the number assessments that they are expected to administer beyond their required curriculum-embedded assessments is an assessment-system audit undertaken in collaboration with school and district leaders. An assessment system includes all the state-required annual achievement tests, school- and/or district-required assessments, classroom summative assessments used for grading purposes, and also classroom formative assessment practices. In other words, the assessment system represents the assessment experiences of a student in a particular grade across multiple subject areas. An *assessment system audit* involves examining the assessments that a student completes in a year, asking whether they are the right assessments, if they are being used for the right purpose, or if adjustments might be necessary. The audit typically involves both an accounting of assessments (which assessments are being used) and an evaluation of those assessments. The initial focus is likely to start with convergent assessments: those that play a more summative role, focusing on whether students have learned specific aspects of grade-level standards.

Leaders in one school district discovered through conducting an audit that the process of asking questions about what assessments were administered for what purpose gave teachers the opportunity and agency to voice their concerns. As a leader observed: "And what we found from these discussions is that schools did these [district mandated] assessments, but they did not use the data. They didn't find it useful. They didn't know how to interpret the data. So what we found is they did the assessments, but then they would turn around and they would do other assessments that they felt useful for their instruction."

By giving teachers the forum to voice concerns, district leaders were able to respond and make significant changes to their assessment requirements, removing the unused district-mandated assessment and building on the assessments that the teachers had developed for their own use.[37]

An assessment system audit may not initially strike readers as a professional learning opportunity, but empowering teachers to ask questions about the components of an assessment system can be an impactful learning experience. To engage in the process thoughtfully requires collaboration among teachers and leaders to develop a clear understanding of the assessment purpose, use, and user of each assessment. The evaluation component necessitates an understanding of what quality assessment evidence is as well as the information needs of various users in the system. Many of the statements in table 1.1 that describe the components required for fair and justice-oriented assessment practices can be turned into questions for an assessment audit. The discussion associated with each of those questions will provide learning opportunities for the participants. For example, asking whether the district-mandated end-of-semester assessment is aligned with meaningful and challenging learning goals requires several layers of analysis to (1) determine whether the instructional goals are of sufficiently high quality; (2) examine the alignment between the rigor and complexity of the learning goals and the assessment; and (3) identify whether any of the learning goals are under- or overrepresented in the assessment.

Considering assessment interpretation entails asking if teachers have access to the kinds of assessment strategies that allow for insights into student thinking to inform daily instructional interactions that are targeted to specific content and skills. In addition, going beyond classroom teachers as users of information, an assessment audit also requires consideration of whether school and district leaders have information that can be aggregated across classrooms or schools to monitor student learning—for example, to help evaluate the impact of a new reading curriculum, or inform an evaluation of summer professional learning focused on mathematical practices. It also requires considering whether teachers are using assessments that fairly evaluate student learning at certain points in time to report to parents/caregivers and students about student achievement of state content standards.

There are common issues that often come to light from such an audit: the use of too many assessments, duplicative assessments, assessment approaches not matched to instructional or monitoring needs, assessments that do not adequately address the depth of the standards, or a mismatch between the kinds of ambitious teaching practices described in chapter 2 and the assessments being used. A critical component of any kind of evaluation, then, is to move from evaluation to an action plan that is clearly communicated to all of those likely to be impacted by change. Thinking about the end point actually informs who should be part of the review process. A school or district team that brings a variety of perspectives and understandings is essential.

Peer observation to embed changes into practice

Across many projects that we both have been involved in over the years, we often hear from teachers that one of the most powerful learning opportunities is being able to visit each other's classrooms, since so much teaching happens in isolation from other teachers behind closed doors. One of the ways to maximize the likelihood of value from classroom observations, so that they are not just interesting visits, is to use the observation as a source of evidence to inform deliberate practice as a means of professional learning.

As part of a year of professional learning in a California school district, the school leadership decided to reinstate classroom walkthroughs for teachers, an activity that they had been doing before COVID-19.[38] As the focus on the professional learning was on formative assessment, the leaders of the professional development created a walkthrough protocol that included teacher and student look-fors, organized by dimensions of formative assessment practice. The language in the protocol echoed the language used during the professional learning opportunities throughout the year.

The postobservation debrief was intended to be descriptive, not evaluative, of observed practices. It was structured to focus first on what participants noticed in terms of student and teacher actions related to formative assessment, and then on questions that the observers had about their colleagues' practice. The final reflection was for individual teachers to consider implications for their own formative assessment practice. We observed in later professional learning sessions that the teachers made frequent references back to things they learned from these walkthroughs, both in terms of insights about how mathematics was taught at other grade levels and how that understanding impacted earlier grade levels, and different formative assessment practices that could be more widely adopted in the school across grade levels.

At each professional learning opportunity, teachers had individual action plans or journal documents in which they could think about what they had learned since the last meeting. Those action plans also included reminders to teachers to reflect on what they had observed from the walkthroughs and how it might inform their own future formative assessment practice.

An alternative approach to classroom walkthroughs is more teacher-directed observation requests with a focus on a specific aspect of practice, supporting teacher agency by directing the observation to an area for feedback. An observation protocol with a more defined set of rubrics can support this form of deliberate practice.[39] Observations can be done in person or from a video recording. For instance, a teacher might ask for feedback that focuses on the way in which she starts and ends a lesson using the presentation and discussion of learning goals to provide a road map for students. The observed teacher can reflect on the lesson in conjunction with the peer feedback, make some decisions about future practice, then ask for another observation for additional feedback on the refinements. Observers also benefit from the process of providing feedback.[40]

While the specific structures of walkthroughs can vary by resources available, opportunities to observe and be observed are beneficial for teachers. Engaging in these experiences in the broader context of school-embedded professional development learning communities in which teachers identify challenges and dilemmas to problem-solve and learn together supports meaningful professional learning. We focus in chapter 9 on the role of leaders to support these kinds of teacher learning practices.

A FINAL THOUGHT

We began this chapter with an example of a teacher who was initially daunted by the learning that she needed to do, but had the support she needed to embark on her journey. While this chapter has explored ways to support teacher learning, we end with an observation about the importance of not minimizing the complexity of the process.

Johann Hari writes about the challenges of dwindling attention spans arising from the ubiquitous access to online information through multiple digital devices, and how those on online worlds are structured. He describes many of the proffered solutions to these attention-span challenges as nothing more than *cruel optimism,* which is "when you take a really big problem with deep causes in our culture—like obesity or depression, or addiction—and you offer people, in upbeat language, a simplistic individual solution."[41] Too often teacher learning is also treated as a challenge with simplistic solutions. For instance, schools attempt to provide a "one-size-fits-all" approach that does not take account of how adults learn, or the varying needs represented in any group of teachers. They also consider professional learning as the responsibility of individual teachers to participate in on their own time, or present options do not fit well with the teachers' current contexts.

To enable teachers to engage in collaborative, rich problem-solving approaches to support their learning requires a strategy that is not grounded in cruel optimism, that does not assume teachers will squeeze in some professional learning on their own time, but rather builds learning opportunities into the school day in meaningful ways. However, to do this requires school and district leaders to make a commitment, both financial and practical, to this form of professional learning. A teacher recently described a particular type of professional learning that she found incredibly valuable because it included collaboratively examining student work with colleagues.[42] She contrasted her positive experience with what had been her more typical experience of professional learning time being hijacked by school leaders for communications that "should have been in email." Throughout this book, our aim is to present an antidote to cruel optimism.

SUMMARY: KEY TAKEAWAYS

- Assessment literacy expertise encompasses more than knowing about types of assessment, including the ability to implement and use a wide range of assessment practices, and to adjust them to the content, students, and context of the learning.
- These skills are necessary so that teachers can adapt instruction and assessment to meet specific student needs, elevate students' ways of knowing and doing, notice and meet the needs of all students in a classroom, and be reflective on how one's own personal experiences impact classroom practice.
- Assessment literacy knowledge and skills are acquired starting with preservice experiences and extend throughout a teacher's career.
- Effective professional learning must: (1) provide teachers with insight about teaching and learning, (2) motivate teachers to make changes to their practice, (3) provide techniques for putting these insights to work, and (4) enable teachers to embed change in practice.
- School-based professional learning communities provide a site for collaborative learning among teachers, and often require leadership support to help protect the learning time.
- Critical elements of professional learning community meetings include mechanisms that support teachers to engage in deliberate practice of new ideas, together with feedback, reflection, and action-planning.

CHAPTER 5

Learning Goals: Assessment Literacy Knowledge and Skills

Learning goals specify the aims of teaching and learning and are a prerequisite for assessment design.[1] *Success criteria* describe the performances that indicate that students have met the learning goal. Learning goals and success criteria work in unison to clarify and communicate the intended learning that teachers and students should pursue, and how they will assess success along the way, or at the end of a more or less extended period of instruction.[2]

We described in the preface that assessment literacy means having the ability to engage in a chain of reasoning. Identifying learning goals and success criteria is the first step in this chain of reasoning. Once the goals are clearly defined, next in the assessment process is designing a means for obtaining evidence of student learning relative to the goals. The end point of the chain is interpreting the evidence and then taking asset-based and future-oriented actions to advance student learning. This process is always applicable regardless of the differing contexts, purposes, and timescales of assessment.[3]

Learning goals will differ in grain size and scope depending on the duration of the specific instructional and assessment cycle. Noted assessment expert Dylan Wiliam describes three instruction/assessment cycles spanning different time scales: (1) short-cycle, which take place within and between lessons and occur day-by-day (twenty-four to forty-eight hours) and minute-by-minute (five seconds to two hours); (2) medium-cycle, which occur within and between teaching units and last for one to four weeks; (3) long-cycle, which span units and terms, with a length of four weeks to one year.[4] To help ensure coherence among the assessments of different time scales, learning goals are derived from standards and equity-centered curricula, and based on a vision of learning that reflects modern conceptions of knowing and learning (see chapter 2).[5]

In chapter 3 we introduced the concept of the divergent and convergent classification of assessment. Short-cycle assessments are primarily divergent because, in the main, they are used to provide insights into students' current learning status to guide immediate or near-immediate instructional actions. In a medium cycle, a unit assessment might be both convergent and divergent: convergent in that it could be used to determine what students had achieved at the end of the unit to assign a grade, and divergent because teachers might use the information to plan subsequent units. Long-cycle assessments can be considered as primarily convergent because their purpose is to find out the status of student achievement—for example, the end-of-year state tests in relation to grade-level standards.

Since this book is primarily concerned with the development of teachers' assessment literacy, we devote this chapter to what teachers need to know and be able to do with respect to creating learning goals for the convergent and divergent classroom assessments that they use, and how they can develop that knowledge and skillset. However, as we saw in chapter 3, teachers will likely be required to use a wide array of assessments that are external to their classroom (for example, district assessments). We address assessment literacy competencies with respect to these assessments later in chapter 8.

By way of laying a foundation for thinking about how teachers approach creating learning goals, we begin with examples of how two teachers created learning goals from standards to author ambitious teaching practices described in chapter 2. After these examples, we outline the knowledge and skills that teachers need for creating learning goals and success criteria. Then, drawing on the approaches for teacher learning in assessment literacy in chapter 4, we consider ways in which teachers can develop the knowledge and skills for developing and reviewing learning goals and success criteria for classroom assessment.

PLANNING LEARNING GOALS

This section describes how two teachers, one high school and one elementary school, planned learning goals, instruction, and the assessment of the goals.

High school social studies teacher

Mary Helen Diegel teaches history to a very diverse tenth-grade class comprised of African American, Arab American, Asian American, Hispanic, and White students. Many of her students' home languages are not English, and there are several students in the class who are designated as having special educational needs.

For this particular unit, which occurred at the beginning of the school year, Ms. Diegel started her planning by identifying a cluster of her state's standards that address both content and analytical practices that she will teach in the unit.

Content Standards

- Understand political and intellectual transformations of America to 1877.
- Identify the core ideals of American society as reflected in the documents below and analyze the ways that American society moved toward and/or away from its core ideals:
  - Declaration of Independence
  - The US Constitution (including the Preamble)
  - Bill of Rights
  - The Gettysburg Address
  - Thirteenth, Fourteenth, and Fifteenth Amendments

Analytical Practice Standards

- Compare and contrast treatments of the same topic in several primary and secondary sources.
- Draw evidence from informational texts to support analysis, reflection, and research.

As she thought about planning learning goals from the standards, she was guided by the Inquiry Arc included in *The College, Career, and Civic Life Framework for Social Studies: Guidance for Enhancing the Rigor of K-12 Civics, Economics, Geography, and History* (C3 Framework).[6] The C3 Inquiry Arc, which is consistent with ambitious teaching practices, is a set of interlocking and mutually reinforcing dimensions to frame the way students learn social studies:

1. Developing questions and planning inquiries.
2. Applying disciplinary concepts and tools.

3. Evaluating sources and using evidence.
4. Communicating conclusions and taking informed action.

From her analysis of the content standards, she identified five core ideas of American society: democracy, equality, rights, liberty, and opportunity. She wanted her students to investigate how these ideas are represented in the documents specified in the content standards, and consider how they have evolved since those documents were first written. As Ms. Diegel explained, "I knew some of these core ideas would be a key interest for students, especially with contentious current events flooding their social media." The unit would consist of four lessons, each one lasting for approximately three class periods.

In line with the C3 Inquiry Arc's dimensions, Ms. Diegel framed a compelling question to drive the students' inquiry for the unit: "How successfully has the United States upheld the core democratic values over time?" This question represented the overall goal for the unit and would require students to engage in the analytical practices of examining and interpreting primary and secondary sources that related to different turning points in US history, such as the Voting Rights Act of 1965. To expand the goal and deepen the inquiry, Ms. Diegel planned to pose the supporting question: "What lessons have we learned from the past that we can apply to what is happening today?" The framing of the compelling and supporting questions was intended to help students increase the sophistication of their skills in evaluating and analyzing evidentiary sources, and in understanding the complexities of sustaining core democratic values.

She then determined the following success criteria for their inquiry, which would form the basis for her divergent assessment throughout the lessons of the unit, and also give students guidance for their own self-assessment of progress:

- Show evidence of analyzing each primary and secondary source.
  - Describe the key ideas of each event (think about the who, what, when, where, why, and how).
  - Explain how each event demonstrates a core democratic value, and why it is important to American society.
  - Explain in what way does the event illustrate how the core democratic value has been supported or weakened.

Ms. Diegel then thought about how to break the content down into manageable chunks that students could investigate based on a progression of learning. By creating this progression, Ms. Diegel noted that "students could focus on key elements and build on their previous learning without getting overwhelmed." In lessons 1 and 2, the students would analyze the Declaration of Independence and the Constitution, with Ms. Diegel modeling how to analyze documents and notate their findings. In lesson 3, the students would dissect historical primary and secondary sources in eight different stations. In lesson 4, students would work in smaller groups to research present-day topics related to the historical issues they had previously investigated.

Then she planned the short-cycle, divergent assessment opportunities related to the goal and success criteria during each class period as students were working individually or in small groups. These included, for example, questions or prompts such as "What is your thinking about this event/image/excerpt? Tell me more. How does this event reflect the core democratic value? What evidence shows this? How does it connect to today? How does it connect to the historical events you analyzed earlier? Why is this important? How does this show how successful the United States has been in upholding the core democratic value(s)?" At the end of each class period, Ms. Diegel planned to provide some reflection time for students prompted by a range of questions, including "What helped you understand the ideas?," "How might you further your understanding of the ideas?," "What are some ways to improve your analysis?," "What worked well?," and "What needs improvement?" Student responses would inform her ongoing instruction, and also guide students' own next steps.

From the outset of their investigation, students knew that the end-of-unit assessment (medium cycle) would be a presentation of their research findings communicated through a choice of a digital poster, a movie, an essay, or an art piece. Ms. Diegel noted that "students reported they felt more excited to engage in the work knowing they could demonstrate the change over time in different modalities." For scoring purposes, each student would rate their work on a four-point scale and provide an explanation for their rating. Ms. Diegel also planned to rate the students' work and give feedback to each student. Those students who did not achieve the highest level would have the chance to revise their work.

Elementary mathematics lesson[7]

Gabriela Cárdenas teaches a class of third-grade students who all have Mexican or Central American backgrounds, and most of them are classified as English learners. She is planning to teach this mathematics standard:

> Interpret whole-number quotients of whole numbers, e.g., interpret 56 ÷ 8 as the number of objects in each share when 56 objects are partitioned equally into 8 shares, or as a number of shares when 56 objects are partitioned into equal shares of 8 objects each. *For example, describe a context in which a number of shares or a number of groups can be expressed as 56 ÷ 8.* (Italics added.)

She first determined that the core idea of the standard is dividing groups into equal parts, which will build on students' prior understanding of multiplication as combining equal groups to find the total number of objects. Ms. Cárdenas wanted to introduce division to her students as partitioning a total into equal groups. Her thinking about the learning goal and success criteria was informed by two questions: What are the students going to learn in this lesson (over three class periods)?, and What are they going to do that will show evidence of their learning?

She formulated the learning goal for the lesson, which she will discuss with the students, like this: "As mathematicians, we are learning how to partition a whole into equal parts and explain our solutions." Notice how she begins the goal with the phrase *as mathematicians*. This is a very deliberate practice for all learning goals in mathematics because she wants her students to develop identities as individuals who can do mathematics. Next, she thought about the success criteria—what students will say, do, make, or write that indicates they are meeting the learning goal. She sets a lot of store on students being able to explain their thinking as both a means for their sense-making in mathematics, and to provide her with evidence of their learning status. Ms. Cárdenas also uses students' models and representations for supporting their understanding and, again, for providing evidence. Along these lines, she identified three success criteria that will guide her in eliciting evidence as students are engaged in problem solving:

- I can model and explain how a whole can be partitioned into equal shares.
- I can describe the unit for the equal parts that make up the whole.
- I can represent and explain why the unit fraction matches the equal parts.

Ms. Cárdenas explains her thinking about success criteria as follows: "Students are invited to model, describe, and represent their understanding of the problem in the way that makes sense to them. When the success criteria are open-ended, students do not feel forced to show evidence of understanding using a set approach or specific set of strategies. This allows me to see where the student is in their thinking, and helps students see themselves as doers of mathematics."

Notice, too, how these criteria are formulated as statements for the students to assess how their understanding is developing as they are working on a task. Before the students engage in problem solving, Ms. Cárdenas will discuss the criteria with the students to ensure they fully understand what meeting them entails. She will also draw students' attention to the criteria throughout the lesson, so that they do not lose track of their intended learning.

Once Ms. Cárdenas determined the lesson goal and success criteria, she thought about the context for the partitioning problem that she wants the students to solve. Because of their cultural backgrounds, most, if not all, of her students will be familiar with a quinceañera, the celebration of a girl's fifteenth birthday, so she decided to relate the problem to ordering tables for that event, given the total number of guests and the number that can be seated at each table. As she says, "Using this event for problem solving will help my students see themselves reflected as someone who does mathematics and will also help them see that mathematics is everywhere around us."

Ms. Cárdenas also planned to give students a choice of which numbers they can use for the problem. She and the students refer to these as the "just right numbers" and they have jointly developed a set of criteria that they use to choose numbers that are at the right level for them–not too easy and not too challenging. For this problem they are invited to select one of these number pairs, where the first number is the total guest count and the second the number of guests seated at each table, that they think is the most appropriate for them:

(36, 6) (63, 3) (85, 5)

Of course, Ms. Cárdenas monitors the choice of numbers very closely, but finds that the students generally select what is right for each of them.

After an initial class discussion of the problem, she intends to invite the students to solve the problem in a way that makes sense to them, using their choice of manipulatives, drawings, diagrams, or conversations with their peers. As they work, Ms. Cárdenas plans to intentionally observe the students' solutions and ask questions to obtain evidence of their thinking, such as "Can you tell me why you used this strategy?," "Can you explain your thinking to me?," or "How well do you think you are meeting the success criteria?" Based on the evidence from these divergent assessment opportunities, she plans to make in-the-moment decisions about when to intervene to support student thinking.

One feature of every lesson that she will also include in this one is for students to share their solutions with a peer, receive feedback, and then make revisions as they deem fit. She will also use these peer feedback conversations as another source of evidence about student thinking related to the goal. An additional lesson feature she also plans to use at the end of the lesson after she has reviewed the success criteria with the class is students' individual self-assessment of how well they have met the goal, based on this protocol:

- I've got it!
- I need more practice.
- I need more time.
- I need to work with a partner to get this right.
- I need help from my teacher.[8]

With this background on learning goals and success criteria and how they specify the aims of teaching, learning, and classroom assessment, we now turn to a consideration of the knowledge and skills that teachers need to be able to develop effective learning goals and related success criteria.

KNOWLEDGE AND SKILLS FOR LEARNING GOALS AND SUCCESS CRITERIA

In chapter 1, we noted that to be consistent with advances in the learning sciences assessment should encompass three dimensions of learning and development: cognitive, cultural, and socio-emotional. These dimensions need to be considered when teachers are creating learning goals for their own assessment practices; otherwise, opportunities for fair and justice-oriented assessment are diminished.

Returning to the two prior examples, we saw how the teachers created goals that integrated cognitive, cultural, and socio-emotional dimensions of learning. From the cognitive perspective, Ms. Diegel's learning goal incorporated the distinct ways of knowing and reasoning specific to a discipline, supporting students to behave like historians, experiencing history as a process of investigating questions, and constructing interpretations of historical events from reading primary and secondary sources. The cultural and socio-emotional perspectives were integrated with the cognitive because students were able to select a current event to investigate that was important to them personally, such as racism, discrimination, or the wealth gap. They were able to use their own lived experiences to help them with their analysis of past and present, and had agency over how they would demonstrate their learning at the end of the unit. As a result, students would perceive the goal as worthwhile and relevant, a factor contributing to their motivation.

In terms of a cognitive perspective, the learning goal and success criteria that Ms. Cárdenas established for the lesson were appropriately challenging for all students, and they were situated within a progression of learning so that they built on students' prior knowledge (of multiplication). The goal and criteria also prompted an apprentice-style approach to learning mathematics, reflected first in her statement "As mathematicians, we are . . . ," which from a socio-emotional perspective positioned the students as competent doers of mathematics. In terms of the cultural dimension, Ms. Cárdenas tailored the problem-solving context of the goal to make connections to students' lived experiences and funds of knowledge (a quinceañera), elevating and legitimating the students' linguistic, cultural, and substantive practices.

DEVELOPING THE KNOWLEDGE AND SKILLS

In this section we focus first on how teachers can acquire knowledge of the cognitive, cultural, and socio-emotional dimensions for learning goals, and second on how they can develop and refine their skills to integrate this knowledge into learning goals.

Table 5.1 below presents a summary of the knowledge and skills that teachers need related to the cognitive, cultural, and socio-emotional dimensions of learning and development in order to create fair and justice-oriented learning goals for instruction and assessment.

In the next section, we elaborate on ways in which teachers can develop their knowledge outlined in table 5.1.

Cognitive dimension

Knowledge of the cognitive dimension entails deeply knowing standards, curriculum, and learning progressions within a discipline. Pointing to the value of teachers working together to deepen their understanding of the standards they

TABLE 5.1 A summary of knowledge and skills for developing learning goals

Learning goals and success criteria are rigorous, high quality, meaningful, and challenging for students. They are informed both by a trajectory of learning (building on prior knowledge) and by disciplinary knowledge including how students learn.[a]	
Cognitive	• Knowledge of standards, curriculum, and learning progressions within a discipline • Knowledge of distinct ways of knowing/reasoning specific to a discipline and how students come to learn these distinct ways • Skills in creating worthwhile and rigorous learning goals, aligned to standards, progressions, or curriculum materials that challenge each student based on their current learning status
Learning goals and success criteria that integrate the cultural dimension of assessment are informed by local circumstances and students' lived experiences and funds of knowledge.[b]	
Cultural	• Knowledge of students' family/community beliefs, values, culture • Knowledge of students' interests and gifts they bring to the classroom • Skills in leveraging this knowledge to create learning goals that connect to students' lived experience and that support students gaining insight into experiences different from their own
Learning goals and success criteria that integrate the socio-emotional dimension of assessment foster identity development, motivation, and self-regulated learning.[c]	
Socio-emotional	• Knowledge of self-regulation, metacognition, motivation, and self-efficacy and their impact on development • In-depth knowledge of students emotionally • Skills in leveraging these constructs when making decisions about learning goals (e.g., will student be motivated by this goal; will all students be able to access this goal?) • Skills in creating goals that apprentice students to the discipline (e.g., behaving as a mathematician/writer, etc.)

[a] Lorrie A. Shepard, "Ambitious Teaching and Equitable Assessment: A Vision for Prioritizing Learning, Not Testing," *American Educator* (Fall 2021): 28–48, https://files.eric.ed.gov/fulltext/EJ1321974.pdf; David P. Ausubel, *Educational Psychology: A Cognitive View* (Holt, Rinehart, and Winston, 1968); Paola Sztajn, Jere Confrey, P. Holt Wilson, and Cynthia Edgington, "Learning Trajectory Based Instruction: Toward a Theory of Teaching," *Educational Researcher* 41, no. 5 (2012): 147–56, https://doi.org/10.3102/0013189X12442801; National Academies of Sciences, Engineering, and Medicine, *How People Learn II: Learners, Contexts, and Cultures* (The National Academies Press, 2018), https://doi.org/10.17226/24783.

[b] Kris D. Gutiérrez and Barbara Rogoff, "Cultural Ways of Learning," in *Knowledge, Values and Educational Policy: A Critical Perspective*, ed. Harry Daniels, Hugh Lauder, and Jill Porter (Routledge, 2009); Luis C. Moll and James B. Greenberg, "Creating Zones of Possibilities: Combining Social Contexts for Instruction," in *Vygotsky and Education: Instructional Implications and Applications of Sociohistorical Psychology* (Cambridge University Press, 1990), 319; National Academies of Sciences, *How People Learn II*.

[c] Carole Ames, "Classrooms: Goals, Structures, and Student Motivation," *Journal of Educational Psychology* 84, no. 3 (September 1992): 261–71, https://doi.org/10.1037/0022-0663.84.3.261; Mary Helen Immordino-Yang and Antonio Damasio, "We Feel, Therefore We Learn: The Relevance of Affective and Social Neuroscience to Education," *Mind, Brain, and Education* 1, no. 1 (March 2007): 3–10, https://doi.org/10.1111/j.1751-228X.2007.00004.x.

are required to teach, Australian researchers Valentina Klenowski and Claire Wyatt-Smith suggest that "standards provide a common set of stated reference points for teacher use, and acquire meaning through use over time. This is because standards, written as verbal descriptors, require interpretation and application within a community of practice."[9] Notice that these researchers stress that the standards acquire meaning over time, clearly indicating that understanding the standards is not a one-off activity. Teachers and those who support them cannot claim to have "done the standards" after one or several sessions of professional learning. Rather, over time teachers use their professional learning community (see chapter 4) to interpret the standards and how they are applying them to teaching and learning. Collaboratively, teachers can analyze a standard or cluster of standards to determine the outcomes contained in the standards, and how they build incrementally within the grade level and from one grade level to the next. We saw an example of this practice in chapter 2 when Dr. Wendy Johnson and her colleagues broke down three science performance expectations related to a core idea in science into five chunks of learning that would progress in a connected way over the course of the unit. They also referenced a research-based learning progression to inform the order of the chunks. After teaching the unit, Dr. Johnson and her colleagues could reflect on the progression they had identified to determine if changes needed to be made to it for future teaching. This kind of analysis and reflection can be an ongoing activity for a professional learning community to increase teachers' knowledge of the standards so that the learning goals they develop for teaching, learning and assessment are of sufficient depth and rigor to author ambitious teaching practices described in chapter 2.

Klenowski and Wyatt-Smith's point of view on standards can be applied to curriculum as well. Even if learning goals are provided in the curricular materials, teachers can benefit from analyzing how the concepts, skills, and analytic practices progress so as to deepen their understanding of what they are to teach and what students are to learn. With a knowledge of standards, teachers can also consider if the curriculum is sufficiently aligned to them, or if learning goals need to be refined or revised to guide ambitious teaching. Reflecting on the goals in a professional learning community after teaching a lesson or a unit can help teachers strengthen their curriculum knowledge, their understanding of what learning the curriculum content entails, and whether future learning goals for the lesson or unit need to be modified.

We know from learning science research that learning with understanding is facilitated when new and existing knowledge is structured around the major ideas and principles of the discipline.[10] For this reason, disciplinary knowledge is foundational to the cognitive dimension for constructing learning goals. Disciplinary knowledge involves knowing that each discipline has its own structure that represents interrelated core ideas and specific modes of inquiry. For example, in history students may consider core ideas such as power and how societies organize themselves for the purpose of government. In the study of literature, students consider the core ideas of theme, character, and plot.[11] These core ideas recur so that students encounter them at different levels of sophistication across their school experience. The structure of a discipline also determines the inquiry skills that are important and how students should learn and apply them. For instance, students need to learn how to estimate in mathematics, to make predictions in science, to plan their writing, and to recognize specific text structures while reading.[12]

Teachers need to understand the core ideas of the discipline they are teaching and how the ideas connect to one another. In the context of a professional learning community, examining standards or the curriculum to identify the core ideas that inhere within them, and how inquiries are carried out, can help teachers deepen their understanding of disciplinary structure and the central inquiry approaches and habits of mind that students need to develop. In a learning community, more veteran and expert teachers can serve as mentors to their less experienced colleagues to help them expand their disciplinary knowledge.

Also, reading and discussing documents about disciplinary core ideas and inquiry from professional organizations such as the National Council of Teachers of Mathematics, the National Science Teachers Association, the National Council for the Social Studies, and the National Council of Teachers of English can be a useful strategy for identifying important core ideas in a discipline and how students come to learn them.

Cultural dimension

Before teachers can incorporate students'cultural background, including their funds of knowledge, into either lesson or unit goals, they must have some familiarity with the communities to which their students belong. Leaders can assist their teacher colleagues to develop a deep understanding of the local community and the students they are teaching by providing time for them to take neighborhood learning walks, to participate in community events, to lead parent and student focus groups, to engage in informal meetings with parents, and to patronize local restaurants. Providing time for this knowledge building would be a valuable investment for the individual teacher and for the school as a whole. Teachers could pool information to create a deeper and fuller picture of the communities that they serve. In this regard, one group of high school teachers found that driving around the area where their students lived, visiting local stores, places of worship, and locations of community events, helped create a resource they could use to tailor learning goals to their students' lived experiences. This group of teachers also used the first week of school exclusively to get to know their students and to find out about the students' out-of-school interests and activities.

A more involved project, possibly undertaken over several years, could entail teachers working together in a professional learning community to create an ethnography of their school community, drawing on interviews with families and community leaders about the demographics of the area, families' roots, languages, religious observances, food, and local industry and businesses, for example. Once completed, it might need updating every year, but it would serve as a valuable resource, particularly for new teachers or teachers new to the area.

Another practice that assists teachers to understand their students' cultural background and funds of knowledge is an early parent-teacher conference. One school we have worked with conducts these "intake" conferences in the first few weeks of the new school year with the objective of understanding what their students' parents value about their culture and community, and what they want the teacher to know about their child.[13]

Reading about methods that other teachers have used to understand their students' funds of knowledge can also be a valuable activity in a professional learning community. For example, the Michigan Assessment Consortium's work on model assessment systems provides rich portraits of early literacy development and assessment that illustrates what it means to understand students' funds of knowledge.[14] In these examples, activities such as family picnics, home visits, "all about me" activities, family phone calls, and a neighborhood bus tour are described in accessible langauge. Such resources can act as a springboard for teachers to collectively share what they know about their students' funds of knowledge, and develop local strategies for enhancing their knowledge.

Moisès Esteban-Guitart and Luis Moll expanded on the original concept of funds of knowledge to include funds of identity, defined as "historically-accumulated, culturally-developed and socially-distributed resources that are essential for people's self-definition, self-expression and self-understanding."[15] To a greater or lesser degree, students may incorporate elements from their family's and community's funds of knowledge in the construction of their identity—for instance, the language, the people, and the experiences that they consider significant and that define and characterize them.[16] They may also incorporate other elements in their self-definition that are not drawn from their families and communities, such as their hobbies, their musical preferences, and their friendship groups.

Students' funds of identities can be explored by inviting students to produce identity artifacts that can help deepen teachers' understanding of who their students are and what defines them. For instance, one strategy is for students to create an autobiography through a self-portrait. Students are asked to draw who they think they are right now. Those who are reluctant to draw can choose other ways to represent who they are such as symbols, words, or phrases. If they wish, they can add what for them are the most significant, important things, people, places, and institutions. In the case of younger students, the emphasis is on the things, people and places they like the most.[17] Discussing these portraits with individual students would provide further insights into how they self-identify, and what they value. Imagine the depth of conversations that teachers and students could have if these autobiographies were a focus during the getting-to-know-you first week of school. Another strategy is to invite students to create "all about me" books called *My Compass Guide*, which include personal and familial research, hopes and dreams, maps of family birthplaces, and special stories about parents/caregivers and living or ancestral grandparents.[18] Students share their unique books with their teachers and peers to provide insights for teachers about their students, and to build confidence and self-awareness among students.

The importance of taking time to get to know students cannot be overstated. As the high school teacher Ms. Diegel explains, "I've been fortunate to have real conversations with students about their experiences. I've taken the opportunity to learn about different cultures, traditions, systemic barriers and privileges, learning differences, while finding ways to honor each student's talents and funds of knowledge." The work described in this section will pay off as teachers work to increase the connections between academic learning goals and students' identities, families, and communities.

Socio-emotional dimension

A confluence of recent research and experience makes it clear that children learn best when their socio-emotional needs, as well as academic ones, are attended to.[19] While teachers have always been concerned about the well-being of their students, there is a renewed imperative for them to know about the socio-emotional facets of their students. These facets also bear on the broader goals of schooling, which call for students to develop competencies, such as collaboration, perseverance, setting goals, monitoring learning, problem solving, and understanding different perspectives, all of which are necessary for success in school, careers, and life.[20]

What all of this means for teachers is that they need knowledge about the socio-emotional dimensions of learning and development, particularly in relation to the constructs of self-regulation, metacognition, motivation, and self-efficacy, and their impact on learning and development. Self-regulation enables learners to proactively orient their actions to achieving goals—academic, personal, and behavioral.[21] Metacognition involves learners in actively paying attention to their thinking processes while they are working toward a goal, and obtaining internal feedback about their learning status along the way. In the context of classroom learning, motivation can be thought of as wanting to learn, being willing to engage in learning, increasing effort, persisting in the face of challenges, and deriving satisfaction from accomplishing one's goals. Self-efficacy refers to people's beliefs in their capacity to perform actions that lead to accomplishing a specific goal.[22] Each one of these constructs plays a role in academic achievement.[23]

Gaining knowledge about these constructs can be accomplished by reading and discussing articles in a professional learning community. We recognize that teachers are doers and have a preference for spending time thinking about concrete actions that they can take to advance learning. However, our suggestion to read about these constructs does not entail plowing through extensive tomes of research. Instead, district and school leaders can provide resources that address these topics in short but substantive ways, then teachers can consider how they apply to actual classroom practices, share ideas, and learn from one another.

In addition to knowledge of the constructs, teachers also need an in-depth knowledge of their students, socially and emotionally, so that they can make decisions about how to promote the constructs that materially impact academic learning, and equip students to achieve the broader goals of schooling referenced earlier. Knowing about the students' funds of knowledge and their funds of identity will contribute to gaining social and emotional knowledge, but teachers need to go further to create a fully comprehensive picture of their students.

When teachers observe how students interact with one another in the formal setting of the classroom as well as outside—for instance, in the lunch room—they can gain insights into both students' positive and avoidance behaviors and feelings. Observing students' participation and affect in class can also be a source of information about the socio-emotional dimension. Teachers can use simple, brief techniques at the beginning of a lesson to take stock of how students are feeling. For instance, asking them to quickly share something positive they are feeling about the day and something they feel less positive about, or a one-word share around the class about their emotions that day. From their observations and student responses to these techniques, teachers may uncover some issues that they want to follow up about in a deeper one-on-one conversation outside of the classroom context.

Asking students to complete entry and exit tickets before or after a lesson, whether anonymously or with student names, can probe their affective anticipation and response to the lesson. Inviting students to complete periodic surveys at a grade, department, or school level related to how they feel about school can provide expanded information about the socio-emotional dimension and where students stand in relation to the constructs. For instance, a survey could ask questions such as: Which subjects do you feel strong or weak in and why?, What do you do when you feel stuck in your learning?, Do you have friends who care about you at school?, Can you solve conflicts with your friends when they arise?, Do you feel safe with the other students at school?, Do you feel welcome at school?, Do you like going to school?, and Why, or why not? These kinds of questions can be adapted to accommodate more or less sophisticated levels depending on the age of the students.

Similarly, a survey or extensive conversation could be focused on one of the constructs. For example, students could be asked about their motivation: What interests you in school?, What makes you want to learn?, What makes you not want to learn?, What stops or reduces your motivation?, What else would you like me to know about what makes you want to learn?, or How do you like me to help you when you are learning? Again, these questions can be modified according to the grade level of the students. Students will more likely see the value of completing these surveys if teachers demonstrably act on the information and discuss their actions with their students, so that they know that their teachers are being responsive to the information they are providing.

Pooling information with colleagues can augment each teacher's knowledge of their students, and assist them to understand how students feel and behave in different settings. Having conversations with parents about their observations and knowledge of their children can offer points of comparison or difference between social and emotional states at home and at school. Acquiring socio-emotional knowledge about students is not a simple one-time activity. Instead it is a form of continual inquiry that can be updated as teachers gain more information and insights, which they can share among their colleagues.

DEVELOPING SKILLS FOR CREATING LEARNING GOALS.

In chapter 1, we discussed that fair and justice-oriented goals need to address three dimensions of learning and development—cognitive, cultural, and socio-emotional—so that they are: (1) meaningful and challenging for all students; (2) aligned to standards and curriculum and situated in a progression of learning that leads to growing conceptual understanding and analytic practices; (3) reflective of the distinct ways of knowing and reasoning with a specific discipline; (4) informed by students' culture, language, lived experiences, and interests; and (5) worthwhile and motivating to students. Using the sources of knowledge of the three dimensions we have described so far to create and modify learning goals effectively is a continuous process of planning, review, and refinement to ensure that these elements are fully represented and are reflective of who the students are.

Our experience of supporting teachers suggests that it is a tall order for individual teachers to develop these skills on their own, particularly if they are early-career educators. Working with a grade-level peer or collaborating with colleagues in a professional learning community can be productive environments to plan lesson, unit, or end-of-course goals, reflect on their effectiveness, and make future modifications. An equity-oriented curriculum that allows teachers to refine goals to better reflect their students' lived experiences, funds of identity, and motivations can provide foundational support so that teachers do not have to create their own goals from scratch. Teachers who are using the same curriculum materials can examine together whether or not the goals address cognitive, socio-emotional, and cultural dimensions. Identifying some exemplar goals that address the socio-emotional and cultural dimensions can then inform expansions and revisions to learning goals in their curriculum.

There is no single prescription for creating learning goals, but a useful first step for teachers could be to use the knowledge gained from their analysis of standards, from tracing the pathway for learning outlined in a learning progression, and from their examination of the core ideas of the discipline, to identify cognitive goals of an appropriate grain size or chunk, depending on the assessment cycle they are planning for—short, medium, or long. When identifying these chunks of learning, it will be important to ensure that the goal builds on the students' prior knowledge and reflects the Goldilocks principle: it should be matched to the current edge of student learning so that it is appropriately challenging, not too easy and not too hard. In this regard, the goal or goals need to contribute to, not undermine, students' feelings of self-efficacy such that they are willing to persist with a challenge and not give up in the face of any difficulty. The goal or goals also need to feed forward so that they are a component of growth toward later outcomes. For example, in chapter 2 we saw how Wendy Johnson planned a series of lessons about air particles that laid the foundation for a more sophisticated level of understanding about specific molecules in air, and how atoms are rearranged in chemical reactions to make new molecules.

The goal will then need to be shaped so that it resonates with the students' funds of knowledge and their personal funds of identity. Again, teachers can draw on their accumulating knowledge of their students for this purpose. They can also use this knowledge to decide if they think their students would be motivated by the goal. For example, an eighth-grade teacher set the goal as "understand art as a form of storytelling," which was connected to the visual literacy strand of her district's art curriculum. Many of the students' families had roots in Mexico and the teacher knew that quite a few of her students had visited relatives in various parts of that country. So to make connections to their Mexican heritage, and to broaden the cultural understanding of those students who did not share that heritage, she contextualized the unit goal as "understand art as a form of storytelling in the works of the Mexican Muralism Movement." Based on her knowledge of

Callout Box A

Questions to Guide the Development of Learning Goals

- Are the goals aligned to the standards, progression, or curricular materials?
- Are they appropriately challenging and rigorous for all students?
- Is it clear from the learning goals what instruction and assessment are aiming for?
- Do they apprentice students to the discipline?
- Do they build on and are they coherent with students' prior academic learning?
- Do they combine cognitive, socio-emotional, and cultural dimensions—for example, by reflecting the students' family- and community-based funds of knowledge, and nurturing students' identities?
- Are they at the appropriate grain size for a course, a unit, or a lesson?
- Will the goals be motivating for students?
- Will the goals author rich learning experiences and equitable assessment opportunities?

her students, she thought this goal would pique their interest and be motivating for them to pursue.[24] The knowledge and interpretive skills related to composition, color, and perspective that the students acquired from this experience would be generalizable to other forms of visual narrative.

Sharing learning goals with peers in a professional learning community, and discussing together ways to incorporate funds of students' funds of knowledge, can strengthen teachers' skills in connecting learning goals to students' lived experiences and their funds of identity.

One final consideration is to make sure that the goals are contributing to students' identity development and self-efficacy by apprenticing them to the discipline. Recall from chapter 2 that as apprentices students learn the models of thought, the practices, and the language of the discipline. This apprenticing aspect was clearly present in Mary Helen Diegel's overall driving question that was the goal for her unit described earlier: "How successfully has the United States upheld the core democratic values over time?" This question requires students to behave like historians by engaging in the analytical practices of examining and interpreting primary and secondary sources. Similarly, Gabriela Cárdenas' lesson goal began with the words "As mathematicians . . . ," a deliberate, consistent practice to contribute to students' identity development, which was followed by a problem-solving goal reflecting the work that mathematicians do. Teachers can use the questions in callout box A to guide them in developing learning goals.

Establishing success criteria

Clarity of criteria is foundational for good assessment no matter whether it is for classroom assessment, including grading, or end-of-year assessment. The Australian scholar Patrick Griffin explains, "Humans can only provide evidence [of their learning] in the form of what they *write, make, do* and *say* [italics added] and it is from these four observable actions that all learning is inferred. This is the basic and fundamental role of assessment—to help interpret observations and infer learning."[25] In other words we can never "see" into a student's head to understand their learning. We can only infer their learning status from what they produce.

Success criteria are an interpretive framework for teachers so that they can draw inferences about student learning in relation to the goal. As we saw in our earlier two-classroom examples, one of Mary Helen Diegel's success criteria in relation to her goal was for students to "explain how each event demonstrates a core democratic value, and why it is important to American society." In Gabriela Cárdenas's lesson, a success criterion was that students "[could] represent and explain why the unit fraction matches the equal parts." From their observations of what students were writing, making, doing, and saying, both teachers would be able to draw inferences in relation to the criteria about their students' learning status from which they could decide on actionable next steps.

In addition to acting as an interpretive framework for teachers, the learning goal and success criteria supply learners with the opportunity to monitor their own learning. They promote student involvement and self-regulation, as well as giving students self-assessment language that they can use to communicate effectively with their teacher and peers about their understanding, reasoning processes, and their skills.[26]

Callout Box B

Questions to Guide the Reflection of Success Criteria

- Are they connected to the learning goal?
- Do they describe learning rather than assignment completion?
- Can they be applied to more than one performance or assignment?
- Are they appropriate to students' level of understanding, observable, and definable in student-friendly language?
- Are they distinct from one another?
- When taken together do they describe the whole of the learning outcome?
- Do they exist along a continuum of quality?

Once teachers have determined the learning goal(s), they need to establish the related success criteria—what students will say, do, make or write. Assessment experts Connie Moss and Susan Brookhart identified seven characteristics of highly effective success criteria, shown in callout box B.[27] In their professional learning communities, collaborative planning sessions, or even individually, teachers could use these characteristics as guides to creating the success criteria.

To generate observable actions, teachers might begin the success criteria with the following words:

- Explain . . .
- Represent . . .
- Describe . . .
- Clarify . . .
- Justify . . .
- Compare . . .
- Determine . . .
- Make . . .
- Create . . .
- Model . . .
- Use . . .
- Distinguish . . .
- Support . . .
- Relate . . .
- Interpret . . .

This is not an exhaustive list, but rather gives ideas of how to make the criteria concrete and learning observable.[28] For instance, the following are success criteria related to different learning goals in a range of grade levels that use some of the words above:

- Represent functions in a variety of ways.
- Use mathematical models with linear functions to reason about real world situations that involve linear functions.
- Explain what the author's purpose is and how you know.
- Support your analysis with textual evidence, including quotations.
- Describe the similar or different ways society responded during the pandemics.
- Make an inference about what is happening in the picture.
- Based on your inference, make a prediction about the story—what will it be about?

We can learn an important lesson about creating success criteria from the reflection of a teacher who was participating in a professional learning about this very topic: "In the first learning cycle for success criteria, I had the misunderstanding that success criteria could be a list of steps that students might take to find a correct answer. My lesson did not go well in terms of the students using the success criteria, much less taking ownership of them."[29]

It is easy to make this mistake when first starting to think about success criteria. Success criteria are not a checklist of steps to complete a task. As Moss and Brookhart stress, they describe learning rather than assignment completion or describe what students are going to do. Learning, not doing, needs to be kept at the forefront.

Again, teachers' sources of knowledge described earlier will come into play in creating success criteria and, again, ongoing deliberate practice will be a factor in how well they advance and hone their skills.

In chapter 4, we described several techniques for addressing the "knowing-doing" gap: instruction, practical social support, modeling, rehearsal, and feedback. Some of these techniques can be applied to developing skills in creating learning goals and success criteria. For example, in terms of modeling, colleagues who are more experienced and skillful can share goals and criteria that they have constructed, talk about their process for developing them and any difficulties they have encountered, and describe how they addressed them.

For the purposes of rehearsal and feedback, teachers could ask a peer or an administrator to observe a lesson, using the questions in callout boxes A and B to guide their observation. After the lesson, the observer could provide feedback about the effectiveness of the goals and success criteria. Practical social support could occur as they work together to make refinements for future use.

Reflecting on learning goals and success criteria

An important part of developing skills for creating learning goals and success criteria is to reflect on their effectiveness after implementing them in either a lesson, unit, or course. In professional learning communities, teachers can employ a "create, implement, review, and refine" process as a component of deliberate practice. A review after implementation could take the form of teachers sharing how effective they thought the goal and success criteria for a week of learning or for a unit were for the purpose of instruction and assessment, using questions such as those in callout box C. A personal reflection might sometimes be sufficient for such an analysis, but if teachers have taught a lesson or unit with the same learning goals they can profit from a collaborative review. Once these questions have been addressed, teachers can make any revisions they think are necessary to improve the goals for subsequent use. A similar process can be used to evaluate the accompanying success criteria for the specific goal or goals, using the questions in callout box D. Sharing answers to these questions with colleagues and getting feedback can help in making revisions and refinements to the success criteria for use in future lessons or units.

Callout Box C

Questions to Guide the Reflection on Learning Goals

- Did the learning goals embody effective disciplinary representations (concepts and analytic practices)?
- Did they lead to rich, productive learning experiences?
- Were they accessible and meaningful for all students?
- Did they effectively build on students' prior learning, including their lived experiences?
- Were they at the appropriate grain size for a unit or a lesson?
- Were they motivating to students?

Callout Box D

Questions to Guide the Reflection of Success Criteria

- Were the success criteria sufficiently well aligned to the learning goal statement?
- Did they describe learning and not doing?
- Did they provide appropriate and useful indicators of a successful performance?
- Were students able to understand what meeting the criteria entailed?
- Were they accessible and meaningful for all students?
- When I used them as an interpretive framework, did they lead to insights into the students' learning status?
- Were students able to use them for self- and peer assessment?

A FINAL THOUGHT

While teachers may think that developing goals that incorporating the three dimensions—cognitive, cultural, and socio-emotional—is time consuming, it is worth reiterating that this work is in the interests of fair and justice-oriented assessment. It is imperative to shape learning goals for instruction and assessment that are going to support all students' learning, regardless of any racial, social, economic, cultural, or linguistic factors, and to ground assessment opportunities for students to show what they know and understand as they pursue high quality educational outcomes. In this vein, it is also worth recalling that deliberate practice (see chapter 4), which entails specific and sustained efforts to do something that a person cannot do well, can lead to higher levels of expertise over time, especially when undertaken in collaboration with colleagues.

Once quality learning goals and success criteria have been created, with some modifications in response to changes in who the students are, they can be reused in future school years, so that the upfront work reduces after the first year. A focus for school and district leaders on providing high quality curricula gives teachers a good starting point to do this work.

The stakes for our students are just too high for teachers and those who support them not to invest time and effort in acquiring the knowledge and skills for developing learning goals and success criteria, the foundation for fair and justice-oriented assessment.

SUMMARY: KEY TAKEAWAYS

- Learning goals specify the aims of teaching and learning and are a prerequisite for assessment design.
- Learning goals and success criteria work in unison to clarify and communicate the intended learning that teachers and students should pursue, and how they will assess that learning.
- Learning goals are derived from standards and equity-centered curricula, and based on a vision of learning that reflects modern conceptions of knowing and learning.
- Learning goals differ in grain size and scope depending on the duration of the specific instructional and assessment cycle—long (convergent assessment), medium (convergent and divergent assessment), or short (mostly divergent assessment).
- To be fair and justice-oriented, learning goals should reflect three dimensions of learning and development: cognitive, cultural, and socio-emotional.
- To create effective learning goals, teachers need to build a corpus of knowledge about standards, disciplinary core ideas, the curricula they use, and their students' funds of knowledge and identity, and about self-regulation, metacognition, motivation, and self-efficacy.

CHAPTER 6

Eliciting Evidence: Assessment Literacy Knowledge and Skills

Recall from earlier chapters that we conceptualize assessment as a chain of reasoning about the status of student learning. In this chain, quality assessment practices follow a series of logical connections: first clear learning goals are defined, then a way to collect evidence of learning relative to those goals is designed, and finally the evidence is interpreted to decide on next instructional or learning steps.[1] The focus of this chapter is on the middle link of the chain: *eliciting evidence of student learning relative to high quality, meaningful learning goals.* If this chapter had a subtitle to supplement the focus on eliciting evidence, it would likely be "Know your purpose!" This subtitle emphasizes that there is no value in collecting evidence of student learning without first being clear on the specific purpose for using that evidence. Purpose should inform the nature of evidence collection, and as we noted in chapter 3 the continuum of divergent to convergent assessment information will inform the design process.

To illustrate how assessment purpose informs design, consider third-grade students working on a mathematics unit about multiplication. The teacher's unit goals for students include both the development of a conceptual understanding of multiplication and of computational fluency. Partway through the unit, she asks students to respond to an open-ended task to represent the following situation in as many ways as possible using drawings and number sentences: "In the classroom we have seven round tables with six students at each table. Represent this situation in as many different ways as you can using drawings and number sentences to show how many students are in the class." After students have had time to work on this problem, either on their own or in pairs, she then invites them to share out their ideas so that all the representations are pooled together for everyone to see. In contrast, at the end of a unit one form of assessment she uses is a fill-in-the-blank worksheet with simple multiplication problems such as 7×6. The assessment purpose of each assignment is different. For the former, the goal is to understand students' conceptual sense-making of multiplication, and an open-ended, divergent task best serves that purpose. When the assessment goal is determining students' fluency with multiplication facts, a worksheet is an efficient vehicle for collecting that information.

Depending on purpose, evidence of learning can vary from a quick-write targeting a key idea within a class period (short-cycle assessment) to a more complex performance task that provides evidence of multiple learning goals for a longer lesson sequence (medium-cycle assessment).[2] In this chapter, we consider how teachers and students can participate in obtaining different kinds of information needed for particular purposes. To this end, we return to two important ideas first introduced in chapter 3: (1) instructionally useful assessment information and (2) convergent and divergent assessment. We begin with an examination of the features of instructionally useful assessment, and then follow with several examples of practice, focusing on meeting teachers' and then students' evidentiary needs. Finally, we examine how teachers can develop the knowledge and skills to elicit high quality evidence of student learning.

INSTRUCTIONALLY USEFUL EVIDENCE OF STUDENT LEARNING

As we noted in chapter 3, Carla Evans and Scott Marion offer ten features of assessment evidence in their book *Understanding Instructionally Useful Assessment*.[3] Each of these features exist along a continuum, and when they are more strongly present, the assessment evidence is more likely to be instructionally useful. We provide a brief explanation of each feature in table 6.1. We will illustrate these assessment features in more detail with the examples that follow.

Let us start with a few introductory comments. It is helpful to think about how external state summative assessments differ from the classroom assessment in terms of purpose, design, and administration, which impacts where each of the ten features from table 6.1 fall on the continuum of possibilities. For example, large-scale assessments are intended to be administered to broad student populations (e.g., statewide) during some common time period of necessarily

TABLE 6.1 Features of assessments that can improve the instructional usability of information

Feature	*Explanation*
1. Cognitive complexity and associated item types	Assessment prompts and tasks can vary in the level of cognitive complexity or level of thinking demanded. One common framework for categorizing the different levels, Depth of Knowledge Framework, was developed by Norman Webb. It comprises four increasingly complex levels: level 1: recall and reproduction; level 2: skills and concepts; level 3: strategic thinking; and level 4: extended thinking.[a] More complex levels of thinking generally require more open-ended question types rather than multiple-choice questions.
2. Coherence with the enacted curriculum	Often curriculum materials have embedded assessments, which we consider curriculum-specific assessments that are most likely to be tightly aligned with the content just taught. At the other end of the continuum are curriculum-agnostic assessments (e.g., state summative assessments). Regardless of what curriculum students experienced in grade 5, they should be familiar with the knowledge and skills assessed in the state summative assessment. Assessment tools and practices that are most tightly aligned with the curriculum are likely to be the most informative to teachers for deciding how to respond to the insights about student learning.
3. Breadth of content standards and resulting grain size of results	Breadth refers to how many content standards are being assessed within one assessment. The state summative assessment is required to address all the grade-level standards and so the results will be at a large grain size (i.e., reports focus on overall grade-level proficiency and subscores that represent understanding on a significant grouping of standards). By contrast, an exit ticket (final question students answer just before leaving the class) is more likely to target a specific aspect of one standard, and so will provide information at a small grain size (i.e., qualitative insight into a specific aspect of student understanding).
4. Type of results	Results can come in a quantitative form of a score (scaled score, simple number correct, or a score level on the rubric), or in a qualitative form such as a description of what students do and do not understand based on a review of an oral response or piece of work. Often, more qualitative descriptions of what specifically students know and can do, and do not yet know, or cannot yet do, will provide greater insight into next instructional steps.

(*continued*)

TABLE 6.1 *continued*

Feature	*Explanation*
5. Timing of results	Timing ranges from almost instantaneous (e.g., when a teacher recognizes initial, incoming ideas from a student comment during a discussion) to several months later (e.g., state summative assessment results). Information that is more immediate can be responded to in the natural progression of instruction.
6. Administration and scoring conditions	Conditions can range from highly inflexible (e.g., state summative assessments are generally administered under highly comparable conditions for all students, unless a student is allowed a specific accommodation under an Individualized Education Plan, to more flexible conditions that might allow for student collaboration or choice in task.
7. Allowable student responses	Multiple-choice questions typically have a single correct answer that students must select. Students might respond to performance tasks in a variety of ways, and a high quality performance task will also have a rubric that describes the range of student performances that would demonstrate less to more sophisticated thinking, while allowing for a variety of approaches to the response.
8. Student choice	State summative assessments typically have little student choice as by their nature they are quite constrained, whereas classroom assessment can offer students a variety of ways to demonstrate their understanding.
9. Collaboration	State summative assessments typically do not allow for student collaboration since they are required to provide a report for each individual assessment. Teachers have more freedom in classroom assessment, and may design assessments that offer students an opportunity to complete part of the assessment together, along with a component to be completed on their own. Alternatively, a teacher may design an assessment with a peer feedback and revision opportunity prior to students completing the work.
10. Real-world and culturally relevant connections	While state summative assessments can use real-world and culturally relevant contexts for questions, classroom assessment may provide greater opportunities to connect both learning and assessment to the specific cultures and communities represented in a specific classroom.

[a] Norman L. Webb, *Criteria for Alignment of Expectations and Assessments in Mathematics and Science Education*, Research Monograph No. 6 (Council of Chief State School Officers, 1997).

limited duration. These assessments aim for standardization of content and administration, and therefore cannot be aligned to local curricula. Interim assessments also tend to be based on grade-level standards rather than aligned to the curriculum, unless they have been developed by the school district that is requiring their administration. When information is more removed from instruction, it generally will require teachers to engage in additional work to uncover more specific details in order to inform next steps.

For example, seeing student results from the previous year's state summative assessment might allow the current grade-level teacher to conclude that some students struggled with an area of the curriculum last year such as the number system. However, that knowledge is insufficient to inform instructional planning except in the broadest sense. A teacher might decide to pay more attention to eliciting student ideas at the start of each new unit to understand the specific strengths and weaknesses within the class to appropriately scaffold and build on each student's strengths. But it is the in-class assessment that will be most instructionally useful, not the state summative assessment. We say more about the uses of the state summative assessment in chapter 8.

These instructionally useful features are not binary. Rather, each exists on a continuum. Assessments can vary in their level of complexity from a series of simple recall questions to less defined problems that offer the possibility of multiple solution strategies or perspectives that can be brought to the problem. Using these features, when we contrast end-of-year summative assessments or other external interim assessment against the range of classroom assessment practices, we can see why classroom assessment is more instructionally useful. For instance, classroom assessments can be coherent with the curriculum in a way that standardized external end-of-year or interim assessments are much less likely to be, given the need for them to be appropriate assessments of grade-level standards, regardless of the specific curricula being used. Classroom assessment practices can target a small aspect of a standard, while, by their nature, external end-of-year or interim assessments must address the breadth of grade-level standards. This feature of scale relates directly to the one that follows in table 6.1, since the reports will necessarily be much broader and more general for the external end-of-year or interim assessments than for a focused classroom assessment. Assuming the teacher has the time to examine the responses to her classroom assessment, the information will be immediately available rather delayed for weeks or even months while all the quality control processes associated with external assessments are completed. Classroom assessment offers greater flexibility compared to large-scale summative assessments in terms of how it is administered, how students respond, the level of choice in task selection, and whether students are offered the opportunity to collaborate. Finally, teachers can develop or modify classroom assessments to meet the specific interests and experiences of students in their classrooms in a way that external end-of-year or interim assessments cannot.

ELICITING EVIDENCE OF STUDENT UNDERSTANDING

This section presents three classroom examples of eliciting evidence of student learning, using both divergent and convergent assessment approaches, and analyzing each one through the lens of instructional usefulness.

Fifth-grade science example

The NYU (New York University) Science and Integrated Language (SAIL) Research Lab developed an award-winning unit in collaboration with a group of teachers that illustrates how assessment opportunities are integrated into the flow of the unit, giving teachers ongoing insights into student thinking as their ideas become increasingly sophisticated.[4] The fifth-grade unit spans about nine weeks and targets aspects of three performance expectations from the New York State (NYS) P-12 Science Learning Standards:

5-PS1–1. Develop a model to describe that matter is made of particles too small to be seen.

5-PS1–2. Measure and graph quantities to provide evidence that regardless of the type of change that occurs when heating, cooling, or mixing substances the total amount of matter is conserved.

5-PS1–3. Make observations and measurements to identify materials based on their properties.[5]

In this unit, student learning is anchored in the phenomenon of garbage, an everyday experience from students' homes, school, and community, which grounds their scientific explorations.[6] The unit description helps teachers understand how exploring this phenomenon will provide rich learning opportunities to address the science performance expectations, including student understanding of the conservation of matter. The unit draws on the use of science and engineering practices as students make observations, develop questions, and conduct investigations of those questions, while incorporating crosscutting concepts such as patterns to assist students in their investigations.

One of the NYU SAIL Research Lab briefs describes how one teacher used the assessment practices within the unit.[7] The unit begins with students exploring a pile of garbage from their school cafeteria (curated by the teacher to remove any dangerous items and with appropriate safety gear worn by students). Small groups of students collaborated to develop categories that they use to sort the garbage. While the teacher observed the students working together, she found occasions to introduce more precise language, such as *patterns* that students were using to identify similarities and differences in pieces of garbage, and *properties* of the different materials such as color, size, and texture. At the end of this lesson, students wrote in their science and engineering notebooks the categories that their group came up with, and the properties of the garbage in each category. Once they heard from other groups, students reflected on their categories and decided if they needed to make any changes.

After beginning the unit with a very concrete, familiar experience, in the next lesson students took a virtual field trip to a landfill by watching a video. Students started to generate questions of interest about garbage from these two experiences. For homework they repeated their sorting exercise with garbage at home, using the categories they generated from the opening lesson, and then continued to generate more questions about garbage during the next lesson. These questions provided the teacher with a starting point for a whole-class discussion during which the students grouped similar questions together, and with support and guidance from the teacher collaboratively determined an overall driving question for the unit: "What happens to our garbage?"

This opening sequence of lessons provided the teacher with multiple, rich divergent assessment opportunities, including listening to the students' discussions about how to sort and group the pieces of garbage, and eliciting questions that the students had about garbage after the first two lessons, before finally settling on a driving question. Reviewing students' written responses in their science and engineering notebooks gave the teacher insights into individual students' thinking, specifically attending to whether students were able to create distinct categories, and if they could identify patterns in the properties of the garbage. This assessment was not focused on whether students had a specific set of correct answers, and it was not graded, nor did the teacher correct student responses. Rather, it was intended to help her obtain an overview of the range of student understandings near the start of the unit that she could build on, and to identify students who may need additional support during future activities.

In a later lesson within this unit, students investigated whether and how properties of food and nonfood materials change over time, and drew models to represent their initial thinking. Students codesigned an investigation with the teacher: they put food and nonfood in containers, one closed and one open, modeling a landfill. Students made observations at three time points of the properties of the items in the containers and the weight of the two containers. Students noticed by the second observation that the open container was starting to smell badly, which raised some new questions about what the smell was and its nature. The teacher asked students to model what they thought was happening in each of the containers, and then provided them with a series of investigations to help them understand that the smell is really a gas made up of particles that are too small to see. As students worked in small groups with their investigations the teacher interacted with groups, probing their thinking, and asking questions to help them articulate their new understandings about the idea that a gas that they cannot see takes up space. The teacher materials for this unit provide examples of teacher probes to help support students' evolving ideas. For example, after observing a video illustrating that a balloon filled with air was heavier before it was punctured and the air released, there are the following suggested teacher prompts:

- Now that we have observed that air also has weight, what does that tell us about air?
- Think about how the data in the investigation matches your ideas about What is that smell?

As part of the landfill bottle investigation, when students weighed their bottles, they discovered that the open container was losing weight at the second and third timepoint, while the closed container was not. Combining their observations of the containers with what they had learned about the nature of gas, students were able to revise their landfill models. The teacher also provided time for students to look at another group's model and to give feedback on that model to help them revise it further, using a checklist shown in figure 6.1.[8]

FIGURE 6.1 Student self and peer model checklist

☑ **SELF AND PEER CHECK! Group Model of Landfill Bottle Systems**

Does the model include the following components?	YES
Open and closed landfill bottles	❑
Garbage materials	❑
Gas particles (smell)	❑
Does the model include the following processes?	
The properties of the food materials changed over time.	❑
The weight of the closed system stayed the same, but the weight of the open system decreased.	❑
Gas particles (smell) are produced in both system and move freely out of the open system.	❑
Does the model follow modeling conventions	
Components and processes are clearly identified using labels and/or a key.	❑

Identify one area for improvement in your peer group's model.

____

____

____

____

After students had completed their third observation of the containers, the teacher asked them to develop a scientific argument to answer the question "Does the amount of matter change in a landfill bottle?" This task required students to use the more formal argumentation structure of claims and evidence and associated language. To help students with this process, the teacher provided a worksheet with separate sections for students to write their claim in response to the question, cite evidence from their investigation, explaining why they chose the data that they did, and finally a section to articulate their reasoning based on the evidence (see figure 6.2).

The teacher used a task-specific rubric that outlined what a correct claim would be, the evidence that a student should include from both the closed and the open system, and the reasoning that linked the evidence to the claim. The rubric informed the brief comments she wrote for each student.

This later lesson illustrates more ways in which the teacher elicited evidence of students' developing understanding. Listening in on the small group discussions as they completed the various investigations related to the nature of gas provided the teacher with insight into student reasoning and on-the-spot

FIGURE 6.2 Structured student worksheet to support scientific argumentation

☑ **INDIVIDUAL CHECK! Arguing About the Amount of Matter in Landfill Bottles**

Arguing from Evidence	
Question: Does the amount of matter change in a landfill bottle?	
Claim: The amount of matter changes in the open system but it	
stays the same in the close system.	
Evidence:	**Why did you use these data?**
According to my system weight	I chose this data because
table the open system was 2.38	the open system kept losing
in timepoint 1 and in timepoint 3	weight and the closed system
was 0.877. My closed system	stayed the same.
weight in timepoint 1 was 1.2	
and in timepoint 3 was 1.2	
Reasoning: Since our open system lost weight and our close system	
stay the same then whe know the amount of matte changes	
only in the open system.	

opportunities to use questions and probes to help students articulate more sophisticated understandings and use more precise scientific vocabulary, building off their everyday language register. Observing the students discuss the models of another group and develop feedback for that group also offered the teacher insights into student thinking. Finally, the last activity in which students developed a claim statement and supported it with evidence and reasoning gave the teacher a more formal opportunity to observe how individual student understanding had progressed.

All of the instances of eliciting evidence in this example were intended to be formative, and shifted over the course of the unit from more divergent to convergent. For each assessment, the primary purpose was to inform the next question the teacher would pose to an individual or group of students, to help her plan for the next investigations, or to identify a model or explanation that the whole class would benefit from seeing and discussing. To summarize, the assessment practices in this unit illustrated short-cycle assessment; the teacher collected informal evidence from observations of students organizing and classifying the garbage items, from asking questions about what was puzzling them, and from discussions with students during small group work on a series of investigations to understand the nature of a gas. The written assessment (medium-cycle assessment) toward the end of the unit provided a more formal piece of evidence about students' understanding of scientific argument and their ability to connect claim, evidence, and reasoning together. The features of instructionally useful assessment practices evident in this 5th grade science unit are described in call-out box A.

End-of-unit assessment

The purpose of an end-of-unit assessment is to provide a teacher with an overview of student learning from the unit, using open-ended response and multiple-choice questions. In our case, the multiple-choice questions (convergent assessment) provided the teacher with information about student learning of key vocabulary and concepts. The open-ended questions gave more insight into students' reasoning and conceptual understanding. A few of the open-ended questions were similar to those that students had already experienced during the unit, while others required students to demonstrate whether they could transfer knowledge from a context they experienced during the unit to a new context (e.g., in the unit they were asked to explain whether the weight of a closed carton of ice cream would change over time, but in the end-of-unit assessment a different context was used). The end-of-unit assessment provided information about students' ability to write about phenomena using the language and structure of claim-evidence-reasoning, to draw models of a system, and to make predictions, all important foci of the unit. We saw a similar approach in chapter 2 from Dr. Johnson, who asked students to apply the core science ideas and practices

Callout Box A

Features of Instructionally Useful Assessment Practices Evident in the Fifth-Grade Science Example

- *Cognitive complexity*: All of the examples engaged students in complex thinking, connecting ideas and drawing on multiple sources of evidence.
- *Curricular coherence*: The assessment opportunities occurred as a coherent part of the curriculum, rather than separate from it, so that information obtained by the teacher could inform how she supported students in the next step of learning.
- *Breadth of standards/grain size of results*: While the performance expectations for this science unit are comprehensive (e.g., 5-PS1-2), the unit focused on understanding the conservation of matter in the context of decomposition only, which influenced both the learning activities and assessment opportunities.
- *Type of results*: The type of information that the teacher gained was primarily qualitative in nature, relying on observations, and providing her with insight into student thinking as it was unfolding. The argumentation task and rubric was a more systematic assessment approach, and yielded information from students' writing or drawings that the teacher could interpret directly, rather than trying to draw conclusions about why a student might have selected a particular option on a multiple-choice item.
- *Timing of results*: Information was available to the teacher in real time or near real time, depending on how long she took to review and write feedback to students.
- *Administration and scoring conditions*: Much of the formative (divergent) assessment evidence was collected in very informal ways; students likely do not consider a class discussion as assessment. For the claim-evidence-reasoning assessment, the process was more standardized, with every student working from the same structured worksheet, and the use of a rubric to help the teacher attend to critical features of every student's response in the same way.
- *Allowable student responses*: When students wrote in their science and engineering notebooks, the teacher encouraged the use of students'

home languages on their drawings, in addition to writing in English, to enable students to communicate their thinking.

- *Student choice and collaboration*: Student choice and collaboration was evident in how students formed small groups to work together for various investigations, and how they determined initial sorting categories for the garbage items.
- *Real-world connections*: The real-world connections were apparent with the use of garbage directly from the school cafeteria, then using home garbage in the follow-up activity.

they had learned during the unit to explain a new phenomenon in the end-of-unit assessment.

A set of scoring criteria accompany the end-of-unit assessment, with the correct answer for each multiple-choice item, and a two- or three-point rubric for each constructed-response item. The rubrics also have examples of student responses at each level, or examples of student models to show the varying levels of complexity. The unit materials do not provide any specific guidance about interpreting scores on the assessment or next steps. We suggest, as we do for any end-of-unit or other form of consequential assessment, that teachers review the student results with colleagues to identify patterns across students and across classes, of strengths and weaknesses and to consider implications for the future in two ways:

1. Next year, are there lessons that might need extra time, emphasis, or alternative examples because students struggled with the concepts?
2. For this year, based on the results, are there students who need extra support in order to be able to demonstrate their learning more effectively? For these students, are there key ideas from this unit related to the science and engineering practices, the crosscutting ideas, or the disciplinary concepts that can be revisited or reinforced in future units?

EIGHTH-GRADE ENGLISH LANGUAGE ARTS PEER FEEDBACK

The previous science example briefly touched on peer feedback as a source of evidence of student thinking as one component of eliciting evidence. We observe this source of evidence more fully in an example from an eighth-grade English Language Arts (ELA) class.[9]

The students had been working on informational writing over multiple class periods on topics of personal interest. They gathered research and then developed a summary of what they learned. Students chose to work on their topic individually or in pairs. In the observed lesson, their teacher, Ms. Marshall, wanted the students to determine whether their summaries would make sense to someone not familiar with the topic, and to use insights gained from their peers to inform revisions to their drafts. Ms. Marshall described what she called *backyard-barbeque* feedback, a process intended to stimulate informal conversation among students about their research, with the explicit goal of identifying holes in their summaries so that they could make them better.

Ms. Marshall communicated the purpose of the structured process to the students and provided them with a note-taking sheet to guide them. Students began by finding a partner to talk to about their research. Ms. Marshall explained that she was going to set the timer for ninety seconds during which time one student (or the pair) would describe their research, and they were to keep talking for the entire ninety seconds. The other student was not allowed to interrupt, but was to take notes about questions they had about aspects of the research that were unclear. Once the allotted time was up, the student who was initially listening then had sixty seconds to ask their questions to the presenting student. The presenting student was not allowed to answer the questions in the moment, but to use them to consider how they could more clearly describe what they had learned in their research. Ms. Marshall recognized that asking questions can be difficult but provided encouragement noting that, "the best questions come when someone has run out and is really having to think." After that, the roles swapped and the process repeated with the second student having ninety seconds to describe their research, followed by another sixty seconds of questions from the first student.

Ms. Marshall had students repeat the process with another partner so that every student had two opportunities to present their summaries, and to hear questions about unclear aspects. She asked students to reflect on the experience of summarizing their research and the questions that they received, and to use those reflections to refine their summaries. She let them know that they would not have enough time to write out clean versions of their summaries during this lesson, but that they should make notes on the margins of their drafts about things they needed to reorder, clarify, provide more detail about, and so on. After five minutes of revision time, Ms. Marshall asked students to do one more round of backyard-barbeque feedback in order to try out the revisions they had just made with another student whom they had not previously talked to.

Students completed this final feedback round, and then had some extra time at the end of class for one more round of revisions to their summaries. As the class was wrapping up, Ms. Marshall collected the summaries and note-catcher forms in order to review and provide students with one more round of feedback before they would make final revisions to this piece of writing.

During this lesson, Ms. Marshall was serving as a timekeeper to make sure the process kept moving. From an assessment perspective she also was listening as students summarized their research, or asked their peers questions about things that were unclear. She had to remind the students occasionally of their roles as listeners rather than responding to the questions. She recognized that questions coming from peers would be seen as less threatening or critical than if she were to ask similar questions of the students. She also understood the value of making sure that each writer had multiple perspectives on their drafts. These conversations allowed her to get a sense of which students might still be struggling to communicate their research in a coherent way, which she would then be able to look at in more detail when she read their individual summaries.

Recall the ten features in table 6.1. The instructionally useful features of the peer feedback process are described in callout box B.

From our observations, it is clear that Ms. Marshall has established a productive classroom culture with a collective orientation among students. Reflecting aspects of ambitious teaching (chapter 2), the teacher and students share responsibility for learning and use classroom routines to facilitate that shared responsibility. In summary, the teacher recognized that she would not be able to provide individual feedback to every student during a single class period and that the backyard-barbeque feedback process would provide multiple perspectives for each student. Students benefit from being both givers and receivers of feedback; the feedback process gave students the opportunity to hear how other students had approached the same task.[10]

Callout Box B

Features of Instructionally Useful Assessment Practices Evident in the Eighth-Grade ELA Example

- *Cognitive complexity*: The peer assessment task, requiring students to listen to their peers' oral summaries of their research topics and findings, was a complex one and so worthy of students' attention.
- *Coherence with the enacted curriculum*: The peer feedback task was directly part of the curriculum and not separate from it.
- *Breadth of standards/grain size of results*: While the writing task represented an important aspect of eighth-grade standards, students were given a more narrowly gauged task, which required them to listen for holes or lack of coherence in their peer's research.
- *Type of results*: The results from the assessment came in a qualitative form (questions from the listening students about aspects of the presentation that were confusing) and were also provided immediately as part of the discussion process. The informal process did not have scoring associated with it; rather, peers were providing their questions back to the presenting student for consideration.
- *Student choice and collaboration*: Students had choice and collaboration opportunities in this assessment process, in terms of the research topic they selected, whether to work on their own or with a partner, and also in the selection of peers for feedback.
- *Real-world and culturally relevant connections*: The topics the students chose were personally meaningful to them.

High school mathematics example

In chapter 5, we gave an early elementary example of a *just right* problem in which students self-select the number combination that they will use. This practice enables all students to select an entry point that is appropriate for them. We draw on a pair of high school performance tasks from the Mathematics Assessment Resource Service (MARS) bank to illustrate how a teacher might use them to support finding the appropriate entry point from which to elicit evidence of student understanding.[11] Figure 6.3 illustrates the modeling task that targets two high school CCSSM (Common Core State Standards for Mathematics) standards:

H.G-GMD: Explain volume formulas and use them to solve problems.
H.M: Model with mathematics.

Students need to bring a practical perspective as they work through the problem, using a graphing or calculation approach to try several options for the radius to identify that a radius of approximately 3 cm will result in the smallest surface area. Students who are still developing mathematical modeling skills may struggle with the open-ended version of this task (figure 6.3). The teacher or students could elect to begin with the more scaffolded version of this task which

FIGURE 6.3 Modeling task

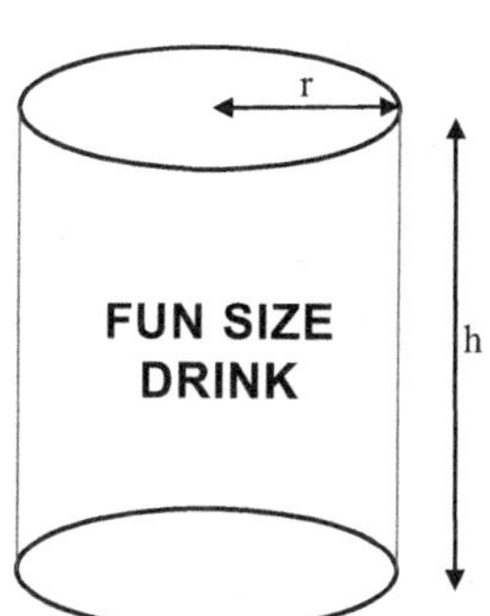

The Fresha Drink Company is marketing a new soft drink.

The drink will be sold in a can that holds 200 cm^3.

In order to keep costs low, the company wants to use the smallest amount of aluminum.

Find the radius and height of a cylindrical can which holds 200 cm^3 and uses the smallest amount of aluminum.

Explain your reasons and show all your calculations.

provides some initial questions to support student thinking. The question posed in figure 6.3 is the last part of the scaffolded version of the task. However, first students are asked to find the height of the can for two given radii, and to contrast the practical implications of a can with radius 2 cm and 5 cm. They also calculate the surface area for those radii. Having had that experience, students are then presented with the question in figure 6.3. The scaffolding questions help a student to recognize that even though the volume is kept constant for different sizes of can, the surface area will vary for different radii. The two radii also bound the options that a student might consider in the open-ended final part of the task: neither a can with a radius less than 2 cm nor one that is more than 5 cm is practical because either the can will be too tall or too wide to drink from. We highlight features of instructional usefulness in this example in callout box C.

Callout Box C

Features of Instructionally Useful Assessment Practices Evident in the High School Math Example

- *Cognitive complexity*: The pair of tasks require students to engage in complex thinking rather than routine application of algorithms.
- *Coherence with curriculum*: The tasks are aligned with the curriculum.
- *Breadth of content standards*: The tasks provide a summative (convergent) assessment at the end of a unit rather than trying to address the breadth of grade-level standards as in large-scale assessments.
- *Type of results*: The teacher will have access to student explanations and reasoning as well as summary scores for each student, allowing for decisions about where to move instructionally in a short period of time.
- *Administration and scoring conditions*: The two linked tasks provide flexibility in administration and the teacher can select—or allow students to select—which version of the task is most appropriate for them.
- *Real-world connections*: Uses a familiar context (soda cans) even if students are not regularly engaging in design processes.

KNOWLEDGE AND SKILLS FOR ELICITING EVIDENCE OF STUDENT LEARNING

We now consider the three dimensions of learning and development (cognitive, cultural, and socio-emotional) in relation to the process of eliciting evidence of student learning. From the cognitive perspective, the elicitation of assessment evidence must be aligned with the learning goals, and provide students with multiple ways in which their knowledge and reasoning can be displayed.[12] In the mathematics and science examples, we saw opportunities for students to write, draw, and talk about their understanding of what they were learning in ways that were tightly aligned to the learning goals. The collection of evidence took place shortly after when learning was happening, rather than a distant event after learning has been *completed*.[13] Some of the opportunities were more divergent than convergent, depending, in part, on how far into the unit of learning students had progressed. The collection of assessment evidence across examples was sufficiently rich to be instructionally useful by providing tractable insights to guide subsequent pedagogical moves.[14]

The science unit on garbage began with a very familiar experience for students, illustrating how assessment evidence that integrates the cultural dimension of assessment is collected from tasks that both reflect students' lived experiences and give insight into experiences different from their own (often described as *mirrors* and *windows*), and that provide opportunities for the integration of students' funds of knowledge into assessment.[15]

Assessment evidence that integrates the socio-emotional dimension of assessment is obtained in a classroom context of trust and requires that students understand the purpose of the assessment and that they perceive the task as worthwhile and relevant.[16] The writing task in the ELA example that incorporated peer feedback was based on a topic of personal interest to students, so that while all students would provide evidence of their ability to synthesize and summarize information, students had freedom to explore a topic that they considered personally valuable and meaningful. Additionally, the use of multiple entry points to the assessment permitted students to demonstrate where they were in their learning. Giving students choice among prompts has a positive impact on both student perception of competence and outcomes.[17] The two mathematics tasks which would allow either the teacher or the student to select a version of the task, and hence the level of challenge, illustrates one way to provide multiple entry points to allow all students to experience success while still giving the teacher clear evidence of their current skill level. Opportunities for students to contribute evidence of their own learning or that of their peers (e.g., metacognitive activities) promote students' sense of agency and purpose, as we saw in the way that the ELA teacher gave students multiple opportunities to get feedback from peers and to apply it to their own work.[18]

Developing the knowledge and skills to elicit evidence of student learning

This section focuses on the acquisition of knowledge of the cognitive, cultural, and socio-emotional dimensions for eliciting evidence, as well as the application of that knowledge to the development of divergent and convergent assessment practices.

Table 6.2 presents a summary of the knowledge and skills that teachers need related to the cognitive, cultural, and socio-emotional dimensions for eliciting evidence of student learning in ways that are fair and justice-oriented.

Developing knowledge related to the cognitive, cultural, and socio-emotional dimensions

Developing knowledge related to the cognitive dimension of eliciting assessment evidence builds directly on the work that teachers can do to deepen their disciplinary knowledge to support the development of learning goals and success criteria, as described in chapter 5. In other words, to create, modify, or select assessment opportunities that address the breadth and depth of the standards, a teacher must understand the structure and nature of the discipline, and how knowledge builds from less to more complex ideas.

There are some core assessment literacy concepts that are important for teachers to possess, some of which have been already identified in table 6.1. Also, there are important concepts related to the quality of an assessment that teachers need to be aware of:

- validity, the concept of a task, probe, or discussion prompt assessing what it is intended to assess; and
- reliability, ideas related to the consistency and sufficiency of assessment evidence.

An assessment course during preservice education may take a formal approach to the concepts of validity and reliability as are appropriate for high-

TABLE 6.2 A summary of the knowledge and skills for eliciting evidence

Assessment evidence that addresses the cognitive dimension is aligned with the learning goals, and provides multiple ways in which knowing and reasoning can be displayed.[a]	
Cognitive	• Knowledge of the importance of coherence among learning opportunities, classroom formative and summative assessment • Knowledge of how assessment purpose will inform how evidence of student understanding is produced (validity) • Knowledge of how to align sufficiency of information with purpose (reliability) • Skills in planning situations, activities, tasks, or questions to elicit prior knowledge and evidence of progress toward the current learning goal(s), with shared indicators of successful performance that will be instructionally useful in the here and now of learning; and, in the case of summative assessment, at the end of a period of learning • Skills in planning authentic and worthwhile tasks that: ◦ have multiple modes (e.g., written, oral, performance); and ◦ require students to engage with powerful disciplinary ideas and practices
Assessment evidence that integrates the cultural dimension of assessment is collected from tasks that both reflect students' lived experiences and provide insight into experiences different from their own (often described as *mirrors* and *windows*) and that provide opportunities for the integration of students' funds of knowledge into assessment.[b]	
Cultural	• Knowledge of how to create assessment opportunities that sustain the specific local cultural and linguistic diversity present in each classroom and support students' ways of knowing/being • Skills in planning authentic and worthwhile tasks that incorporate students' funds of knowledge and interests that they bring to school from their homes and communities
Assessment evidence that integrates the socio-emotional dimension of assessment is obtained in a classroom context of trust, and requires that students understand the purpose of the assessment and perceive the task as worthwhile and relevant.[c]	
Socio- Emotional	• Skills in creating an optimal climate for learning and assessment, generating an atmosphere of trust and purpose, and ensuring a collective orientation to learning and development • Skills in planning authentic and worthwhile tasks that ◦ have sufficiently broad entry points to provide all students with the opportunity to show where they are in their learning in ways that situate them as competent; ◦ are accessible to students with disabilities and those who are English learners • Skills in ensuring metacognitive skill development (including goal setting and self-monitoring) and promoting the ongoing use of these skills in the classroom to help students understand their own learning status and performance

(*continued*)

TABLE 6.2 *continued*

	• Skills in identifying and collecting other sources of information (such as student surveys or interviews, attendance information) to support deeper insights into student learning compared to solely considering assessment data

[a] Robert Glaser, Naomi Chudowsky, and James W. Pellegrino, eds., *Knowing What Students Know: The Science and Design of Educational Assessment* (National Academies Press, 2001).

[b] Carla M. Evans and Catherine S. Taylor, *Culturally Responsive Assessment in Classrooms and Large-Scale Contexts: Theory, Research, and Practice* (Routledge, 2025), 409.

[c] Paul Black and Dylan Wiliam, "Developing the Theory of Formative Assessment," *Educational Assessment, Evaluation and Accountability* (formerly: *Journal of personnel evaluation in education*) 21 (2009): 5–31.

stakes and large-scale assessments. That approach, however, does not meet the needs of teachers who primarily deal with the design, selection, and use of classroom assessment practices. Teachers need a more general understanding of these concepts and how they impact classroom assessment design. The concept of validity comes into play whenever evidence of learning is being elicited. It is important for teachers to ask whether the assessment, including everything from a discussion probe to an end-of-unit assessment, is targeting what it is intended to target. This inquiry should be informed by the success criteria for the unit (or lesson), which lay out what a student should be able to do if they have successfully achieved the content of the unit or lesson. Teachers can examine whether there is an alignment between the intended outcomes for the period of learning and evidence being collected. The education scholar Frederick Erickson argues that for assessment to be formative, it must both be timely and produce information that can inform instruction during its ongoing course. For this reason the immediate or proximate timing of evidence is a key component of formative assessment validity.[19]

One way to examine the validity of interpretations made about student learning based on any formative assessment opportunity is to review the verbs used in the success criteria and to consider whether discussion questions, tasks, or other forms of assessment are a reasonable match for those verbs. Table 6.3 presents the list of verbs suggested as a starting point for success criteria in chapter 5, and names the format of an assessment task, question, or discussion that would be required to assess the verb.

Some of the verbs in table 6.3 suggest recall or declarative knowledge, such as "*determine* the area of a right-angled triangle," which could be assessed using a

TABLE 6.3 Assessment implications for different kinds of success criteria

Success criteria verbs	*Assessment items or tasks*
Compare	• Classroom discussions and tasks that ask students to make comparisons • Multiple-choice or matching questions that ask students to group like ideas
Determine	• Classroom discussions and tasks that ask students to calculate an answer • Multiple-choice questions that ask students to select a correct answer
Use	• Classroom discussions and tasks that ask students to use a concept in context • Multiple-choice questions that ask students to select the correct usage
Distinguish	• Classroom discussions and tasks that ask students to describe similarities and differences between concepts
Support	• Classroom discussions and tasks that ask students to provide evidence for a claim • Multiple-choice questions that ask students to select the strongest evidence for a claim from a list of options
Relate	• Classroom discussions and tasks that ask students to make connections among ideas • Multiple-choice questions that ask students to select the response that best connects to the idea in the stem
Interpret	• Classroom discussions and tasks that ask student to provide an interpretation of evidence • Multiple-choice questions that ask students to select the best interpretation from a list of options
Explain	• Classroom discussions and tasks that ask students to develop an explanation
Describe	• Classroom discussions and tasks that ask students to describe a situation
Clarify	• Classroom discussions and tasks that ask students to clarify or further develop an idea
Justify	• Classroom discussions and tasks that ask students to provide a justification for a claim or explanation
Represent	• A task that asks students to draw a representation or image to show their understanding of an idea or set of ideas
Make	• A task that asks students to make something
Create	• A task that asks students to create something
Model	• A task that asks students to model or approximate a situation

multiple-choice item, a short constructed-response item, or a class question with a single correct answer. However, other verbs such as *explain* or *describe* would not be well served by an assessment that relies only on multiple-choice items. This distinction gets to the heart of the validity concept. If a unit assessment or classroom interactions only address the factual recall aspects of the success criteria and omit other higher-order aspects of the learning, the validity of conclusions about student learning based on those assessments are weakened.

Assessment expert Lorrie Shepard has argued that reliability is less critical for classroom assessment because errors in instructional decisions can be rectified quickly through gathering more evidence of learning (see also chapter 7 for more on reliability in classroom assessment).[20] However, there are some important conceptual understandings that teachers should have related to reliability. For one, they should know that all assessments have a degree of error, and that a small number of items might not be sufficient to provide stable insight into what students know and can do.[21] Teachers have to be confident that they have enough information about the student's learning to make a reasonable judgment about the current status of that learning. One way to think about this is to ask whether a teacher would get the same result if they collected similar evidence about student learning—in other words, whether the conclusion about student learning that she drew from the assessment evidence is characteristic of the student's level of performance, or a chance outcome or "fluke." From a teacher perspective, the idea of sufficiency of evidence could be reframed as: "How do I know this isn't a fluke or artifact of what is going on today—including whether the student may have gotten up on the wrong side of the bed. Do I know enough to rule that out, or do I have to try again on another, brighter day?"[22] This conception of reliability argues for multiple sources of evidence before a teacher makes an instructional decision. The wider the range of information, and the more frequently the information is collected, the more accurately learning can be inferred.[23] For example, a teacher might not be sure if a student understood a concept if they just responded to one question in a class discussion correctly. However, the teacher would be more convinced by a collection of evidence from that student that included a correct explanation of their reasoning in a discussion, most questions on a worksheet answered correctly, and a response to a class exit ticket that focused on the key concept of the lesson. Depending on the type of decision to be made based on evidence, a teacher can decide the level of information that she would consider sufficient to support the judgment.

There are a variety of assessment literacy resources that are available to help teachers deepen their understanding of basic test design concepts, including assessment literacy standards for teachers and associated learning tools—for example, the Classroom Assessment Literacy Standards and associated learning module, the Michigan Assessment Consortium standards, and the Center for Assessment's assessment literacy modules, as well as no shortage of books on classroom assessment design.[24] These resources can be used by individual teachers, or by groups of teachers learning together. Teams can use these resources as an extended book study with frequent reflections on how the information challenges some existing practices and validates others. Taking time, particularly with identified challenges to current practice, to create action plans for changes is important. The team can then serve as a forum for providing feedback on those changes and support for making refinements.

The knowledge learned about students' cultural backgrounds, communities, interests, and motivations to support the development of relevant and meaningful learning goals will be directly applicable to developing or modifying assessment tasks to ensure that they are relevant and meaningful to students. All of the strategies described in chapter 5 focused on getting to know students and their families in deep ways will form the knowledge base needed to create tasks that are locally relevant, meaningful, and engaging to students.

Developing skills related to eliciting assessment evidence

As should be clear from the preceding chapters, we firmly believe that teachers will hone their assessment elicitation skills by working together as a community. The skills described in table 6.2 can best be developed and deepened through practical application to assessments that teachers are using in their day-to-day practice. Some teachers likely will have stronger disciplinary content knowledge or may be more effective at making assessment tasks more meaningful to students. By pooling knowledge and resources, the collective grade-level team or department will benefit, and ultimately so will students.

We suggest four ways that teachers might review current assessment practices in collaboration with peers to deepen knowledge and develop skills in eliciting evidence of student understanding: (1) skill-by-skill, (2) by teacher questions, (3) by assessment type, and (4) by unit. We discuss each in turn below.

Skill-by-skill discussions The skills described in table 6.2 lend themselves to a structured review, particularly when the learning community is composed of teachers across grade levels or content areas. Teachers can identify one or more of the skill statements as the focus of their next, upcoming investigation. Prior to the meeting, each teacher should collect one or two examples of assessments that they think illustrate the particular skill in practice. When they meet they can engage in a structured discussion of the assessment, and how it exemplifies the focus skill. For example, the community might decide to share examples of assessments that they developed, used, or modified that illustrate "authentic and worthwhile tasks that incorporate students' funds of knowledge they bring to school from their homes and communities." This discussion requires teachers to make explicit connections between the knowledge that they have accumulated about students' families, community, cultures, and interests (see chapter 5 for how teachers can develop this knowledge), and specific aspects of the assessment questions. For instance, during the meeting teachers should initially take turns sharing an assessment activity or task with an explanation of how it reflected the specific skill. For the initial review, other teachers could ask clarifying questions about student background, the learning goal, or the context of the task, but not yet discuss the specifics of the assessment task, or whether it did or did not illustrate the specific skill in question. Once everyone has shared their initial findings, the group could then move to a more general discussion of commonalities in the examples, patterns of strengths, and areas for potential improvement. The wrap-up discussion could then focus on more general strategies that teachers could employ to increase the inclusion of students' funds of knowledge to future tasks.

Alternatively, the community might decide to focus on sharing examples of how they use assessment to elicit prior knowledge from students near the beginning of a unit. Using a similar structure as described above, teachers could take turns to share discussion prompts or open-ended tasks designed to understand students' prior knowledge. These discussions would be an occasion for teachers to draw on their understanding of the progression of learning expected from the previous grade to the current grade, and how the prompt or task provides an opportunity for students to show that knowledge in partial or complete ways.

Review of teacher questions Teacher questions and student discussions are an important source of assessment evidence, as we have seen in previous examples—for instance, the teacher dialogue with third-grade students in chapter 1, or the extended questioning and discussion around equal and even numbers presented in chapter 3. While questioning and discussions in class have a more momentary aspect to them, to be effective as a source of evidence, they still require planning to ensure they are well aligned to the learning goals, support student thinking, and can yield insights into learning. One approach to examining the quality of teacher questions is to review a video of classroom practice in a learning community setting.

Within the learning community there should be established norms for reviewing video so that it is a safe and supportive environment. Teachers should be given time to video record multiple lessons in order to identify a segment of practice that they feel comfortable sharing with peers. A short five- to ten-minute segment is likely sufficient. The teacher sharing should provide sufficient context for peers in terms of learning goals for the lesson, where in the unit sequence the lesson occured, and any other contextual information, such as the rationale for this being a whole group, small group, or individual student discussion.

Examining questions used to support meaningful discussions with students will require teachers to draw on their content knowledge, to examine the alignment between learning goals and questions, and to consider the kinds of question structures that are being used, for instance open- or closed-ended. The group should review the video and consider the prompts in callout box D, ask clarifying questions, and then provide an opportunity for the teacher whose class was

Callout Box D

Questions to Guide the Teacher Questioning Review

- Do the questions provide evidence of prior knowledge or progress toward the learning goals in ways that give instructionally tractable insights?
- Do the questions draw on students' funds of knowledge?
- Do the questions and teacher responses contribute to an atmosphere of trust?
- Do the questions have broad entry points?
- Do the questions help students understand their own learning?
- Are all students engaged in the questioning process or only a few?

recorded to share some initial reflections about the questions she posed in the recorded segment and/or questions that she has about how to make improvements. The group can then identify areas of practice that demonstrate the skills or ways to improve. A timekeeper should monitor the discussion, ensure that it adheres to community norms, and, if multiple videos are being shared in the session, allow sufficient time for each person.

Reflecting across multiple videos can enable teachers to identify different ways in which they use questions to uncover student thinking and help students develop their understanding toward important learning goals. Teachers will benefit from identifying a specific aspect of questioning practice that they want to work on during upcoming lessons and share progress with the group at the next meeting.

Review of assessment tasks This approach and the following suggestion both work best when teachers are from the same grade level or department in a learning community and have common instructional materials.[25] While the skill-by-skill approach can be useful for a group beginning this work of improving classroom assessment, ultimately these skills need to be integrated across assessments rather than treated in isolation. While it is unlikely that every assessment opportunity will exemplify all of the features described in table 6.2, across a set of assessments these features should be present.

One way to begin an assessment review is to select a particular assessment task to examine with peers. This review could focus on start-of-unit explorations used to establish what students already know about the topic from previous grade levels, and from their own individual experiences. Alternatively, the group might begin with the more formal end-of-unit assessments used across the units with a grade-level, or examine the self- and peer assessment opportunities that students experience across units.

The questions in callout box E are derived from the skills in table 6.2 and could be used to examine the quality of each assessment task. Some of the questions in callout box E require the group to examine student work examples from the assessment to consider, based on how students responded, whether the task was accessible to students, if they seemed to understand what they were being asked to do, and whether students responded in a way that was intended. Teachers can also focus on the ways in which the assessment task produced instructionally tractable information, one aspect of which is timing: At what point during the lesson was the evidence of student learning collected? Teachers can consider

Callout Box E

Questions to Guide the Assessment Review

- Does the assessment task align with the learning goals?
- Is the task providing evidence of prior knowledge or progress toward the learning goals in ways that provide instructionally tractable information?
- Is the task authentic and worthwhile?
- Does the task draw on students' funds of knowledge?
- Does the task contribute to an atmosphere of trust?
- Does the task have broad entry points?
- Is the task accessible to all students?
- Does the task help students understand their own learning?

whether the timing of the collection of assessment information occurred at a point in the lesson that appropriately balanced allowing students to productively struggle, as well as gaining insight into student understanding in time to keep the forward momentum of learning going.

Teachers could work in pairs to review each task and make notes, and then share their reflections with the larger group. Once each pair has shared their initial findings, the group could then move to a more general discussion of the strengths and weaknesses of this particular set of assessment tasks and areas for future revision. Depending on the size of the group and the extent of revisions, pairs of teachers may take on revisions of a subset of tasks and bring those revised tasks back to a future learning community meeting for review. The wrap-up discussion could then focus on more general strategies that the group could use for future assessment development or modification.

This process can benefit from a department chair or other individual taking the lead on logistics to plan out which types of assessment will be reviewed, collecting examples, and tracking schedules for future follow-up on revised assessments.

Review by unit This final approach to reviewing a set of assessments is similar to the previous but uses a complete unit as a focus of analysis rather than a specific assessment type. The questions in callout box B still apply, but could be used to consider the range of divergent and convergent assessment opportunities within a unit, using the same process of an initial paired review, whole group share out, and reflection on observations.

One of the features of instructionally useable assessment information, listed in table 6.1, is coherence with the enacted curriculum. A review of the main assessments from a unit, or a representative sample, is an opportunity to analyze coherence. Drawing again on the disciplinary knowledge described in chapter 5, the following questions can be considered:

- Did the instruction during this unit support students to engage with the depth and breadth of the learning goals and success criteria?
- Does the set of assessments similarly reflect the depth and breadth of the learning goals and success criteria?
- Do the assessments use a variety of question types that allow students to demonstrate what they know and can do beyond recall of knowledge?

It is likely the group will identify some potential areas for revisions, and again it will be helpful to have one person serve in the coordinator role to help ensure that revisions are made and reviewed by the group.

Teachers' learning needs will vary by their overall teaching experience. But when circumstances change, whether through a new curriculum adoption or perhaps an assignment to different grade level, even experienced teachers may need to reexamine how they elicit evidence of student understanding. The knowledge- and skill-building strategies suggested in this chapter are not intended to be worked through in a linear fashion, never to be revisited again, but to be drawn on as new assessment dilemmas present themselves.

A FINAL THOUGHT

Across multiple chapters we have referenced the importance of teachers having support in the form of high-quality instructional materials so that they are not burdened with designing units of instruction while also engaging in all of the assessment practices that we have described in this book. It is also important that teachers are critical consumers, and are able to select or modify assessments as needed in order to improve either their instructional utility through an increased use of open-ended questions, for example, or to provide greater opportunities for students to make personal and meaningful connections to the assessment content. We also recognize that not all teachers have access to such instructional materials, and that wholesale revisions during a busy school year is not practical. We encourage teachers to take a unit-by-unit approach. They might not be able to tackle revisions to every unit and associated assessments within a single school year, but in collaboration with colleagues, they could start with the one unit that seems most in need of revision and work on that one first. It might also be a good time to have a conversation with school leadership about support for summer work to review additional units outside of the hustle and bustle of the school year.

In this chapter we focused on the importance of aligning assessment purpose and structure with how evidence is elicited, and the concept that not all assessment information is instructionally valuable. We hope that the ideas of this chapter will empower teachers to have productive discussions with school and district leaders about their assessment systems. Sometimes examining assumptions about who is using each piece of assessment information can uncover redundant or unused information leading to reductions in assessment burdens.[26]

SUMMARY: KEY TAKEAWAYS

- To support coherence among teaching, learning, and assessment, learning goals and success criteria are used to inform how evidence of student learning is elicited.
- The verbs used in success criteria that describe what students can do to demonstrate their learning, in particular, will guide how evidence of student learning should be elicited.
- For classroom assessment, it is important that assessment information is instructionally useful. Some forms of assessment (flexible format, aligned with curriculum, cognitively complex, visible student responses rather than multiple choice) are more likely to yield instructionally useful information than assessment that is disconnected from the curriculum, spans multiple months of learning, and where results are reported only as scores.
- To be fair and justice-oriented, assessment evidence should reflect the cognitive, cultural, and socio-emotional dimensions of learning and development.
- To elicit evidence of student learning effectively, teachers need to build a corpus of knowledge about standards, disciplinary core ideas, the curricula

they use, about their students' funds of knowledge and identity, and about self-regulation, metacognition, motivation, and self-efficacy.

- Assessment purpose will inform design, in terms of whether seeking divergent or convergent assessment information, and in terms of the amount of information that would be required to be considered sufficient.

CHAPTER 7

Interpretation and Action: Assessment Literacy Knowledge and Skills

In our conceptualization of assessment as a chain of reasoning, each link in the chain is dependent on the others. The two prior chapters focused on the first and second links: clear learning goals aligned to standards and determining a way to collect evidence of learning relative to those goals. In this chapter, we address the final link in the chain: interpreting the evidence obtained and taking action intended to progress learning.

As we have previously emphasized, this book is primarily concerned with the development of teachers' assessment literacy. For this reason, we focus in this chapter on what teachers need to know and the skills they need to acquire with respect to interpreting information yielded from convergent and divergent classroom assessments that they use, and the pedagogical action that they subsequently take based on that interpretation.

To establish the context for interpretation and action, we begin by revisiting the idea of teachers' sociocultural consciousness introduced in chapter 1. Although a teacher's sociocultural consciousness bears on all three links in the chain of reasoning, it has particular salience for interpreting evidence and taking action because the interpretations teachers make and the follow-up action they take will have direct consequences for student learning. We suggest ways in which teachers might explore their own sociocultural consciousness in the interests of fair and justice-oriented assessment. Through several examples of assessment practices, we will identify the knowledge and skills teachers need to effectively interpret evidence and determine next steps in learning for their students. In our final section, we will describe ways in which teachers can develop the necessary knowledge and skills for using assessment information effectively to improve student learning.

TEACHERS' SOCIOCULTURAL CONSCIOUSNESS

Developing one's sociocultural identity is ongoing throughout an individual's life.[1] Beginning in preservice programs and continuing throughout their careers, teachers need to engage in autobiographical exploration, reflection, and critical self-analysis. They need to explore the groups to which they belong in terms of race, ethnicity, social class, language, and gender, and reflect on how membership of these groups has shaped and continues to shape their identity.[2] With an openness to self-knowledge, teachers can develop an awareness of any differences between their students and themselves and become sensitive to how those differences might potentially shape their attitudes toward them.

Research suggests that teachers reprimand students of color more often than White students for subjective infractions in the classroom. When teachers omitted homework completion and judgments about behavior and effort from their grades, the difference in grades between White and non-White students lessened considerably.[3] In other words, teachers' perceptions of students impacted how they assessed them.

Teachers also need to take care about how they assess students who are speakers of languages other than English. Teachers need to be conscious as to whether their social identity influences them to be judgmental about the language the students use rather than focusing on the sense students are making of ideas with the linguistic resources they have. The former interpretation can lead to providing less demanding instruction that undermines the students' intellectual capacities and denies them access to quality learning opportunities.[4] In the same vein, teachers must be conscious of their expectations for students and ask themselves if they have high expectations for all students regardless of ethnicity, race, or social class. Ample evidence supports the idea that high expectations is related to student achievement, so it is essential that teachers examine any latent beliefs they might have that leads them to have lower expectations for some students.[5] Such issues may be challenging to confront. Nonetheless, understanding how you are shaped by your life experiences, and how they may influence your perceptions and judgments of students, is vital to the interests of fair and justice-oriented assessment practices.

Teachers may want to examine their autobiographies and factors that have shaped them individually rather than in a group setting, or with others whom they trust and feel they have their best interests at heart. In this regard, exploring characteristics such as ethnic, racial, class, and gender identity, family relationships, family traditions, friendship groups, religious affiliation, personal values and beliefs, interests and hobbies, personal dislikes, and so on can help paint of picture of what makes you, you. Some scaffolds are available for this, such as the Social Identity Wheel, a graphic organizer with a set of related questions. For instance:

1. Which identities do you think about or feel most often? When are you most aware of these identities?
2. Which identities do you think about or feel least often? Why do you think you aren't aware of them a lot of the time?[6]

A critical analysis of these factors can shed light on how teachers interpret and react to the world and, in turn, inform how they shape their perspectives of their students. This awareness could lead to questioning the assumptions that they may have about some of their students, if they are warranted, and if not, why.

Structured workshops can provide a supportive context in which to explore one's sociocultural consciousness. For example, a module on culturally responsive collaboration available from the Collaborative Discussion Project, an Interactivity Foundation Collaborative Learning Program, focuses on a commitment to learning from and relating respectfully to others who are both similar to and different from oneself.[7] Engaging in this module helps individuals within a group to develop an awareness of social identity and to recognize their own limitations and socially constructed understandings. With a deeper appreciation of who they are as individuals, group members can reflect together about assumptions or views that they have about their students that emanate from their own perspectives, and challenge whether they are prejudiced, dismissive, negative, or judgmental.

Lastly, teachers need to take personal responsibility not just for monitoring their own sociocultural consciousness and their attitudes toward students but also for helping colleagues pay attention to how they are viewing and responding to students. As one high school teacher noted about her conversations with colleagues: "I've approached conversations with compassion and tried to understand other's perspectives and experiences. Yet, I am also willing to call out discriminatory practices and beliefs. It's not always easy and it's important."[8]

KNOWLEDGE AND SKILLS FOR INTERPRETING EVIDENCE AND TAKING ACTION

In previous chapters we have emphasized that to be consistent with advances in the learning sciences assessment should encompass three dimensions of learning and development: cognitive, cultural, and socio-emotional. So far, we have considered the knowledge and skills needed for creating learning goals and success criteria (chapter 5), and for eliciting evidence of learning (chapter 6) in relation to these dimensions. We will now apply them to our discussion of the knowledge and skills needed for interpreting evidence and taking action. These are summarized in table 7.1 below. Notice that teachers' sociocultural consciousness both frames and permeates the knowledge and skills required for interpretation and action, underscoring its essential role in this process for fair and justice-oriented assessment practices.

We begin our discussion of the knowledge and skills that teachers need for interpretation and action by examining two classroom examples: a fifth-grade English language arts (ELA) lesson, and a sixth-grade mathematics lesson.

Fifth-grade ELA lesson

The fifth-grade teacher, Ms. Hernandez, planned a lesson comprising four class periods for her students, fifty percent of whom are classified as English learners.[9] The lesson is based on the English language arts writing anchor standard: "Write arguments to support claims in an analysis of substantive topics or texts using valid reasoning and relevant and sufficient evidence."

Prior to this lesson, Ms. Hernandez had taught her students about the structure of argument writing, and she now wanted them to use this structure to write on a topic of their choice related to the environment. She knew this was an important issue for them from prior questions they had raised and from texts they were interested in reading. She noted, "because of their concerns about the environment, I also wanted my students to see themselves as agents of change and to convince their audience to make changes in their own lives."

To start the lesson, the teacher engages the students in what she refers to as an *entry event.* She invited them to respond to this proverb, which has been attributed to a variety of sources:[10] "Treat the earth well; it was not given to you by your parent, it was loaned to you by your children. We do not inherit the earth from our ancestors; we borrow it from our children."

TABLE 7.1 A summary of knowledge and skills for interpreting evidence and taking action

< *Sociocultural Consciousness* >

Interpretation and action that integrates the cognitive dimension of learning requires evidentiary reasoning and asset-based interpretations of what students are able to do and already know.[a]	
Cognitive	• Skills in evidentiary reasoning based on disciplinary content knowledge • Skills in asset-based interpretations of what students are able to do to tailor action to students' current academic knowledge and skills • Skills in using students' ideas as productive starting points for next steps
Interpretation and action that integrates the cultural dimension of learning is based on an understanding of the influence of students' background on learning and knowledge of the cultures, lived experiences, and the communities to which students belong.[b]	
Cultural	• Knowledge of students' backgrounds, cultural frames of reference, and interests • Skills in leveraging cultural knowledge of students into future learning activities
Interpretation and action that integrates the socio-emotional dimension of assessment is based on an understanding of the connection between emotion and cognition and relies on a deep knowledge of students[c]	
Socio-emotional	• Knowledge of students' attitudes to and interest in the instructional/assessment task content • Knowledge of students' sense of self-efficacy with regard to the discipline • Knowledge of whether students are experiencing anxiety from current personal circumstances or have limited attention control • Skills in supporting students to regard assessment as a means for learning and improvement (e.g., using ongoing progress-oriented feedback from teacher/peers/self) • Skills in collaborating with students to understand learning status/performance in ways that enhance feelings of self-efficacy • Skills in teaching self-regulated learning processes to support learning and motivation

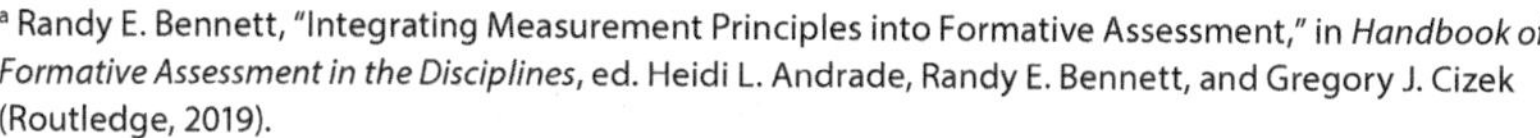

Sociocultural Consciousness

[a] Randy E. Bennett, "Integrating Measurement Principles into Formative Assessment," in *Handbook of Formative Assessment in the Disciplines*, ed. Heidi L. Andrade, Randy E. Bennett, and Gregory J. Cizek (Routledge, 2019).

[b] Luis C. Moll, Cathy Amanti, Deborah Neff, and Norma Gonzalez, "Funds of Knowledge for Teaching: Using a Qualitative Approach to Connect Homes and Classrooms," in *Funds of Knowledge: Theorizing Practices in Households, Communities, and Classrooms*, ed. Norma González, Luis C. Moll, and Cathy Amanti (Lawrence Erlbaum, 2006); National Academies of Sciences, Engineering, and Medicine, *How People Learn II: Learners, Contexts, and Cultures* (The National Academies Press, 2018), https://doi.org/10.17226/24783.

[c] Mary Helen Immordino-Yang and Antonio Damasio, "We Feel, Therefore We Learn: The Relevance of Affective and Social Neuroscience to Education," *Mind, Brain, and Education* 1, no. 1 (March 2007): 3–10, https://doi.org/10.1111/j.1751-228X.2007.00004.x.

She then asks the students to think about what the quote meant to them and what connections they could make to the proverb. Below are responses from two of the students.

> I think this quote is trying to tell us not to damage the earth so that people in the future can live life in a beautiful earth. We should care for mother earth and not allow her to get sick. We can help by stopping air pollution and saving energy.
>
> This quote means to me that we should stop Global Warming because the earth was not given to us to do whatever we want with it. This earth was loaned to us to live in and take care for our children.

Responding to the proverb piques the students' interest and enables them to make an emotional connection to the topic. Ms. Hernandez encourages them to consider what they think should happen to take care of the earth, and what action they would try to convince others to take. They discuss their ideas in small groups as the Ms. Hernandez listens in, intervening when necessary to guide the discussion toward identifying a topic. One group lists several actions such as energy saving light bulbs, solar panels, and unplugging electronics. She prompts the students to think about what the connection is among the solutions they have identified and what their argument would be. At the end of the discussion time, as the class period is about to conclude, Ms. Hernandez tells the students that in their writing class the following day they will begin to construct their arguments, using a graphic organizer of the structure they have previously learned about: claim, arguments, reasons/opinions, and counterarguments.

In the next class period, while the students are making notes for their writing under the headings in their graphic organizer, Ms. Hernandez meets with individuals to discuss their ideas. She uses these conversations as a source of evidence for making decisions about what is next for individual students, or for groups of students if she finds similar needs among them. She sits next to a student and asks: "Could you read me your argument first, just so that I understand what it is." The student responds, "I think people should recycle because like . . . you . . . you could help the earth get well, clean, and healthy." Acknowledging the student's argument, the teacher notices that she has begun to list ideas in the reasons column with "you can stop people by getting injured when they are picking cans, bottles from the street or in the trashcan." The teacher asks her what the purpose of the reasons are. The student replies "to save the earth."

Ms. Hernandez refers to student's argument and explains, "So, your argument is I think people should recycle because that way you could help the earth get well, clean, and healthy, so that's your argument. And I see here that one of your reasons is this is going to help to save the earth, right?" The student responds, "And this is going to save people." Ms. Hernandez interprets the student's response as revealing a possible confusion between giving reasons for her baseline assertion, and the meta-issue of explaining why these reasons are necessary to support her argument. Her response is to focus on the reasons for giving reasons: "You need these to convince people [pointing to the student's list of reasons]. That's why you need this list. This list is so important and you need it to convince people of this [pointing to the argument]. So everything you put here, [pointing to the list of reasons] you have to really be thoughtful, and really think about what you are writing down because these are going be all the reasons why people should listen to you." The student nods and says "okay." Ms. Hernandez asks the student to keep thinking about that as she makes her list of reasons and ends the interaction with a scaffold in the form of a Post-it note that reads, "Why should people listen to your argument?" She took this step "to make sure she [the student] was focused." She then makes notes about her intervention and her plan to give the student a little more time to develop her reasons before she reviews her work again.

Ms. Hernandez then has writing conferences with four other students. She is satisfied that two students have convincing set of reasons, and another has been successfully compiling counterarguments as he reveals in his response to her question, "what are you working on right now?" The student says, "I'm looking for my reasons [points to his arguments on paper] and then sometimes when I find more reasons I . . . like . . . get more counterarguments, and I look for more reasons and I get more the counterarguments—so I keep on adding more." Her action in this case is to provide supportive feedback that he is on the right track and "you are thinking about what people are going to say that is going to be against my . . . what I believe." A fourth student has listed some reasons but appears to have the same challenges as the first student in making clear connections to his argument. She thinks it will be beneficial for her to conduct a mini lesson in the next class period with the students, both of whom are classified as English learners. Reasoning that these students might find the ideas more accessible in Spanish, Ms. Hernandez decides that she will use a Spanish mentor text from the *Yo Opino* series to model the elements of argumentation, and help them apply the structure to their own writing about the environment. While she engages with these two students, the rest of the class will partner with their "writing buddies" to share their work so far and provide each other with feedback, a routine part of her students' writing process.

Sixth-grade mathematics lesson

The next example is from a short lesson unit designed to give sixth-grade students the opportunity to apply their knowledge of the mathematics standard "Represent and analyze quantitative relationships between dependent and independent variables."[11] The unit also has a particular emphasis on four mathematical practices: (1) make sense of problems and persevere in solving them, (2) reason abstractly and quantitatively, (3) construct viable arguments and critique the reasoning of others, (4) model with mathematics.

In the first class period, each student is given an assessment task (figure 7.1), Car Skid Marks, so that Ms. Scott will have information about students' current level of understanding related to the standard and any likely difficulties so she will be better able to target her assistance in the mathematics class.

Ms. Scott introduces the task by asking if anyone has experienced braking suddenly in a car. Did the car skid? Several students recount their experience about what happened. Ms. Scott explains that there are often skid marks at the scene of a traffic accident, even if the road conditions are good. She then asks the students to discuss in pairs if they think that the speed of the car when the driver brakes affects the length of the skid and, if so, how. In the ensuing whole-class debrief, most students think that the higher the speed the car is going means it will slide further when it brakes and so will leave a longer skid mark. Ms. Scott tells the students that accident investigators use the lengths of skid marks to estimate the speed of the car before it starts to brake. She refers to the task, which is shown in figure 7.1.

Ms. Scott observes that some students have difficulty getting started with the task so she asks questions to help them, for instance "What do you need to know? What do you know?" and "For the data in the table, how does the length of a skid mark change as the speed changes?" When all the students have made a reasonable attempt at the task, Ms. Scott tells them that they will have time to revisit and revise their solutions in the next class period. Ms. Scott collects the students' work and makes notes about what it reveals about their current levels of understanding and their different problem-solving approaches.

FIGURE 7.1 Car skid marks task

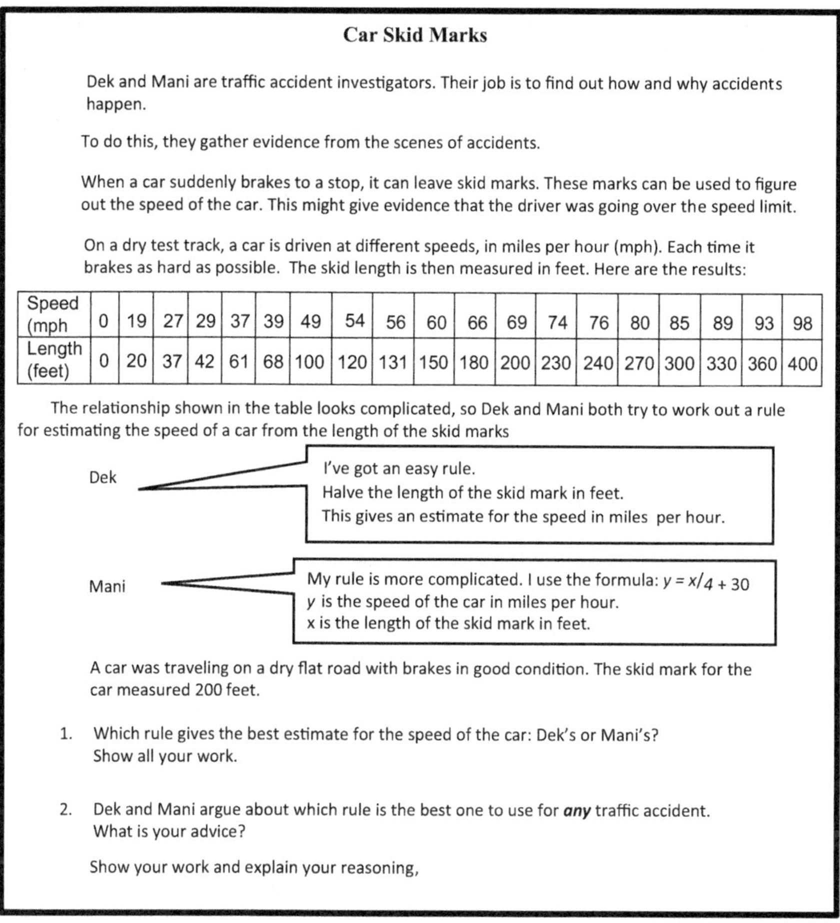

Car Skid Marks

Dek and Mani are traffic accident investigators. Their job is to find out how and why accidents happen.

To do this, they gather evidence from the scenes of accidents.

When a car suddenly brakes to a stop, it can leave skid marks. These marks can be used to figure out the speed of the car. This might give evidence that the driver was going over the speed limit.

On a dry test track, a car is driven at different speeds, in miles per hour (mph). Each time it brakes as hard as possible. The skid length is then measured in feet. Here are the results:

Speed (mph	0	19	27	29	37	39	49	54	56	60	66	69	74	76	80	85	89	93	98
Length (feet)	0	20	37	42	61	68	100	120	131	150	180	200	230	240	270	300	330	360	400

The relationship shown in the table looks complicated, so Dek and Mani both try to work out a rule for estimating the speed of a car from the length of the skid marks

Dek

I've got an easy rule.
Halve the length of the skid mark in feet.
This gives an estimate for the speed in miles per hour.

Mani

My rule is more complicated. I use the formula: $y = x/4 + 30$
y is the speed of the car in miles per hour.
x is the length of the skid mark in feet.

A car was traveling on a dry flat road with brakes in good condition. The skid mark for the car measured 200 feet.

1. Which rule gives the best estimate for the speed of the car: Dek's or Mani's? Show all your work.

2. Dek and Mani argue about which rule is the best one to use for ***any*** traffic accident. What is your advice?

   Show your work and explain your reasoning,

Source: Mathematics Assessment Project. Reproduced courtesy of the BBDSC Trust. Available under the Creative Commons CC BY-NC-ND 3.0 license, https://map.mathshell.org/.

Figure 7.2 is a summary of Ms. Scott's notes about her interpretations of the student responses and the questions or prompts she has written on their work to scaffold students' thinking (table 7.2).

At the beginning of the next class period, Ms. Scott returns each student's work. She asks them to read through the questions and prompts carefully on their own and use them to help them think about ways of improving their work, making notes that they can share with a partner later on. While the students are reviewing their work, she asks questions in cases where she wants to help clarify their thinking.

TABLE 7.2 Summary of teacher's interpretations and responses

Has difficulty evaluating Mani's rule: makes an error when substituting 200 into the formula	• Describe the equation by replacing the variables *y* and *x* with words. • Check your answers. Do your answers make sense?
Evaluates rules based on an inappropriate or insufficient sample of data: only checks the slowest and fastest speeds.	• What assumptions have you made? Can you justify those assumptions? • Is the data in the table linear? How do you know? Does this make a difference to the number of comparisons you need to make? • How do you know you have compared enough values?
Assumes the relationship in the table is linear: only plots two points on a graph of the data in the table.	• Have you made any assumptions when plotting the data in the table? • What do you know about the relationship between the length of the skid marks and the speed of the car?
Checks all values for each rule against the data in the table	• This looks like a lot of work. Can you think of a quicker method?
Does not work systematically and/or their work is disorganized: randomly compares values.	• Would someone unfamiliar with the problem understand your solution? • Can you use a more organized method?
Obtains values for the rules but does not draw conclusions from these values.	• What conclusions can you now make about the two rules?
Concludes that either Dek's or Mani's rule is always the best.	• Is this rule always the best? When is the other rule better?
Does not consider a graphical approach.	• Can you think of an alternative method that could help you see when one rule is closer than another?
Uses an inefficient method when plotting the two rules on a graph: plots several points for each rule.	• What do you know about the two rules? How can you use what you know to think of a more efficient method to plot the two rules?

Once the students have completed this task, Ms. Scott organizes them into groups of two and three and tells them that they are going to work together on the Car Skid Marks task to produce a joint solution that is better than their individual work. She then invites the students to discuss what they have learned from reviewing their individual solutions. She reminds them to listen carefully to each other, asking questions if they do not understand, and to notice similarities and differences between the respective methods that they describe. Her purpose in the discussion is for all students to actively engage with another group's reasoning, as well as voice their own thinking.

After this discussion, Ms. Scott goes over the joint task directions with them, which she has projected on the white board:

1. In your group agree on the best method for completing the problem.
2. Produce a poster that shows a joint solution to the Car Skid Marks task that is better than your individual work.
3. State on your poster any assumptions you have made.
4. Give clear reasons for your choice of method.

While the groups are working on the joint task, Ms. Scott observes how they are progressing and, if they are struggling, asks questions to help them identify strengths and weaknesses in their solutions—for example, "What decisions have you already made?," "Why did you make those decisions?," "What else do you need to find out?," "Have you used all the information given in the task?," "Why/Why not?," and "What do you now know that you didn't know before?"

When the students have finished their posters, Ms. Scott asks them to visit another group and share their work. The students are to explain their work to each other, giving reasons for their choice of method. They can ask each other clarifying questions and discuss any similarities between their methods. Their final job is to write on a Post-it note suggestions for how the work could be improved. After the group discussion, the students have the opportunity to revise their work based on the peer feedback. The class period ends with Ms. Scott giving them time to make any revisions they deem necessary. In subsequent mathematics classes, working in the same small groups, students evaluate and comment on sample responses, identifying strengths and weaknesses in each approach, and comparing them with their own work. In a whole-class discussion, students compare and evaluate the methods they have seen and used. Lastly, students reflect on their work and what they have learned.

Reflecting on the teachers' interpretation and use of evidence

In both examples, the teachers used a divergent, short-cycle approach to assessment. Their purpose was to gain insights into their students' thinking so that they could make instructional responses intended to nudge it forward from its current status to where students could go next, a distinctive feature of classroom formative assessment. None of the assessment opportunities was designed to provide information as to whether the students had achieved a particular curricular goal, as in the case of convergent assessment for summative purposes, including grading. The assessment was integrated into ongoing teaching and learning, with the purpose of guiding the next steps for both teachers and students.

When we consider the role of the teachers' sociocultural consciousness in their practices of interpretation and action, it is evident that they respect and value their students and take a constructive view of the students' competencies, no matter their current levels. Their interpretations and actions are designed to support every student to move from where they are to where they can go next. When students are able to accomplish their next steps in learning, they are positioned as competent individuals who can continue to make progress. The teachers' actions indicate that they have established a safe environment for students in which each one can feel a sense of belonging. Without such an environment for learning and assessment, fair and justice-assessment practices will not be possible.

What knowledge and skills do these teachers draw on?

In these two examples, we saw the teachers employing much of the knowledge and many of the skills for interpretation and action detailed in table 7.1. From the cognitive perspective, both teachers used their skills in evidentiary reasoning based on their disciplinary knowledge, which included an understanding of the content the students are learning, an understanding of how students learn that content and the likely difficulties they have, and what constitutes evidence. Applying this knowledge, the ELA teacher identified one of the student's responses as evidence of confusion and used her interpretive skills to make a judgment about its likely cause. She also determined that two other students were making progress in compiling reasons and that one student had moved to successfully assemble counterarguments, while another was having the same difficulties as the first student she met with, resulting in small group instruction for the pair. Similarly, the mathematics teacher understood what meeting the standard entails, and employed that knowledge in combination with her interpretive skills to draw inferences about the range of student responses to the assessment task.

Both teachers' actions in relation to their interpretation were asset-based—crafted to the "edge" of their students' current learning.[12] As noted in table 1.1, asset-based interpretations are key to fair and justice-oriented assessment practices so that future action to advance learning can be scaffolded based on what the students can do currently. The ELA teacher's actions were contingent on her observations of the student's work and on her interactions with her and designed to stimulate her student's thinking about how what she had already written could be framed as arguments and reasons, as was her plan to use a mentor text. Her response to another student directly built on his explanation of how he was compiling counterarguments and offered support for the direction he was taking. The mathematics teacher's actions were also contingent on the students' responses to the assessment task, and similarly designed to stimulate the students' thinking, as were the questions the teacher asked when she determined from her observations that some groups needed additional support in their joint work.

Underscoring the need for assessment literacy knowledge and skills associated with interpretation and actions is that these teachers had to engage in this process either proximate or nearly proximate to when learning was taking place. The ELA teacher was interpreting and acting in real time during her interaction with her students, and the mathematics teacher was doing the same when asking students questions during their group work based on the observations she had made at the moment. Other actions were planned for the next immediate lesson: the mathematics teacher's comments for students on the assessment task would be used in the next class period. Similarly, the ELA teacher made notes immediately after her interaction with students to introduce a new mentor text the following day. Either way, the teachers had to apply their knowledge and skills in the course of lessons to maintain momentum in learning.

In addition to reflecting the cognitive dimension, the next actions the teachers took intersected with the socio-emotional dimension of learning, again an element of fair and justice-oriented assessment practices (see table 1.1). For instance, neither teacher told the students they were wrong, nor provided them with the correct answer, potentially undermining their feelings of self-efficacy related to the discipline. Both teachers' actions preserved students' agency, a component of self-regulation, with regard to their own learning. Specifically, the ELA teacher's account for her request for the student to read her argument "just so I understand what it is that you're . . ." is registering the student's ownership in their work and her own support role. When she identifies what she believes is the source of the student's confusion, she references what the student has already written to provide assistance, using gesture and explanation to concretely connect the argument with the reasons. She maintained her student's agency and commitment to the writing by reinforcing that her reasons should convince others to pay attention to her argument. After this intervention, the student was given the opportunity to think for herself, with the Post-it note serving as a reminder of what she needed to do, again promoting her agency. It is also worth recalling the teacher's comment about the Post-it note helping her to maintain focus, signaling that she understands her student as a learner who might need support in attention control. In her interaction with the student about his counterarguments, she showed interest in his ideas and offered comments that helped him constructively understand where his learning stood in relation to the desired goal and, in doing so, bolstered his feelings of self-efficacy.

Using her disciplinary knowledge, the mathematics teacher's written responses to the students' assessment task specifically targeted the sources of difficulty she identified, with the intention of providing assistance for them when they reviewed and revised their thinking. Note that the majority of her comments are in the form of questions, rather than direct suggestions that would limit student thinking. The questions nudge each student along from where they were in solving the problem. From a socio-emotional perspective, her comments positioned students as competent: they could take their own action for improvement and subsequently share their work with peers, noting what they had learned from reviewing their individual solutions. In this way, each student was first able to exercise agency, and then contribute to the learning of others in a collaborative way.

When the teacher observed that some students were having trouble getting started with the assessment task, she provided assistance. Her aim was to find out what students know, not to subject them to a stressful situation. After they completed the task, the teacher encouraged students' agency by giving them time to review and revise their own work based on her comments. Students' agency was also promoted when they were offered opportunities to provide feedback to each other and then to make improvements to their joint work. A hallmark of fair and justice-oriented assessment practices (see table 1.1) is enabling students to take an active stance in their learning as in the ways that both teachers fostered.

We observe the cultural dimension of interpretation and action in the ELA teacher's decision to harness the English learner's Spanish language competence to support her understanding of argument structure. She views the students' language as an asset that can be leveraged in their learning, another feature of fair and justice-oriented assessment practices (see table 1.1). While the mathematics teacher did not incorporate students' culture in an explicit way, she chose a task related to a phenomenon that would likely to be familiar to them, made sure that they understood what happens when a car skids, and couched the assessment's protagonists' roles in a real-world context.

USING CONVERGENT ASSESSMENT

Most evidence that classroom teachers will draw from to support instruction will come from the use of short-cycle divergent assessment approaches. However, recall from chapter 3 that we encourage teachers to manage the balance between convergent and divergent assessment and action within an agenda of learning for all students to ensure that they make progress in ways that build on their knowledge and competence within the discipline. Throughout the chapters, while emphasizing divergent approaches, we have seen a number of examples of convergent assessment: for example, hinge-point questions, the end-of-the-week checkpoint, and the use of a portfolio in chapter 3; the history end-of-unit assessment in chapter 5; and the science end-of-unit assessment in chapter 6. Classroom convergent assessment is generally medium-cycle assessment and is summative in nature because it is primarily intended to provide summary information about students' achievement of the unit or course goals. These assessments can be created by teachers or be included in curricular materials or be provided by the district. The results of this type of assessment will generally be in the form of a score from multiple-choice items, or a score derived from a rubric used with constructed-response items. For these assessments to be of any value, teachers need to interpret the scores and take action intended to improve learning. Questions in callout box A can be used by individual teachers, or by grade-level teams who are teaching the same units and using the same assessment to interpret the scores.

There is a range of actions that teachers can take based on interpretation of scores, including reflecting on their own teaching or the unit design and obtaining corroborating information from other assessments. Whereas teachers mainly take action that is proximate to teaching and learning when using short-cycle divergent assessment approaches, their actions based on convergent assessment may take place immediately, for instance in the next class period to address a problem that many students are having or later, for example, in plans for a subsequent unit. Table 7.3 shows some of the actions teachers might consider in relation to the questions in callout box A.

TABLE 7.3 Possible Actions Based on Interpretation of Evidence

• Which students have met the learning goals of the unit and which have not?	• Provide additional support for students who have not met goals before moving to next unit • Spiral back to concepts/skills/ practices that students need help with in subsequent units • Provide feedback to students • Reflect on effectiveness of teaching
• What are the overall strengths and needs of the class? • Are there any areas where students are performing well or are struggling?	• Reflect on effectiveness of teaching • Further investigate particular students' or groups' performance to examine reasons • Allocate additional time for lessons in these areas next time unit is taught • Adopt a different pedagogical approach next time unit is taught; include additional resources; change resources • Provide additional support for students who are struggling before moving to next unit • Spiral back to concepts/skills/ practices that students need help with in subsequent units • Make plans to draw on students' strengths • Provide feedback to students
• Are there any surprises for me in these results?	• Reflect on teaching: what worked, what didn't, why? • Use lens of sociocultural consciousness to consider results • Further investigate particular students' or groups' performance to examine reasons
• Are there any trends or patterns in the scores?	Depending on trends/patterns: • Change or repeat instructional practice • Change or repeat unit plans • Introduce additional resources • Give additional assessments to corroborate scores • Further investigate particular students' or groups' performance to examine reasons
• How do my students' scores compare with other students' scores on the same assessment in my grade-level?	If other students' scores are higher: • Discuss teaching approaches with colleagues • Make adjustments to teaching • Make adjustments to unit plans
• Do the scores indicate that my students are on solid ground to move on to the next unit?	• Make plans to build on student strengths in next unit • Provide feedback to students

Callout Box A

Questions to Guide the Interpretation of Convergent Assessment

- Which students have met the learning goals of the unit and which have not?
- What are the overall strengths and needs of the class?
- Are there any areas where students are performing well or are struggling?
- Are there any surprises for me in these results?
- Are there particular students or groups whose performance I need to investigate further?
- Am I seeing any trends or patterns in the scores?
- How do my students' scores compare with other students' scores in my grade level?
- Do the scores indicate that my students are on solid ground to move on to the next unit?

Providing feedback to students is specifically noted in several instances in table 7.3, either individually, or if appropriate to the whole class. Students should be helped to understand the results of their assessments and, in collaboration with their teachers, be able to set future goals for improvement.

DEVELOPING THE KNOWLEDGE AND SKILLS FOR INTERPRETATION AND ACTION

As we have seen, integrating cognitive, cultural, and socio-emotional dimensions when interpreting evidence and taking action is dependent on teachers' knowledge and skills in two main areas: disciplinary knowledge and knowledge of their students. We have previously discussed disciplinary knowledge in chapters 4 and 5, and we now turn to teachers' knowledge of their students.

Teachers' knowledge of their students, their interests, motivations, cultural backgrounds and references, and so on is essential for fair and justice-oriented interpretation and action. The knowledge that they have accumulated by using the ideas and strategies described in chapter 5 can be applied to developing skills in interpretation and action, and deepened as they reflect on their effectiveness in progressing student learning.

In addition to knowing about the students' funds of knowledge and their funds of identity, a comprehensive understanding of who their students are requires gaining socio-emotional knowledge about them. Chapter 5 has described a range of ways through which teachers can better come to know their students socially and emotionally. In the interests of fair and justice-oriented interpretation and action, this knowledge can also be brought to bear when teachers are interpreting evidence and deciding on action to improve learning.

Throughout the book's chapters, we have advocated for teacher learning communities as an optimal way to support teachers' ownership of and agency in their professional learning. We propose this as the primary forum for increasing knowledge and skills with respect to interpreting evidence and taking action. In this section, we offer several activities for learning communities, which in general can be thought of as *deliberate practice* described in chapter 4. As teachers engage in the activities, we suggest that they use the interpretation and action sections in table 1.1 as a reference for assessment quality components and fair and justice-oriented teacher actions. In the two examples in this chapter, much of the interpretation and action happened in real time during the lesson. The activities we suggest to deepen interpretive skills take place outside of the classroom, but over time will enable a teacher to become more nimble in their pedagogical moves during a lesson.

Using protocols

To develop interpretive skills and determine appropriate next steps, teachers could use a protocol in their learning communities to examine student work or responses to assessment tasks.[13] For instance, the fifth- and sixth-grade teachers whose lessons were described earlier could take a sample of their students' argument-writing graphic organizers or the responses to the car skid marks tasks for discussion and analysis.

The protocol begins with one teacher briefly sharing the context, goals and requirement of the task. Then other teachers participating in the community read the work silently and make their own notes. A discussion follows, stimulated by these questions:

1. What do you actually see in the work itself?
2. Where in the work do you see thinking? What aspects of the work provide insights in students' thinking?
3. What questions does this work raise for you?
4. What might be the next instructional steps for this/these student(s) to build thinking?

About five minutes is allotted for discussion of each question, while the presenting teacher listens. After the participant's discussion, the presenting teacher spends about five minutes describing what they have gained from listening to their peers.

Discussing questions 2, 3, and 4, in particular, provides teachers with the opportunity to share disciplinary knowledge, including what they know about the progression of learning for students relative to specific skills, conceptual understanding, and analytic practices. Less experienced teachers can benefit from hearing the perspectives of their more veteran colleagues who can provide insights drawn from their knowledge of working longer with state-required standards and using them for instructional and assessment purposes.

Teachers could make a commitment at the beginning of the school year to regularly devote meeting time to using the protocol so that all members of the group can both be presenters and participate in discussion and analysis. Presenting teachers could also follow up after using the protocol to report on the action they took in response to the group's suggestions, how effective they thought it was, if they would take different action in the future based on the same evidence, and why.

Many professional organizations have protocols for teacher use. For example, similar to the one above, a *Tuning Protocol* published by ASCD features time for the presenter to talk while participants are silent, and time for the participants to talk while the presenter is silent. It provides three levels of depth: presentation, participant discussion, and presenter reflection, finalized by a general debriefing that can extend the conversation.[14] The recommended time for using this protocol is one hour, which makes it very manageable in the context of a teacher learning community.

Another protocol for use in a learning community is the *Rounds Protocol.* It is very similar to the *Tuning Protocol*, except for the participant discussion, which consists of three rounds. It could be adjusted slightly so that the focus is on interpretation and action. During the first round, participants describe what they have seen in the student work examined (for assessment purposes). During the second round, participants reach some conclusions or generalizations about what they have described (draw inferences about what the work is revealing about the status of learning). During the third and final round, participants base a set of recommendations on what they have concluded and generalized from the second round (what actions would match the edge of student learning and move it forward).[15]

One further protocol for use in a learning community is the *Collaborative Assessment Protocol.* This protocol encourages teachers to examine student work without any information about the student or classroom. The protocol aims to help deepen teachers' perceptions of student work by looking at it carefully without judgment, develop the habit of looking for strengths, share perspectives with others, and encourage conversations among teachers about what the work shows, and how they can act individually and collectively on their interpretations to benefit their students.[16] The suggested time allocation for this protocol is between forty-five and ninety minutes. This protocol could also be modified to emphasize evidence, interpretation, and action.

It is important to remember that all discussions generated by the protocol should be nonevaluative. The goal is to listen to peers' thinking and collaboratively increase individual knowledge and skills by using each other as professional resources, not to put colleagues on the spot or pass judgment on their practice.

By focusing on student work with the use of these protocols, teachers can deepen their pedagogical content knowledge, "that special amalgam of content and pedagogy that is uniquely the province of teachers, their own special form of professional understanding."[17] Through the process of analysis, they learn to see the predictable and nonexpert ways in which students think, and to recognize students' common incoming ideas or partial understandings. With this knowledge, teachers are able to interpret evidence and take action more quickly in situ during teaching and learning.

Inquiry-cycles Inquiry-cycles provide a structure within which a learning community can engage in repeated rounds of inquiry to examine evidence and the action teachers took based on the interpretation of the evidence. This form of an inquiry-cycle shares the characteristics of effective professional learning

Callout Box B

Questions to Guide Inquiry

- What did you learn from the evidence?
- What action did you take?
- Was it effective? How do you know?
- What future action will you take to support learning?
- How will that action support students' feelings of self-efficacy?
- How will the action promote students' self-regulation?
- How are you promoting fair and justice-oriented assessment?
- What changes might you make to your assessment practices in the future?

described by Sam Sims and his colleagues in their meta-analysis, mentioned in chapter 4.[18] Using both their disciplinary knowledge and their socio-emotional knowledge of their students, teachers could take turns sharing one or more examples of evidence and responding to the questions in callout box B.

Using the questions in callout box C, teachers could change the focus of the questions to stimulate discussion and gain a deeper understanding of the cultural dimension of their interpretations and actions. Of course, they will need to draw on their knowledge of their students' funds of knowledge to be able to fully address them.

Repeating this process once a month or per quarter allows for an in-depth experience in interpreting evidence and considering the effectiveness of the action taken that will help teachers increase their individual knowledge and skills.

Analysis of video recordings Teachers may want to take turns in video recording segments of their lessons—for example, their conferences with students—so that they can obtain feedback from their peers. As noted in chapter 6, when teachers are viewing video recordings of each other within the learning community, there should be established norms so that it is a safe and supportive environment to ensure that teachers comfortable sharing their practices with their colleagues. Prior to watching the video, the presenting teacher will need to provide sufficient context for peers in terms of learning goals for the lesson, where in

Callout Box C

Questions to Guide Analysis of the Cultural Dimension

- Does the evidence show that students have drawn on their funds of knowledge? In what ways?
- Does your interpretation take account of students' cultural references and fluencies revealed in the evidence?
- How did/could you leverage the students' funds of knowledge or their cultural references and fluencies in taking next instructional steps?
- How are you promoting fair and justice-oriented assessment?
- What changes might you make to your assessment practices in the future?

the sequence the lesson occured, and any other contextual information, such as the rationale for this being a whole group, small group, or an individual student discussion. It is also helpful to focus peers on a particular aspect of practice that the teacher wants to improve. For example, the teacher might ask them to pay attention to the questions she asks during an interaction with students, and any actions that she took based on the evidence she had elicited. She may be asked to provide a rationale for her interpretation and action to help others better understand what she did and why. Peer feedback can then be an occasion for her to reflect on her practice and consider possible improvements.

Alternatively, the teacher might show the group the evidence she interpreted that prompted her teaching points shown in the video segment. For instance, based on her interpretation she may have decided to do some modeling, share ideas and approaches from other students, use metaphors or representations, engage in a think-aloud, use student ideas as productive starting points for conceptual development, or other options. Peers may ask questions about the teacher's interpretation of evidence to clarify their understanding. There may also be a discussion that allows teachers to add their perspectives on the interpretation, which can lead to deepening all participants' understanding and skills in this regard. After viewing the video segment, group participants can provide feedback about the teacher's actions, including how well they thought it matched the edge of students' learning, and also provide feedback on any student responses they observed that might shed light on the effectiveness of the teaching point and method of moving learning forward. It would be helpful to identify a facilitator for the meeting to ensure that it adheres to community norms, and if multiple videos are being shared in the session to allocate sufficient time for each person.

If some teachers initially find it too intimidating and stressful to share their practice in a learning community, they could invite a trusted peer to observe a lesson in person, or view a recording and provide feedback. This process could involve discussing the evidence and the teacher's plan of action based on their interpretation ahead of the observation, with an observation of the action the teacher took in real time. Jointly discussing the observer's feedback and the teacher's thoughts about what they did could be of benefit for both participants. Building confidence about sharing practice with peers in this way could lead to a willingness to share a lesson video segment with a larger group, thereby benefiting from the different perspectives and experiences of their colleagues.

Examining feedback Skills in providing feedback to students as a contingent action based on the evidence, particularly in the context of formative assessment, can be developed by sharing and critiquing examples of feedback that teachers bring to a learning community. Practicing giving individual feedback on the same pieces of work then sharing, discussing, and revising the feedback if needed can be valuable way for teachers to hone their skills in taking action. For example, the sixth-grade mathematics teacher could share the chart of feedback questions for her students, along with examples of evidence, to prompt a discussion about the comments, leading to increased disciplinary knowledge, in addition to enhancing skills in providing feedback to students.

Collaborative consideration of how students' funds of knowledge can be included in feedback can also be beneficial in strengthening the utility of the feedback, as can sharing examples of how teachers have provided feedback that draws from their knowledge of their students' interests, motivations, and backgrounds. Examining how students have used feedback to improve their work can also be a way to review the quality and effectiveness of the feedback first provided to them. If the improvements are not in line with what the teacher expected, then a discussion of how to revise the feedback would be beneficial.

Secondary school teachers, in particular, can share strategies for how they manage to provide some form of feedback to all their students, such as comment markers linked to specific criteria on a particular piece of work. For example, a history teacher gave her students this criterion for supporting their conclusions about why an event occurred: "All your conclusions should be backed by evidence." When she reviewed their work, she used check marks to identify where the students had used the evidence appropriately. When the work was returned to the students, she asked them to now find statements that were not backed by evidence and provide it.[19] Examining a sample of the checkmarked work could stimulate a discussion about why the teacher placed the marks where she did, and deepen their peers' collective understanding of historical reasoning.

As we noted in chapter 4, there is no shortcut to acquiring assessment literacy, and there is certainly no quick route to becoming skilled in interpreting evidence and taking action based on the interpretation. The suggestions above are intended to be used on an ongoing basis with colleagues and not as a one-shot event. Developing the knowledge and the skills required to be effective in this particular assessment practice will require a long-term commitment to engage with colleagues in collaborative endeavor. However, we can be sure that students will be the beneficiaries of this course of action.

A FINAL THOUGHT

As the late, renowned psychologist Jerome Bruner famously observed, "Good teaching is forever being on the cutting edge of a child's competence."[20] The successful accomplishment of keeping students working at the edge of their competence—or *edge work*—constitutes the core objective and outcome of classroom assessment and, in particular, on teachers' ability to interpret evidence and make sound instructional decisions based on that evidence.[21]

Earlier in this chapter, we presented two student responses to a proverb that the teacher used to connect students intellectually and emotionally to the issue of the environment. We end this chapter with reference to another quote, attributed to the Greek Stoic philosopher Epictetus, among others, to connect us to what interpreting evidence and taking action entails: "We have two ears and one mouth so that we can listen twice as much as we speak."[22]

If we apply this wise saying to interpreting evidence and taking action, we can understand that we need to pay attention to listening to students, whether it is by listening to them talk, or listening to what they are saying in their writing, drawings, or responses to assessment tasks, we can infer what they are telling us about where they are in their learning so that when we talk (the various ways in which we take action) we are on solid ground. Talking without listening or talking more than listening is not going to get us to ambitious teaching practices grounded in sound assessment practice that are fair and justice-oriented for all students.

SUMMARY: KEY TAKEAWAYS

- Interpreting evidence and taking action is the third link in the chain of reasoning for assessment.
- While teachers' sociocultural consciousness bears on all three links in the chain of reasoning, it has particular salience for interpreting evidence and taking action.
- To interpret assessment information, teachers use their skills in evidentiary reasoning based on their disciplinary knowledge in combination with their knowledge of their students.
- Teachers take asset-based actions, crafted to the edge of their students' current learning, that leverage the students' cultural knowledge, interests and lived experiences.
- Teacher learning communities are an optimal context for developing the knowledge and skills for interpretation and action.
- Using protocols and inquiry-cycles to analyze student work, and analyzing video recordings of practice and examples of feedback, are strategies for developing knowledge and skills for interpretation and action.

CHAPTER 8

Beyond Classroom Assessment

In the previous chapters of this book, we have been primarily focused on teachers' fine-grained observations of students' learning from what they say, do, make, and write during the course of learning, and on classroom assessment that occurs at the end of a period of learning, such as an end-of-unit summative assessment. However, there is a wide range of assessments that students complete beyond those that are either designed or selected by the teacher. Unlike much of the assessment that teachers do, which give qualitative data, these assessments provide a numerical score to indicate students' level of achievement and so are categorized as quantitative data. In the interests of fair and justice-oriented assessment practices, and to be assessment literate, teachers need to understand the purpose of quantitative assessment data and the kinds of decisions that quantitative data can and cannot inform.

Educators Shane Saffir and Jamila Dugan, in their book *Street Data,* categorize the data that schools and teachers have access to in a three-level analogy: (1) satellite data; (2) map data; and (3) street data.[1] The *satellite* view is akin to looking down from space and seeing major features such as oceans and mountain ranges on Earth, but without the level of detail that would allow you to navigate from one city to another. In Safir and Dugan's taxonomy, state assessments and district or school interim assessment provide satellite data that are quantitative—the results are expressed numerically.

The *map* view allows you to plan a route between two locations but will not capture all the details of what you observe on the journey. These data are also generally quantitative and come from sources such as student running records or rubric scores on common assessments. (See chapter 3 for a brief discussion on using rubrics to collaboratively score common assessments.) Examining scores across students and classes may provide some insights into curricular modifications or groups of students who may need additional learning opportunities, either to extend or consolidate learning. Teachers may also learn more from sharing observations about patterns they have noticed in student work while they were scoring it. Those qualitative insights will support more nuanced reflections on either adjustments to curriculum materials or learning experiences for students.

Street data are full of observations that get missed in these other views: you notice a new coffee shop that just opened, a road that is closed due to street repair, or a beautiful mural on the end of a building. Street data are full of qualitative observations, in the same way that teachers' classroom assessment practices provide qualitative insights about student learning.

In chapters 3 and 6 we have already discussed instructionally useful information from street data. We have also argued that satellite data—for example, state summative assessments—are not suitable for day-to-day instructional purposes because of their assessment design, type of items, timing, and nature of results. So, if they are not intended to be instructionally useful for day-to-day decisions about student learning, what ought satellite data be used for in general, and how ought they be used by teachers? We plan to answer these questions in this chapter.

First, we introduce a process for examining quantitative assessment data, whether a single source of data or multiple sources together. Then we focus on three types of assessment that provide satellite data that teachers have access to. For each, we will examine the purpose and primary users, design, reporting, and use from the perspective of the classroom teacher. We will return to the data review prompts to examine how using it supports appropriate interpretation and use of the assessment results.

DATA REFLECTION PROMPTS

The Data Reflection Prompts (DRP) are a set of questions drawn from work by the Network for College Success that can be used to help make sense of assessment data:

1. What do we know?
2. What do the data suggest?

3. What more do we need to know?
4. What are the implications?[2]

There are two things to notice in these questions. First, the language references suggestions and implications. This choice of language is a reminder that assessment results are not precise results and always contain a degree of error (see also chapter 6's discussion of error). Second, the DRP invites the teacher to consider additional data sources. This is an action we will return to several times within this chapter because different data sources provide different perspectives, and major decisions about students should not be made solely on the basis of one source. Learning to triangulate across data sources or use one source to help calibrate judgments and expectations is an important part of using data for fair and justice-oriented assessment practices.

Let us now review a description of teachers examining data and then apply the DRP to the example.

An example of teachers examining data

The grades 4 and 5 teachers at Riverview Elementary School met near the beginning of the school year to review how their students had performed on the previous year's state accountability assessments.[3] Teachers observed that in both grades, students' proficiency rates were higher in language arts than in mathematics, so they decided to look more closely at particular mathematics skills. Examining the results on each mathematics content strand, the teachers noticed that although students were performing adequately in arithmetic, the geometry subscores were lower for many students. This observation surprised them because, consistent with state standards, teachers taught shapes and measurement in both grades. They also recognized that without more information they could not make any decisions about how to move forward.

Because students had already taken their first district-created interim assessment of the school year, the teachers were able to review how students had performed in geometry on that assessment. They noticed that students struggled most with measuring perimeters of polygons. Since calculating perimeters was a matter of adding, and students had performed well on the arithmetic strands of both the annual and interim tests, the teachers were perplexed. They decided to collect additional data on students' geometry skills, using questions from the supplemental workbooks of their standards-based math curriculum.

When teachers brought their students' workbook responses to the next meeting, they gathered in small groups to examine the students' work and generate hypotheses. As they shared the classwork examples, they noticed a pattern. Students performed well on simple perimeter problems when the shapes were drawn for them, but on word problems that required them to combine shapes before adding, they largely faltered. The teachers hypothesized that students' difficulties were not with calculating perimeters but with considering when and how to combine polygons in response to real-world problems. They further hypothesized that students would benefit from opportunities to apply basic geometry skills to novel situations.

Working together in grade-level teams, the teachers devised tasks for their students to work on in small groups that would require them to use manipulatives and online interactive simulations to solve perimeter problems about floor plans and land use. At their next meeting, the teachers brought their observation notes and samples of student work from the perimeter tasks that they had planned together. Most teachers reported that students were engaged in the tasks but needed additional practice. They decided to continue with perimeter tasks for a while longer and to collect more evidence of how the students' learning was developing and review the work at their next meeting. They also discussed examining the geometry sections of their curriculum more closely to see if they could make some modifications for future years so that less remediation might be required in the future.

Applying the DRP to the example

Although the teachers in this example did not explicitly name each step of the DRP in their discussion of data, the steps are apparent in their approach. They began by describing what they learned about students (response to DRP 1) from the state assessment data in terms of overall proficiency levels in both mathematics and English language arts (ELA) and the subscores for mathematics. In terms of what this information suggested (DRP 2), they appreciated that although the data showed that students were struggling with some aspect of geometry, there was little else that they could infer about the specifics of what that struggle might be.

Recognizing that they needed to know more about the situation (DRP 3), they were able to draw on the first round of interim assessment results. These data provided some additional insights, but the teachers realized they still needed more data to fully understand what students were struggling with. It was only when they were able to look closely at student work together that they fully understood what the problem was and the implications (DRP 4) for supporting student learning in both the short and long term.

It is clear from this example that satellite data by themselves will not directly lead to specific actions but will suggest areas that might need more supports or interventions than others, or where additional information is needed to understand the situation. The four-question DRP is a reminder that classroom data are often needed to understand the implications of quantitative data.

In the next section, we discuss three specific assessments that teachers have access to (1) end-of-year state accountability tests, (2) state assessments for English learners, and (3) district-mandated assessments in core content areas.

End-of-year state accountability assessment: purpose and uses

The purpose of state accountability assessments is, in part, to meet federal requirements as enacted first in the 2001 No Child Left Behind (NCLB) Act and then in the 2015 Every Student Succeeds Act (ESSA), which requires that states collect, disaggregate, and report data on

- students from major racial and ethnic groups,
- students with economically disadvantaged backgrounds,
- students with disabilities,
- students of military parents,
- foster children,
- homeless students,
- migrant students, and
- English learners.[4]

ESSA calls for states to assess students in mathematics and ELA each year in grades 3 through 8, and once in high school. It also calls for students to be assessed three times in science: once in each specific grade span (3 through 5, 6 through 9, and 10 through 12). A wide range of accommodations is generally available for students who need them (e.g., read-alouds, Braille forms, extra time, etc.). However, for students with the most significant cognitive disabilities, the general education assessments are neither appropriate nor accessible. ESSA allows for states to have 1 percent of accountability testing include students identified as having the most significant cognitive disabilities. These students are assessed on alternate achievement standards (abbreviated AA-AAS) aligned to grade-level and state standards.

The purpose of the ESSA assessment requirements is to ensure that states collect evaluative data about student performance against grade-level standards that can be aggregated and used to summarize what groups of students have learned. In this way, these assessments play a monitoring and evaluation role, which is very different from the informing instruction role of classroom assessment. These assessments are not intended to be diagnostic, in the sense that they do not identify *specific* strengths and weaknesses, nor diagnose particular learning challenges.

State accountability assessment: design

Regardless of which specific state assessment is used, there are some commonalities in their designs. The assessments, typically administered online, use a combination of item types:

- multiple-choice items;
- technology enhanced items (TEIs), which include items such as drag-and-drop or other kinds of matching items or some graphing items for mathematics; and
- short or longer constructed-response items.

The assessments must cover all of the grade-level standards that can be feasibly assessed by summative assessment using the item types previously described. As a result of this requirement, state assessments tend to rely on multiple-choice items and TEIs because they take less time for students to answer, which allows for greater content standards coverage without extending the length of the assessment. Short and longer constructed-response items are reserved for standards that cannot easily be assessed by other means, such as writing in ELA and argumentation and modeling in mathematics. There is a tension in the design of state accountability assessments: assessment designers want students to have rich and engaging tasks while, at the same time, they recognize the concerns about the amount of time that these tasks require to complete.

We should note that unlike classroom assessments, state accountability assessments are subjected to rigorous technical reviews to establish their validity and reliability (see chapter 6). Information about the technical quality of the assessments is available from the assessment developers.

State accountability assessment: reporting

State assessment score reports place students in one of four categories depending on their total score: exceeded standard, met standard, nearly met standard, and did not meet standard. The names of proficiency levels vary from state to state, but generally the top two categories represent student performance at or beyond grade-level expectations, and the bottom two categories represent student performance below those expectations. The proficiency levels are provided for the grade level in a school and for individual students. Sub scores are also provided; for example, an ELA assessment has four groupings of items within the assessment: Reading, Writing, Listening, and Research and Inquiry.

Item-level or standard-level scores are not provided for these assessments. To help us understand why, imagine being at a table quiz night with a team of friends. A question comes up asking which amendment granted women the right to vote in the United States and you blurt out that it is the Fifteenth. Based on your incorrect answer one of your teammates says, "Wow, you really don't know any US history, do you?" That would seem pretty unfair for a number of reasons. First, you realized as soon as you blurted out "Fifteen" that you had mixed up two amendments and that you should have said Nineteen. You really did know the correct answer, but nerves got the better of you. Second, your friend made a broad generalization from a specific question on the US constitution to US history writ large. And third, your friend's conclusion was based on a response to a single item, rather than a more extensive survey of your knowledge of US history.

Every item on the state assessment is mapped carefully to state standards, but each standard likely only has a very small number of items assessing it, so the breadth of the standard may not be fully assessed. Reporting student performance at the level of each standard would not provide a reliable reflection of what students know and can do. In other words, there is insufficient evidence to feel confident in an interpretation about student understanding at that individual level.

State accountability assessment: Uses

Referring back to table 6.1, we can see how most of the features related to instructional utility are either not present or present to a much-reduced extent in state accountability assessment compared with classroom assessment:

- *Cognitive complexity*: While many state accountability assessments use some constructed response questions, not all do, due to time constraints and the requirement to cover statement standards.
- *Coherence with the enacted curriculum*: The assessments are intended to be coherent with the state standards, but not aligned with a specific curriculum.
- *Breadth of standards/grain size of results*: These assessments are intended as a measure of grade-level standards so the grain size of results is large.
- *Type of results*: Results are in the form of total scores, subscores and proficiency levels.
- *Timing of results*: Reporting generally happens at least two to three months after testing windows close.
- *Administration and scoring conditions*: Very standardized conditions in order to support comparisons across students, schools, and districts.
- *Allowable student responses*: Responses will be either selecting answers in the form of multiple question items or written responses for open-ended items, with no options for other presentation forms.
- *Student choice and collaboration*: Very little choice available and no collaboration.
- *Real-world connections*: Item contexts will vary with some real-world connections but not specific to a particular class of students.

While they are not instructionally useful, results from state assessment do have utility, primarily for school, district and state leaders for the purposes of program evaluation and monitoring systems. State assessment results allow leaders to identify trends and patterns across grade level, content areas, student groups, and/or schools. This is because satellite data from these assessments provide a reliable information source that is comparable over years and are available for every student in the tested grades and subjects. For example, a state leader might use satellite data to gauge school quality across the state and identify which schools or districts need additional support. A district leader might look at historic ELA results across the elementary grade levels to see whether the three-year teacher professional learning focus on early reading and the new reading curriculum has had an impact on student outcomes in ELA. A school principal might look at mathematics results by subscores to begin a conversation about whether the current curriculum is providing sufficient learning supports in all areas.

Positive and negative consequences

State assessments send both intended and unintended signals to leaders and teachers that can impact behavior in both positive and negatives ways. For fair and justice-oriented assessment practices, it is important to understand both.

From a positive perspective, state assessments can amplify aspects of standards that could be ignored in instruction (e.g., mathematical practices) by including them in the assessment. State assessments also illustrate some of the ways of assessing the state standards. As we noted earlier in the design section, time limitations on state assessments mean that the number of constructed-response items tends to be low (and for some state assessments zero), so it is important to remember that there are many other ways of assessing the standards when time limits and standardization of responses is less of an issue. Another positive outcome has been expanded expectations for students with disabilities as a result of broader inclusion requirements in state testing programs. State testing has also increased attention to the alignment of standards, curriculum, and classroom practice by grade level, and can potential raise equity issues by highlighting performance differences across groups.[5]

Although there are some positive impacts on classroom practice, educators must recognize the potential harm that can be done when the signal from the state assessment is allowed to overwhelm other signals. For example, there is significant evidence of ways in which accountability assessments have influenced teacher and leader behavior in largely negative ways, such as documented reductions in time spent on subjects that are not part of the accountability testing, which in elementary school means reducing time on everything except mathematics and ELA. High-stakes assessments have also led to some teachers only using item types common to the state assessments and teaching test-taking strategies, reducing students' opportunities to engage in more complex disciplinary problem-solving or analysis. In some schools, principals have encouraged teachers to primarily focus on students close to meeting standards and ignore those who are further from meeting proficiency levels. Furthermore, while group differences on assessments can indicate that not all students are well served, it is also important to recognize that the results can reinforce stereotypes. This is because results are not reflective of students' knowledge and skills due to assessment and item design that privilege White, middle-class ways of thinking.

To conclude this section on positive and negative consequences, we return to a quote from chapter 1: "To what degree and in what ways does this assessment—its content and practices—support or hinder rich and equitable classroom learning environments?"[6] This quote is important for all assessment designers and users to consider in the interests of fair and justice-oriented assessment practices.

State accountability assessment: Classroom teacher use

From the perspective of assessment literacy, it is important that teachers are familiar with the state assessment most relevant to their grade and content area. In particular, newer teachers might want to spend a little time on their State Department of Education's website to review the general information about the specific assessment design and how results are reported to parents and caregivers (see callout box A). Teachers can apply the DRP introduced at the start of this chapter to satellite data from state accountability assessments in several ways.

At the beginning of the year Teachers can use state assessment results to both reflect on the previous school year and look forward to the new school year. They

Callout Box A

From the Department of Education website for your state, locate information about the state accountability assessment for your grade level and content area (if math, ELA, science).

- How many proficiency levels are there?
- What are the proficiency levels labeled?
- What are the reporting categories in addition to the total score?
- How do your grade-level standards map to the reporting categories?
- What do parent reports look like?

can first review the results for a group of students they taught the previous year, applying the DRP. They can repeat the process, examining the assessment results of the current students to see how they performed the previous year. To make this more concrete, let us consider a sixth-grade ELA teacher looking at results in late August from the spring administration of the state summative assessment. She will have data from her previous sixth-grade students, and the fifth-grade data from her incoming sixth-grade students.

Starting with the results of last year's sixth-grade students (who have moved on to seventh grade), she can ask the first DRP, "What do I know?" She can describe what she notices in the data in terms of overall achievement, the spread of proficiency levels, and students' subscores. Moving to the second DRP, when asking what the data suggest, some subquestions she might consider are:

- Did students last year appear to learn based on my instruction?
- Do the data suggest that I have taught some things well and some less well?
- Are there areas of the curriculum that I identify as my strength or as an area for growth? Do those areas seem to be reflected in last year's sixth-grade students' results?

Considering the third DRP, "What more do I need to know?," she can explore whether there are other data sources to consider to assist in refining the implications for this current school year. For example, she might want to collect data based on questions such as, "How did students perform during the year based on classroom assessment or other interim assessments?" and "Are there similar patterns of strengths and areas for growth across data sources?" The fourth DRP then asks her to consider the implications of the results. Some of the subquestions to also consider are:

- What are the implications for using the curriculum materials next year? Are there units or subunits I want to spend more time on?
- What are the implications my own professional learning? Are there areas of the curriculum I feel less sure about?
- How can my colleagues support me in areas of growth?

So far in this example, we are illustrating that when teachers examine data from the previous year's students, it supports their reflection on their own practice. Let's continue with our hypothetical teacher: she has a fresh group of sixth-grade students who will start the new school year in a few weeks. The teacher can look at their fifth-grade summative results to inform her preliminary planning for the start of the year. Responding to the initial DRP, she will go through the same process of describing what she notices in the data (i.e., overall achievement, the spread of proficiency levels, and students' subscores). Moving to the second DRP, when asking what the data suggest, the subquestions she might consider are a little different from the previous set:

- What seem to be the relative strengths and weaknesses of this incoming group of students?
- Did this class of students perform similarly to incoming classes in previous years?
- Are there students who might need more support or more extension opportunities?

Considering the third DRP, "What more do I need to know?," and to help ensure that their perspectives on students are not limited to their summative test performance, teachers may also draw on nonassessment information, such as home surveys or student interest inventories, to develop a more rounded view of a new cohort of students. Finally, in answering the fourth DRP, the teacher will consider whether she needs to make any adjustments to the first unit of the school year. For example, if she notices that students' reading scores are lower than she typically sees, she might think about whether some of the texts the students will read require additional scaffolding. Or she might realize that she can introduce some more challenging writing topics, given higher than normal writing scores. She might also choose not to make any initial changes but identify some students to prioritize in terms of observations to better understand how she can support their learning. Of course, as the school year gets underway, there will be many other sources of observation and assessment data that will refine these initial observations and help modify ongoing teaching and learning opportunities accordingly.

Two final notes in terms of teachers' use of state assessment data. First, it can be helpful for all teachers, not just those who teach ELA, to get a sense of students' reading and writing skills by looking at students' previous year's ELA scores, since writing occurs in all content areas. Second, the timing of when teachers get access to this information is critical. If they are well into the school year, it is much less relevant as they will have had access to other kinds of classroom summative and observational data.

Meeting the needs of all students Teachers may also want to discuss results with colleagues across their department or grade-level team to consider how they are meeting the needs of all students. They could examine the percent proficient of a cohort of students over several grades, or longitudinally look at the percent proficient of a particular subgroup over time. They might explore whether there are particular groups of students that are struggling to meet proficiency levels, and whether the school is getting better over time at meeting those needs. As we noted in the opening example in this chapter, the data themselves will not suggest particular solutions to these questions, but provide a starting point or impetus for other kinds of action, such as a curriculum review to identify ways to increase student engagement, or to make more concrete real-world connections for students, or to leverage their funds of knowledge more effectively.

Curriculum and instructional quality State accountability assessment data can be used as one source of information to help evaluate the impact of changes to curricula or instructional strategies. School or district leaders will likely lead the discussions around the impact of previous decisions, such as a new curriculum. However, teachers have the most relevant perspectives on this topic and can help interpret data or bring additional insights to the conversations. For example, when considering the impact of the new curriculum on student results overall, or by specific reporting categories, teachers may have insights into whether all of the curriculum was implemented in the first year as intended, or if the timing of the associated professional learning had an effect on implementation, which could impact student results.

Teachers can also explore differences in assessment results across classrooms. Focusing on questions such as "Are there any teachers in a grade level or content area whose students are outperforming other classes?" could inform opportunities for classroom walk-throughs or additional ways to share classroom practices that might benefit other teachers and their students.

ENGLISH LANGUAGE PROFICIENCY ASSESSMENT

English language proficiency assessment: Purpose and users

Just as federal regulations require annual accountability assessments for students in ELA, mathematics and science, these regulations also mandate the inclusion of English learners in state assessment systems. The 2001 NCLB legislation called for states to first develop English language proficiency (ELP) standards and then use ELP assessments to measure students' progress in and mastery of these standards in four domains: reading, writing, speaking, and listening.[7] The 2015 ESSA legislation continued that focus and, for the first time, required states to submit their state English language proficiency assessments to the US Department of Education for peer review as a quality control function.[8]

The purpose of the ELP assessments is to meet the federal accountability requirements, to provide a measure of progress of English learners in four domains, to support reclassification decisions about whether a student can exit English language support services, and to inform decisions about placement for students to support their continued learning of English.

When students start school, they are administered a home language survey. Questions and policies around this process vary but in general if a student is from a family who use a language other than English at home, the student will then have to take an ELP screener, results of which will determine whether a student is designed as an English learner. Once classified in this way, the student will continue to take an annual ELP assessment until they are reclassified out of English learner status, a decision that is largely based on results of the annual ELP assessment.

English language proficiency assessment: Design

The focus of the ELP assessment is on reading, writing, speaking and listening in English. The ELP assessments use a wide variety of items, including standard multiple-choice, drag and drop items, items that require students to record themselves speaking a short answer, and items that prompt a written response. Items draw on content that students may have experienced in school, but from grade levels significantly below the grade level of the assessment so that what is being tested are students' English language skills, rather than the mathematics that might be part of the item content. In addition to ELP assessments for general education students, states are now also required to develop ELP assessments for students with disabilities, following similar design processes to those used for creating the alternative assessments for ELA, mathematics, and science.

English language proficiency assessment: Reporting

Score reports from different ELP assessment sources vary somewhat, but all of them have common features. Both grade-level and individual student reports provide an overall proficiency score or level along with scores and proficiency levels for each of the four tested domains: reading, writing, speaking and listening. At the individual student level, a score report might also include a general description about what the student can do at the reporting proficiency levels. For example, for the WIDA ELP assessment a student at proficiency level 2 in Reading can:

> Understand written language related to specific familiar topics in school and can participate in class discussions. For example, they can
>
> - identify main ideas in written information;
> - identify main actors and events, in stories and simple texts with pictures or graphs;
> - sequence pictures, events or steps in processes; and
> - distinguish between claims and evidence statements.[9]

This form of reporting represents an asset-based approach to explaining what the proficiency levels mean so that teachers and families can build on each student's strengths rather than focus on what they cannot do. However, the descriptions are at a satellite level, and teachers will need to draw on classroom assessment information to obtain more of a map and street level perspective on what an individual student can and cannot yet do.

English language proficiency assessment: Uses

The discussion earlier in the chapter about the instructional usefulness of state accountability assessments apply directly here. ELP assessments also tend not to use many constructed response items due to time constraints, are coherent with ELP standards rather than local curricula, and report results at a large grain size in the form of total scores, subscores and proficiency levels, with several months delay between testing and reporting. There is very little opportunity for student choice or collaboration, and while items might have some real-world relevance, broadly speaking they are not specific to a particular class of students.

While they are not instructionally useful, results from ELP assessments do have utility, primarily for school, district and state leaders to examine support resources for English learners against the demand represented by the data. Longitudinal results can also provide insight into whether previous English learner supports have been adequate, and if students are exiting out of ELP status at an expected rate.

English language proficiency assessment: Classroom teacher use

Increasingly, teachers are likely to have English learners in their classes and need to be familiar with the ELP assessment reports.[10] To contribute to assessment literacy among teachers, we suggest that less experienced teachers, regardless of grade level or content area, who are not familiar with their state's ELP assessment take some time to understand what the assessment entails using the questions in callout box B.

The ELP assessment results provide a satellite view of students' language proficiency that can be helpful both to teachers who are providing English as a second language support and general education teachers who may need to plan for scaffolds in the content areas for students designated as English learners. Teachers can apply the DRP introduced at the start of this chapter to satellite data from state accountability assessments in several ways. Having a mixture of English learner specialists and general education teachers can be particularly helpful when it comes to responding to the question about implications.

Teachers should address the first question in the DRP about what is known from the data. Teachers might first just notice differences by student in their relative performances across the four domains. The second DRP asks what these data suggest and teachers can consider students' relative strengths and areas for additional assistance.

The third DRP, which asks teachers what else they need to know, provides an opportunity to consider English learners across the different content areas, and whether they show strengths or struggles in class that might challenge assumptions from the ELP assessment data. Finally, the fourth DRP, which focuses on instruc-

Callout Box B

From the Department of Education website for your state, locate information about the state ELP assessment.

- How many proficiency levels are there?
- What are the proficiency levels labeled?
- What are the reporting categories in addition to the total score?
- What do parent reports look like?

tional implications and the profile of performance across the four domains, along with other insights about students from previous years, can offer some initial insights about student English language learning needs. For example, an ELA teacher might realize that the typical types of reading scaffolds that she provides for English learners may be insufficient in a school year when she has an increased number of English learners with more limited reading skills than in previous years.

While the ELP assessment is a starting point, much like the other state accountability assessments, it is essential to stress two things in particular for English learners. First, researchers have emphasized that language learning should not occur independent of active engagement with rich disciplinary learning.[11] Although the ELP assessment is divided into four domains, English learners should not experience language learning that focuses on discrete skill-building. Rather, language development should be undertaken in the context of rich content learning as exemplified in ambitious teaching practices (see chapter 2).[12]

Second, similar to accountability assessments, ELP assessments provide a snapshot in time, and are particularly helpful to get a picture of group performance, whether of a school, a district, or a particular subgroup of students. However, the results are not of a sufficiently fine grain size to directly inform next instructional steps for an individual student. In other words, while teachers might generate some observations and ideas based on the data, they likely will need more direct observations of students to help explain ELP data that suggest a group of students who have significantly stronger listening skills compared to their writing skills, or stronger reading skills compared to listening skills.

The in-class direct observation of what students are able to say, write, make, and do, along with information about their experiences, interests, and passions, will both shed light on the ELP data and have a much more direct influence on how teaching should proceed from day to day, and unit to unit. For example, in chapter 5 we saw how Ms. Cárdenas used a range of approaches to help ensure that all students, including English learners, were able to be successful: opportunities for students to talk in pairs first before sharing their ideas with the whole class, and for students to use diagrams or writing to explain their reasoning. Her instructional decisions were all based on her most immediate observations of how best to use the language resources from all students to maximize learning, rather than treating students' status as English learners as a deficit and seeing them only in terms of performance on past ELP assessments.

Positive and negative consequences In broad terms, the 2015 ESSA legislation reduced the flexibility established under NCLB for districts to create their own approaches for the identification of English learner supports and the subsequent exiting of services for English language instruction, creating uniform state-level processes. In addition, under the new reporting requirements, English learner subgroups must be disaggregated and English learners with disabilities must be separated from the overall English learner population. Having greater clarity in the data allows for the investigation of the effectiveness of different supports and instructional models for English learners.[13]

However, some English learners do not meet their state's standard for being reclassified out of the English learner group for more than six years, which can impact their access to disciplinary content learning.[14] While there may be harm if students lose out on additional language supports by being reclassified too soon, there is concern that some students are denied access to rigorous grade-level content due to the misconception that English learners need English proficiency first, implicitly signaling that students must be able to use language "correctly" before they can engage with sophisticated content.[15] While this perspective is not the fault of the ELP assessment, if administrators and teachers have this view, then student learning will be impacted negatively.

INTERIM ASSESSMENTS IN THE CONTENT AREAS

Interim assessments: Purpose and users

The third category of standardized, large-scale assessments that we discuss in this chapter are interim assessments. This term was introduced by researchers Marianne Perrie, Scott Marion, and Brian Gong in an attempt to make sense of this category of assessments that emerged in response to the increased testing required by the NCLB legislation.[16] This is the most challenging category to define because there is a wide range of assessments and associated terminology, including benchmarks, diagnostics, and sometimes, to our concern, "formative assessments" that fall under this broad umbrella. For the most part, these assessments are administered to all students within a grade-level at the school or district level to provide standardized, common assessment data across classes and schools.

Part of the difficulty of describing this type of assessment is that the purpose and users can vary. From one vantage point, we can consider that these assessments allow for aggregated information about student learning during the year, primarily for policymakers and school or district leaders, because they provide common assessment information about student progress toward grade-level standards. The multiple data points during the year means that they do not have to wait until the end of the school year for the results from the accountability assessments that we have been discussing up to this point of the chapter. While leaders may believe that they benefit from having more information sooner in the year, it is unclear how often decisions about resource allocation are adjusted during the year based on these results.

Alternatively, we can consider these assessments primarily to inform teacher decisions at the classroom level, but many of the concerns about instructional usefulness that we have discussed throughout this chapter will still apply to these interim assessments as results tend to be given at a fairly large grain size. Some of the assessments in this category will provide a prediction of how students will do on the end-of-year accountability assessments, but that information does not inform teachers about what kinds of instructional changes are needed.

Interim assessments: Design

Interim assessments can vary in purpose, which impacts their design. There are two primary design approaches: mini-summative and modular.[17] A mini-summative design is one where each time the interim assessment is administered (whether two, three or more times per year), the format replicates the state summative assessment design; it assesses all of the grade-level standards in each administration. As a result, students may be presented with content in an assessment administered early in the year that they have not yet had an opportunity to learn. However, from a measurement perspective it may be easier to determine end-of-year performance predictions using this design compared to the modular design because each time the full set of grade-level standards are assessed rather than just a subset.

By contrast, the modular design results in a series of interim blocks of assessment, where each block targets a subset of grade-level standards. This design can allow for a school or a district to schedule specific interim modules to be administered after students have had an opportunity to learn the content assessed by that module.

Regardless of the choice of mini-summative versus modular design, another way in which these interim assessments can vary is whether teachers have access to the specific items used in the assessment and student responses to those items, or if they only see a summary report of student performance. This decision is related to whether the items are considered test-secure, in which case teachers will not have access to this information. If the interim assessment has been developed by the local district rather than by a vendor, it is more likely that teachers will have access to the items themselves.

Interim assessments: Reporting

The reports for an interim assessment will vary depending on the design. If the assessment is a mini-summative in design, the report may look more like a state summative assessment report with some indication of overall proficiency and a breakdown of performance across broad categories.

Assessments with a modular design assess a smaller number of academic targets. Results are reported in terms of whether the student is above, at/near or below standard on the assessed set of targets. This is a finer grained level of reporting and can be considered as map data. However, teachers may not find these data particularly actionable without also reviewing the student responses which are provided in the reporting system. Herein lies the challenge for teachers: whether the time invested in the item-by-item analysis will yield sufficient information, beyond what they already knew about student learning from their classroom formative and summative assessment, to significantly improve their next instructional steps for the students.

Interim assessments: Uses

Similar to the other large-scale assessments discussed in this chapter, the direct instructional utility of interim assessments is limited due to item format, standardization of items, limited coherence with the curriculum, and lack (in many cases) of direct access to student responses. The results will give leaders a pulse check on the system, although given that many decisions about resource allocations are typically made in the spring for the following year, a district or school leader may have limited degrees of freedom available.

Interim assessments: Classroom teacher use

Teachers can use the DRP to examine interim assessment data. Because of the variety of formats it is more difficult to cover the range of possibilities. If the interim assessment follows a mini-summative design, the analysis and use of the assessment data will be similar to what we described in the first section with respect to examining state accountability assessment, but with information midyear. If the interim assessment follows a modular design, then the grain size of the reporting will be much more targeted, perhaps addressing content covered in the last couple of units. Again, the same DRP applies, and teachers can describe the data (DRP 1), consider what the data mean (DRP 2), particularly in the light of other information from the classroom (DRP 3), and identify potential next steps.

As we noted earlier, item-level results for state summative assessments are not provided because those data are not sufficiently reliable. However, some interim assessment reports do provide that kind of data, resulting in the concern that teachers will then remediate item-by-item, which can lead to a series of discrete, disconnected lessons that ultimately do not support deeper student learning.

An alternative approach to how teachers might think about results from the interim assessments is as a tool to help teachers qualitatively calibrate their classroom judgments and expectations of quality work. This calibration process will help teachers to understand student competency development better and to make more informed, appropriate instructional decisions in the future, particularly when done as part of a grade-level learning community.[18]

To explain the idea of calibration, consider someone about to knit a sweater using a pattern. It is important that the knitter uses a similar gauge (stitches per inch and rows per inch) as the pattern designer so that the fit of the sweater will be correct. The knitter will first knit a plain rectangle that is big enough to allow them to measure how many stitches and rows they have per inch. They then compare their measurements to what the pattern says they should be. If they are the same, the knitter is ready to begin the project. If the two are not the same, the knitter is either knitting too tightly or too loosely, resulting in a swatch that is too small or too large. The knitter has some options for how to remediate the issue, either by being more attentive to tension in their yarn or by adjusting needle size. They will likely knit another swatch to confirm that they have resolved the problem. In other words, the knitter is calibrating or standardizing with the pattern designer.

This idea of calibrating can also apply to the use of interim assessment results. At the conclusion of teaching a unit on fractions, a teacher can reflect on how many students in the class she considers as having reached grade-level proficiency in the relevant standards. Let's say she thought that fifteen of the twenty-two students were proficient based on classroom observations, classwork, and the teacher's end of unit assessment. The teacher could also administer an external interim assessment that mapped well to the content of her unit. Based on the results of that assessment, eighteen of the students were reported as above or at/near standard. The external assessment evidence could be considered validation that the teacher's own classroom judgments were quite accurate.

Consider the alternative case if the report revealed that only five of her students were at or above or at/near standard as in a modular design. This time the external evidence suggests a mismatch with the teacher's classroom judgment. While not confirming anything, it raises questions about whether the teacher's expectations for proficiency for these standards are as rigorous as the standards describe. The teacher might decide to explore how other teachers compared their own judgments with the external assessment data, and also look at student work across classrooms to align judgments more closely with the expectations of proficiency communicated by the external assessment. To be clear, this is absolutely not a recommendation to teach to the test, nor is it suggesting that teacher judgment be replaced by the external assessment, but rather that a recalibration occur.

The DRP that we have been using in this chapter can guide a teacher through this process to first observe and describe the data (DRP 1), then consider what that suggests about students' strengths and weaknesses (DRP 2). Considering other sources of data (DRP 3), in particular classroom convergent data, opens the discussion about whether teachers' expectations of proficiency are aligned with the expectations of the interim assessment. Whether or not they are aligned will impact the implications (DRP 4) for next steps. Next steps could include coplanning lessons together and talking about the learning goals and criteria for success, in particular to develop shared understanding of the expectations. Alternatively, using a common prompt or set of questions across classes and reviewing student work together with colleagues can also help develop shared expectations of grade-level standards.

Positive and negative consequences

To summarize, interim assessment data can provide useful check-ins during the year by supplying common data across classrooms. However, if teachers are to use these data meaningfully, they need both time to review them collaboratively, and also sufficient time in their teaching schedules to either return to ideas that are still developing among students or to explore aspects of the content more deeply. If teachers do not have sufficient flexibility in their schedule, often as a result of district pacing plans, then deep analysis of these data is a waste of time.

Somewhat parallel to a comment we made about the ELP assessment, an assessment that uses discrete multiple-choice items to survey content may provide some useful information for teachers about student progress, but should not be taken as a model for how teaching and learning in the discipline ought to unfold (see chapter 2 on ambitious teaching). School and district leaders need to be very careful with their messaging to teachers so that they do not encourage teaching to the test and test preparation in a way that hinders meaningful learning.

A FINAL THOUGHT

Road signs posted at a construction zone might instruct motorists to stay in their lanes, as weaving within the narrow spaces can create a hazard. Athletes who race in marked-off lanes, such as swimmers, might be instructed to remain in those lanes to avoid disqualification. In a business or professional sense, staying in your lane means focusing on your responsibility, or on your own area of expertise.[19] We can apply the same "stay in your lane" direction to the assessments discussed in this chapter. We have pointed out that they can play an important evaluative and monitoring role. This is their lane. For the sake of fair and justice-oriented assessment practices, users should let them stay in it.

Continuing the lane analogy, teachers' use of these large-scale assessments can be comparable to having a two-way left-turn lane on a street. Because this middle lane can be used for drivers making a left turn in either direction, drivers are strongly encouraged not to linger in that lane. Similarly, we are not suggesting teachers never look at these large-scale assessment results, only that they limit the amount of time they devote to that exercise, and make sure the time is worthwhile. Take the results for the satellite view that they are, and then quickly seek out a more continuous lane of information from classroom divergent and convergent practices.

SUMMARY: KEY TAKEAWAYS

- Large-scale assessments can provide decision-makers with an overall picture of student performance that can be compared across classes, schools, or districts, and by various groups of students.

- State accountability assessments in mathematics, ELA, and science for grades 3 through 8 and high school, and alternative assessments for students with significant cognitive disabilities, are intended to assess grade-level standards primarily through selected-response items, given time and scoring cost constraints.
- English Language Proficiency assessments play a high-stakes role in the lives of English learners, as they make a significant contribution in determining when a student exits out from English language support services. Similar to state accountability assessments, the reports are at a coarse grain size of information.
- Interim assessments can take various formats from a mini-summative to a more targeted modular approach.
- While all three of these assessments primarily provide school, district, and state leaders with data that they can use to take a pulse of how the system is working, we encourage teachers to take a little time to look at the data, but not too long, recognizing that once the school year is underway, summary level data will be outdated and replaced by teacher insights from both convergent and divergent assessment.

CHAPTER 9

The Role of Leaders in Supporting Teachers' Assessment Literacy

In the book's final chapter, we turn to the role of school and district leaders in developing their teacher colleagues' assessment literacy competencies. While we have mainly focused on ways in which teachers can take charge of increasing their own assessment literacy and that of their peers within collaborative structures, teachers cannot do this alone. They require system conditions that support their professional learning, which only leaders can provide.[1]

These conditions include school and district leaders establishing a clear and compelling vision for why teachers need to be assessment literate and communicating this vision in ways that persuade teachers of the value of these competencies. If teachers cannot be persuaded that their assessment literacy competencies are valuable and be certain of support in developing them, they are unlikely to pursue any path of professional learning.[2] Above all, school and district leaders need to establish a culture of curiosity and inquiry, and create a sense of safety for productive failure.

We begin by depicting a theory of action that leaders should understand in order to realize the benefits of assessment use for improved student learning. This understanding is fundamental to leaders' ability to provide appropriate support for teachers' assessment literacy development. Then we step outside the realm of education to describe a leadership initiative for creating and sustaining a small business from which we will draw parallels to the actions of school and district leaders who have a vision of assessment literate teachers. Lastly, we will offer specific actions that leaders can employ to achieve their vision.

A THEORY OF ACTION

As a grounding for their role in assisting teachers' assessment literacy development, leaders should understand how convergent and divergent assessment approaches come together to inform teaching and learning in the classroom. They must also understand how to interrogate assessment data to identify learning needs for their students as well as the professional learning needs of their teacher colleagues. Figure 9.1 depicts a theory of action that lays out the connections among the actions teachers and leaders take, based on convergent and divergent assessment opportunities, that lead to the ultimate goal of improved student learning.

The theory of action can be read from left to right, starting with the various kinds of convergent and divergent assessment data that we have been discussing throughout this book. While one could justify adding other arrows to represent other ways in which each form of assessment information could be used, we have elected to highlight the uses that align with the themes of this book. Note that teachers and leaders use assessment information differently. The first box that describes leaders' use of data specifies that they are using *aggregable* data—that is, data that can be easily compared across classrooms, schools or groups of students. Of all the sources of convergent data, leaders are most likely going to use data

FIGURE 9.1 Theory of action for assessment use

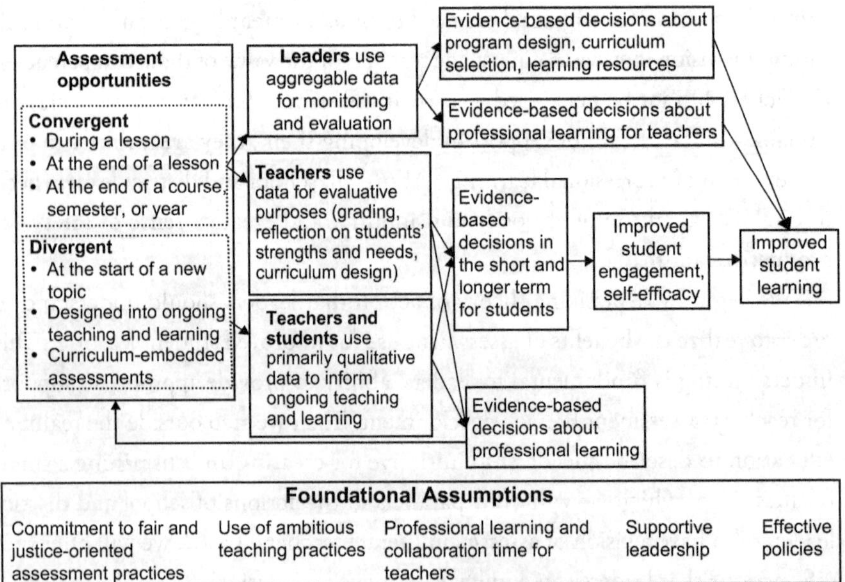

from end-of-course, semester, or year assessments. While leaders do not directly impact student learning in the way that teachers do, when they make sound decisions about resources and professional learning needs there should be a positive indirect impact on students. We also highlighted the importance of teachers using assessment information as one source of information to inform their own professional learning needs.

The theory of action also distinguishes between teachers' use of convergent and divergent assessment information. For the former, we highlighted the opportunities for teachers to reflect on broader considerations, such as future adjustments to the next time the unit is taught. For the latter, the focus is on both teachers *and* students using information to make fine-grained adjustments to teaching and learning in real or near-real time. Ultimately, when students recognize that teachers are using evidence of their own learning, and they have opportunities to also reflect on their learning and make decisions about next steps, student engagement increases and there is a positive impact on student learning outcomes.

Looking at the bottom of figure 9.1, you can see a number of foundational assumptions that we believe need to be in place so that both leaders' and teachers' actions can be successful in achieving the goal of improved student learning. We have discussed three of these throughout the book: fair and justice-oriented assessment practices, ambitious teaching practices, and professional learning and collaboration time for teachers. Two additional assumptions are included in the theory of action: effective policies and supportive leadership. Effective policies for assessment practices prioritize using assessment as a tool for learning, not just for accountability, encouraging the use of different assessment types for a range of purposes, and using assessment for individual student learning as well as for school-wide or district-wide improvement. Supportive leadership entails ongoing assistance for teachers to develop their assessment literacy knowledge and skills through collaborative learning, coaching, and access to resources.

PARALLELS BETWEEN ENTREPRENEURS AND SCHOOL LEADERS

If you live in Mercer County, New Jersey, there is a reasonable chance that you have heard of Joanne Canady, and if not her, then her bakery Gingered Peach, in the sleepy town of Lawrenceville. It first opened in 2015, and Joanne has created a go-to location for lovers of sticky buns and cinnamon rolls. By March 2020, the Gingered Peach had a loyal following. Joanne was determined to find a way to stay open during COVID-19, prioritizing both the safety of her staff and of her customers. She tried several different online-purchasing and pick-up models before settling on an approach that was successful. Her initial attempts at an online commerce site were glitchy and some people complained about not being able to process their bakery orders. However, critics were outnumbered by supporters who were appreciative of her efforts and urged patience. In the years since the shutdown, the Gingered Peach has gone from strength to strength, capitalizing on some unexpected opportunities such as taking over a nearby ice cream shop.

Research highlights what makes a successful entrepreneur: brainstorming and exploring an initial idea, getting organized, building a network, finding investors and partners, marketing and launching, and evaluating and evolving.[3] We can see those steps in how Joanne developed the Gingered Peach, managed through a crisis, and has gone on to expand her business. School leaders need to adopt this entrepreneurial approach as they work with the teachers in their building. To illustrate the connections between the two, table 9.1 below draws some parallels between the bakery and supporting teachers' assessment literacy learning.

TABLE 9.1 Drawing parallels between entrepreneurs and leaders

Entrepreneurs	*Gingered Peach*	*Leaders*
Brainstorm and explore	Had a vision for a neighborhood bakery	Have a clear vision for assessment practices and the literacy skills that teachers need
Get organized	Found a location, developed a business plan	Develop a theory of action
Build your network of investors and partners	Prepared to launch, created a space, trained staff, started with an initial set of offerings	Develop top-down leadership support within the school and bottom-up support with teachers
Form your business, market, and launch	Opened, used paid advertising and word-of-mouth	Decide on an implementation plan: a single grade or department, or volunteer group to start, or whole school
Adjust, evolve, and grow	Found a way to maintain the business during COVID-19, although it required trial and error; the community stuck by her; found new opportunities	Create a supportive culture in which to fail and retry, evaluate and adjust approaches for learning communities Expand into new areas

There are several aspects of the Gingered Peach story that have parallels to the work that leaders do as they support teachers' assessment literacy growth. First, Joanne started with a clear business plan to guide decisions about what she needed to invest in, whether equipment or staff, in order to meet her vision, which she described as "people deserve better food."[4] School and district leaders should not embark on a major assessment literacy initiative without a theory of action, or game plan. The section below contains more details about what that could entail.

Second, Joanne could not have predicted the disruption that COVID-19 brought to her business. While her first attempts to remain open during COVID were not entirely smooth sailing, the willingness of the community to stick with her and to chastise online naysayers was impressive. Similarly, starting up school-based learning communities will not always be simple or straightforward. Federal, state, or district mandates and other local or national circumstances can precipitate sudden disruptions. Having a supportive community within the school or district can help sustain progress through those disruptions.

Third, critical evaluation has been important to the success of the Gingered Peach. During COVID, evaluation of her initial efforts to stay open required Joanne to be nimble and communicative. She used social media to share information about the process for online purchasing and in-person pickup, and when change was needed, she was very honest about it. When it was necessary she closed down completely for a week to regroup and replan. School leaders need to similarly evaluate and adjust approaches to learning. Perhaps a school tries an early close once a month for teachers' professional learning but gets negative feedback from some parents. Collecting information about concerns, focusing on what the desired outcomes are, and engaging the community in problem-solving can help maintain the buy-in for the overall purpose of the initiative while working through growing pains.

Finally, Joanne's initial business plan focused on the bakery. In the years since she first opened the Gingered Peach, she has expanded to take over both a local ice cream shop and a coffee roaster. These opportunities had to be carefully considered in terms of her own bandwidth and her ability to expand her staff while maintaining quality and branding. School leaders may also find that an initial foray into assessment literacy learning may expand into other areas such as schoolwide grading practices, or student self- and peer regulated learning, or other connected opportunities. Finding ways to make these initiatives build on each and be cohesive can help counter "initiative fatigue" and support deeper learning for teachers.

ACTIONS FOR LEADERS TO ACHIEVE THEIR VISION

Our theory of action for assessment use shown in figure 9.1 identifies supportive leadership as one of the foundational assumptions. In this section, we describe six specific actions that leaders can take that together result in supportive leadership for achieving their vision of assessment literate teachers. Again, we can see parallels between these actions and Joanne's outlined in table 9.1.

1. Articulating a clear vision for assessment literacy

Leaders must be clear about their vision of fair and justice-oriented assessment and, as an impetus for teachers' professional learning, consistently articulate the value of those practices for all students. Leaders must be secure in their own knowledge of assessment and what constitutes fair and justice-oriented assessment practices, while at the same time being aware that they, too, are continuous learners in this area. Developing the knowledge and skills for assessment literacy requires a long-term commitment by teachers and they need to know that leaders are convinced of the value of assessment literacy for student learning. Articulating the importance of assessment literacy entails helping teachers recognize that it is not just the flavor of the week, but instead is a hallmark of effective teaching and assessment that takes time to achieve.

2. Develop a theory of action

A theory of action is like a business plan, laying out the steps or strategies necessary to go from initial inputs and desired outcomes. A principal or district leader might not develop one as complex as the one we created for this chapter, but rather take just one aspect of assessment literacy and create the business or game plan for it to be realized. The plan also could get much more specific, particularly thinking about the local assumptions that need to be in place for a certain initiative to be successful. For example, a principal might work with teachers to identify the need for them to come together to examine student work to improve the quality of their written feedback to students. Figure 9.2 is a simple example of a theory of action for that vision.

FIGURE 9.2 Mini Theory of Action

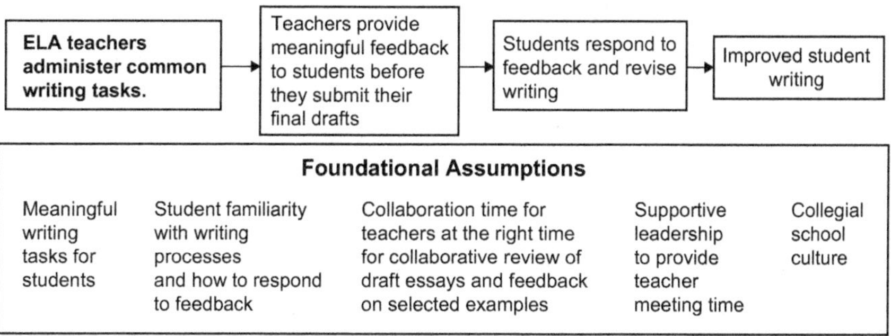

The theory of action is a set of if-then statements that connect a series of actions: if teachers administer a common writing task, and if they provide meaningful feedback to students before they submit final written work, and if students have an opportunity to respond to that feedback and revise, then student writing will improve over time. Being aware of the assumptions that need to be in place for this theory of action to be implemented can help a leader evaluate whether the plan is ready to be enacted, or if additional planning steps need to be established first.

3. Adopt a top-down and bottom-up approach

Research concludes that extending leadership responsibility beyond the principal is an important lever for developing effective professional learning communities in schools.[5] In a top-down, bottom-up approach, leaders set the goals and direction for professional learning around assessment literacy, while at the same time empowering teachers to take responsibility for identifying their own learning needs, and actively pursuing their own pathway to meeting them.

Leaders maintain the press for professional learning. This press entails leaders maintaining an active interest in the development of teachers' assessment literacy competencies. This does not mean that leaders are evaluating teachers, but rather that through collegial communication they are paying attention to how teachers think and feel about their evolving assessment literacy and its impact on student learning, while ensuring that they remain as the drivers of their own professional learning activities.

Leaders must be clear about the alignment among initiatives either at the school or district level in a top-down, bottom-up approach. In our experience, teachers often view professional learning as "just one more thing," leading to feelings of being overwhelmed and a lack of motivation. When teachers have this view, it may be because they have previously experienced incoherent initiatives or professional learning foci that come and go, year by year. Preserving teacher buy-in for developing assessment literacy competencies requires that they perceive an alignment among initiatives rather than viewing them as a set of competing demands. Creating this perception among teachers is a critical aspect of top-down leadership. From the bottom-up perspective, teachers need to understand how assessment literacy development fits in with all the other initiatives in the school or district. For example, leaders can make connections between assessment literacy and ambitious teaching practices, underscoring the importance of building on students' prior knowledge, leveraging knowledge from students' homes and communities in learning, and engaging students in rigorous tasks and activities matched to the edge of their current learning status. They can make connections between schoolwide reading or mathematics initiatives and the use of effective assessment practices to monitor student progress, and then adjust curriculum or teaching and learning based on the results. They can make connections between assessment literacy and the goal of developing student agency through providing actionable feedback based on assessment or helping students to set their own goals. When teachers understand these connections, they are more likely to engage in a bottom-up approach to their professional learning.

In a top-down, bottom-up approach, leaders keep a check on policies that could potentially impede teachers' commitment to assessment literacy development. It is difficult to provide universal guidance about effective and ineffective school or district policies in the absence of contextual information about a specific school or district. However, it is possible that in the course of collaborative professional learning an idea or strategy will get shot down with one or more people saying, "We can't do that. It's against policy." It will take a little investigation to understand whether the proposed action is truly against policy. But in some cases, leaders will identify a policy impediment that they will need to take care of.

Grading is one possible site of conflict between policy and effective assessment literacy development. Some districts mandate the number of grades that must be provided per grading period, and others are even more specific about the types of assessments that can make up those grades. Other districts have a policy that a teacher must grade every piece of work that a student completes. It will be important for teachers to surface such impediments (bottom-up) and for leaders to take responsibility for changing or amending policy to create a more supportive environment for assessment literacy development (top-down).

4. Develop an implementation plan

Articulating a vision for assessment literacy is an important first step in an implementation plan. From that point, leaders need to think carefully about how their vision can be achieved. For instance, in collaboration with their teacher colleagues, they need to decide if all the teachers in the school will be involved from the outset, or if it makes sense to begin with a smaller group, such as a single grade level in an elementary school, or a particular department in a secondary school, or if it would be preferable to start with a volunteer group. Through this process, leaders make clear that developing assessment literacy is not a choice—top-down—but that teachers can be involved in collaborative decision making about how to begin—bottom-up.

There is no prescription for who should be involved first. Such decisions will be made based upon local circumstances, such as the current level of assessment literacy competencies among teachers, the number of teachers in the school, and which teachers are likely to be more amenable to participate in professional learning for this purpose and will be good models for their colleagues' future involvement. Ultimately, in the interests of fair and justice-oriented assessment practices, all the teachers in a building will need to participate in professional learning, but joint decisions about how to begin what will be a long-term commitment can pave the way for accomplishing the vision. Once leaders have established a starting point, they can lay out a plan for increasing the number of teachers over time, if the whole school is not initially involved.

Leaders and teachers will also need to decide how they will keep track of the development of their competencies and across what time scales. Figure 2.2 is a useful reference for defining indicators for this purpose. For instance, will teachers be more aware of what shapes their teacher positioning and how it might impact interpreting assessment information and taking subsequent action? Will assessment content be more recognizable and relevant to students? Will assessments, both convergent and divergent, provide access for all students to show what they know and can do? Will students be adopting an increased agentic stance to assessment? How is assessment literacy impacting other initiatives in the school or district?

In addition to establishing indicators to monitor assessment literacy development, leaders and teachers need to create timelines for review and adjustments. For example, they might decide to focus on one or two indicators per month or per quarter. Working in a longer time frame might result in a lack of momentum and opportunities to rethink professional learning strategies. If these strategies need to be modified, then respecting the top-down, bottom-up approach, teachers will need to determine what those modifications should be in consultation with leaders. Depending on the number of people involved, leaders might want to schedule a periodic check-in meeting just to examine what is working and what could be improved. Alternatively, for a larger group, leaders could use an online survey tool comprised of open-ended questions.

5. Establish and maintain a culture of learning

A learning culture is an environment that demonstrates and encourages individual and organizational learning, prioritizes gaining and sharing knowledge and skills, and promotes collaboration among colleagues.[6] To achieve such a learning culture for teachers, leaders can do a number of things. First, they can give teachers the autonomy to determine their own professional learning needs in connection with assessment literacy. Second, they can safeguard time for the kind of teacher learning communities we have described in this book by removing any obstacles that might stand in the way, showing that they value teacher learning about assessment literacy. Third, leaders can encourage teachers to request resources for their own learning. These might include books on aspects of assessment, video cameras for recording classroom practices, or access to online learning resources or experts. Fourth, they can model behaviors that express the goals and values of a learning culture. These include respectful and open communication with colleagues; showing a consistent interest in what and how teachers are learning, possibly requesting periodic attendance at teacher meetings as a genuine participant, not as an evaluator; expecting successes and failures along the way and regarding them as part of the process; and encouraging teachers to ask questions and share concerns without fear of retribution. Lastly, they can celebrate teachers' achievements individually and as a group at points when they demonstrate assessment literacy competencies in their classroom work.

A FINAL THOUGHT

In an illuminating insight about leadership, the former First Lady of the United States, Rosalynn Carter, observed that "A leader takes people where they want to go. A great leader takes people where they don't necessarily want to go but ought to be." In this observation, she alludes to a harder road for leaders, not just taking people where they want to go, but more challengingly creating a vision and then guiding them to the destination that they might not have initially identified but that they ultimately come to value and desire to reach.

This observation is relevant to educational leaders. As we have discussed, leaders need to have a vision that they can effectively articulate, persuade others of its value, and generate commitment and buy-in to pursuing it; they need to provide the conditions for their teacher colleagues to develop professionally by creating a culture of learning and empowering them to make decisions about their own professional growth. At the same time, they must ensure that they maintain commitment and continuously take action to achieve the goal of assessment literacy for all teachers.

In this book, we have laid out what it means for teachers to be assessment literate in the interests of fair and justice-oriented assessment practices. We hope that this final chapter will spur leaders to take supportive actions with their teacher colleagues so that all students can experience fair and justice-oriented assessment practices that, in the context of ambitious teaching, will assure success in school and beyond for every student.

SUMMARY: KEY TAKEAWAYS

- School and district leader support is necessary for teacher learning communities to focus on assessment literacy.
- Leaders must have a deep understanding of what constitutes fair and justice-oriented assessment practices and how convergent and divergent assessment practices work together.
- Leaders can develop a theory of action as one way to articulate the conditions necessary for teacher learning to thrive.

- Successful implementation requires a combination of a leader's vision for assessment literacy learning together with opportunities for teachers to plot the course of their own learning within some identified boundaries.
- Leaders should proactively consider school and district policies that could derail efforts to improve assessment practices, and be willing to learn about such impediments when identified by teachers.
- Leaders need to develop an implementation plan, periodically evaluate progress toward the goal, and be flexible to modify the plan as needed.
- Leaders need to create and sustain a learning culture for adults in the organization. This can mean everything from protecting time for learning communities to being willing to show up as a learner rather than a leader.

Notes

Preface

1. Carla Evans and Scott Marion, *Understanding Instructionally Useful Assessment* (Taylor & Francis, 2024).
2. Lorrie A. Shepard, "Classroom Assessment to Support Teaching and Learning," *The ANNALS of the American Academy of Political and Social Science* 683, no. 1 (2019): 183–200, https:// doi:10.1177/0002716219843818.
3. Pat Hutchings, "General Education and Assessment: Powerful Connections," *Assessment Update* 4, no. 4: 5–8, 6, https://doi.org/10.1002/au.3650040404.
4. Margaret Heritage and Christine Harrison, *The Power of Assessment for Learning: Twenty Years of Research and Practice in UK and US Classrooms* (Corwin, 2019).
5. National Research Council, *Knowing What Students Know: The Science and Design of Educational Assessment* (The National Academies Press, 2001), https://doi.org/10.17226/10019.
6. See Serafina Pastore, "Teacher Assessment Literacy: A Systematic Review," *Frontiers in Education* 8 (2023): 1217167, https://doi.org/10.3389/feduc.2023.1217167 for a useful set of definitions; Robert J. Mislevy, "Evidence and Inference in Educational Assessment," *Psychometrika* 59, no. 4 (1994): 439–83; James W. Pellegrino, "Assessment as a Positive Influence on 21st Century Teaching and Learning: A Systems Approach to Progress," *Psicología Educativa* 20, no. 2 (2014): 65–77.
7. E. Caroline Wylie and Margaret Heritage, "Assessment Literacy and Professional Learning," in *Reimagining Balanced Assessment Systems*, ed. Scott F. Marion, James W. Pellegrino, and Amy I. Berman (National Academy of Education, 2024), https://doi.org/10.31094/2024/1.
8. James W. Pellegrino, Shuchi Grover, Christopher J. Harris, and Eric Wiebe, "Classroom Assessment in STEM Education: An Introduction to the Report," in *Classroom-Based STEM Assessment: Contemporary Issues and Perspectives*, ed. Christopher J. Harris, Eric Wiebe, Shuchi Grover, and James W. Pellegrino (Community for Advancing Discovery Research in Education [CADRE], Education Development Center, Inc., 2023).
9. Maria Araceli Ruiz-Primo and Erin Marie Furtak, *Informal Formative Assessment of Students' Understanding of Scientific Inquiry*, CSE Report 639 (Center for the Study of Evaluation [CSE], National Center for Research on Evaluation, Standards, and Student Testing [CRESST], 2004).
10. Susan R. Goldman and Carol D. Lee, "Human Learning and Development: Theoretical Perspectives to Inform Assessment Systems," in *Reimagining Balanced Assessment Systems*, ed. Scott F. Marion, James W. Pellegrino, and Amy I. Berman (National Academy of Education, 2024), https://doi.org/10.31094/2024/1.
11. National Academies of Sciences, Engineering, and Medicine, Division of Behavioral and Social Sciences and Education, Board on Science Education, Board on Behavioral, Cognitive, and Sensory Sciences, and Committee on How People Learn II: The Science and Practice of Learning, *How People Learn II: Learners, Contexts, and Cultures* (National Academies Press, 2018), 160.

12. Jill Willis, Lenore Adie, and Val Klenowski, "Conceptualising Teachers' Assessment Literacies in an Era of Curriculum and Assessment Reform," *The Australian Educational Researcher* 40 (2013): 241–56, https://doi.org/10.1007/s13384-013-0089-9.
13. Tyrone C. Howard, *Why Race and Culture Matter in Schools: Closing the Achievement Gap in America's Classrooms* (Teachers College Press, 2020).
14. Django Paris and H. Samy Alim, "What Is Culturally Sustaining Pedagogy and Why Does It Matter?," in *Culturally Sustaining Pedagogies: Teaching and Learning for Justice in a Changing World*, ed. Django Paris and H. Samy Alim (Teachers College Press, 2017).
15. Harry Torrance and John Pryor, "Developing Formative Assessment in the Classroom: Using Action Research to Explore and Modify Theory," *British Educational Research Journal* 27, no. 5 (2001): 615–31, https://doi.org/10.1080/01411920120095780.
16. Miho Taguma, Kelly Makowiecki, and Florence Gabriel, "OECD Learning Compass 2030: Implications for Mathematics Curricula," in *Mathematics Curriculum Reforms Around the World: The 24th ICMI Study*, ed. Yoshinori Shimizu and Renuka Vithal (Springer Cham, 2023), https://doi.org/10.1007/978-3-031-13548-4_32.

Chapter 1

1. François de la Rochefoucauld, *Reflections, or Sentences and Moral Maxims* (Paris, 1665; Project Gutenberg, October 2005), https://www.gutenberg.org/ebooks/9105.
2. Miho Taguma, Kelly Makowiecki, and Florence Gabriel, "OECD Learning Compass 2030: Implications for Mathematics Curricula," in *Mathematics Curriculum Reforms Around the World: The 24th ICMI Study*, ed. Yoshinori Shimizu and Renuka Vithal (Springer Cham, 2023), 479–509, https://doi.org/10.1007/978-3-031-13548-4_32.
3. "Racial/Ethnic Enrollment in Public Schools," *Condition of Education* (National Center for Education Statistics, Institute of Education Sciences, US Department of Education, 2024), https://nces.ed.gov/programs/coe/indicator/cge.
4. "English Learners in Public Schools," *Condition of Education* (National Center for Education Statistics, Institute of Education Sciences, US Department of Education, 2024), https://nces.ed.gov/programs/coe/indicator/cgf.
5. "Students with Disabilities," *Condition of Education* (National Center for Education Statistics, Institute of Education Sciences, US Department of Education, 2024), https://nces.ed.gov/programs/coe/indicator/cgf.
6. *Schools of the Future: Defining New Models of Education for the Fourth Industrial Revolution* (World Economic Forum, 2020).
7. Linda Darling-Hammond, Lisa Flook, Channa Cook-Harvey, Brigid Barron, and David Osher, "Implications for Educational Practice of the Science of Learning and Development," *Applied Developmental Science* 24, no. 2 (2020): 97–140, https://doi.org/10.1080/10888691.2018.1537791.
8. Na'ilah Suad Nasir, Carol D. Lee, Roy Pea, and Maxine McKinney de Royston, "Rethinking Learning: What the Interdisciplinary Science Tells Us," *Educational Researcher* 50, no. 8 (2021): 557–65, 557, https://doi.org/10.3102/0013189X211047251.
9. Fritz Mosher and Margaret Heritage, *A Hitchhiker's Guide to Thinking about Literacy, Learning Progressions, and Instruction*, CPRE Research Reports #RR 2017–2 (Consortium for Policy Research in Education, 2017), https://repository.upenn.edu/handle/20.500.14332/8452.
10. Lorrie A. Shepard, "Classroom Assessment to Support Teaching and Learning," *The ANNALS of the American Academy of Political and Social Science* 683, no. 1 (2019): 183–200.

11. E. Caroline Wylie and Melissa Gholson, "U.S. Federal Assessment Policy Reforms in the Twenty First Century and Their Impacts," in *International Encyclopedia of Education*, 4th ed., ed. Robert J Tierney, Fazal Rizvi, and Kadriye Ercikan (Elsevier, 2023), https://doi.org/10.1016/B978-0-12-818630-5.09027-8.
12. Jenifer Harr-Robins, Mengli Song, Michael Garet, and Louis Danielson, *School Practices and Accountability for Students With Disabilities*, NCEE 2015–4006 (National Center for Education Evaluation and Regional Assistance, Institute of Education Sciences, US Department of Education, 2015).
13. Suzanne E. Eckes and Julie Swando, "Special Education Subgroups Under NCLB: Issues to Consider," *Teachers College Record* 111, no. 11 (November 2009): 2479–2504, https://doi.org/10.1177/016146810911101106; Lynn Olson, "All Means All," *EducationWeek*, January 8, 2004, https://www.edweek.org/teaching-learning/all-means-all/2004/01.
14. Nora Gordon and Sarah Reber, "Addressing Inequities in the US K-12 Education System," in *Rebuilding the Post-Pandemic Economy*, ed. Melissa S. Kearney and Amy Ganz (Aspen Economic Strategy Group, December 2021).
15. Shepard, "Classroom Assessment to Support Teaching and Learning."
16. We use the term *College and Career Ready Standards* as the umbrella term to describe both the Common Core State Standards (CCSS) published in 2010 and other state-specific standards that were developed after the release of the CCSS.
17. "Smarter Balanced," official website of the Smarter Balanced consortium, https://smarterbalanced.org; Partnership for Assessment of Readiness for College and Careers (PARCC), official PARCC website, https://web.archive.org/web/20120220151926/, http://www.parcconline.org/about-parcc (archived).
18. Morgan S. Polikoff, *Common Core State Standards Assessments: Challenges and Opportunities* (Center for American Progress, 2014); Derek C. Briggs, "The Past, Present, and Future of Large-Scale Assessment Consortia," *Educational Measurement: Issues and Practice* (2024): 1–11.
19. Briggs, "Past, Present, and Future."
20. Catherine McClellan, Jilliam Joe, and Katherine Bassett, *The Right Trajectory: State Teachers of the Year Compare Former and New State Assessments* (National Network of State Teachers of the Year, 2015); Catherine McClellan, Jilliam Joe, and Katherine Bassett, *Still on the Right Trajectory: State Teachers of the Year Compare Former and New State Assessments* (National Network of State Teachers of the Year, 2016).
21. Scott Marion, "Accountability as a Roadblock to Assessment Reform," *CenterLine* (blog), Center for Assessment, January 26, 2021, https://nciea.org/blog/accountability-as-a-roadblock-to-assessment-reform/.
22. Linda Darling-Hammond and Jon Snyder, "Authentic Assessment of Teaching in Context," *Teaching and Teacher Education* 16, no. 5–6 (2000): 523–45, https://doi.org/10.1016/S0742-051X(00)00015-9.
23. Jennifer Randall, David Slomp, Mya Poe, and Elena Oliveri, "Disrupting White Supremacy in Assessment: Toward a Justice-Oriented, Antiracist Validity Framework," in *Twin Pandemics* (Routledge, 2023).
24. Erin Marie-Furtak and Okhee Lee, "Equity and Justice in Classroom Assessment of STEM Learning," in *Classroom-Based STEM Assessment: Contemporary Issues and Perspectives*, ed. Christopher J. Harris, Eric Wiebe, Shuchi Grover, and James W. Pellegrino (Community for Advancing Discovery Research in Education [CADRE], Education Development Center, Inc., 2023).

25. Maura Spiegelman, "Race and Ethnicity of Public School Teachers and Their Students," *National Center for Education Statistics (NCES) Data Point*, NCES 2020–103 (US Department of Education, September 2020), https://nces.ed.gov/pubs2020/2020103/index.asp.
26. Ana Maria Villegas and Tamara Lucas, *Educating Culturally Responsive Teachers: A Coherent Approach* (State University of New York Press, 2002).
27. Wayne N. Muller, "The Contribution of 'Cultural Literacy' to the 'Globally Engaged Curriculum' and the 'Globally Engaged Citizen,'" *The Social Educator* 24, no. 2 (August 2006): 13–15, http://hdl.handle.net/10072/13561.
28. Heraldo V. Richards, Ayanna F. Brown, and Timothy B. Forde, "Addressing Diversity in Schools: Culturally Responsive Pedagogy," *Teaching Exceptional Children* 39, no. 3 (2007): 64–68, https://doi.org/10.1177/004005990703900310.
29. Norma González, Luis C. Moll, and Cathy Amanti, eds., *Funds of Knowledge: Theorizing Practices in Households, Communities, and Classrooms* (Routledge, 2006).
30. Source: Mary Helen Diegel, Michigan high school teacher, in discussion with the authors.
31. Villegas and Lucas, *Educating Culturally Responsive Teachers.*
32. James A. Banks, *An Introduction to Multicultural Education*, 2nd ed. (Allyn and Bacon, 1999).
33. Villegas and Lucas, *Educating Culturally Responsive Teachers.*
34. Lorrie A. Shepard, "Ambitious Teaching and Equitable Assessment: A Vision for Prioritizing Learning, Not Testing," *American Educator* (Fall 2021): 28–48, files.eric.ed.gov/fulltext/EJ1321974.pdf.
35. Susan R. Goldman and Carol D. Lee, "Human Learning and Development: Theoretical Perspectives to Inform Assessment Systems," in *Reimagining Balanced Assessment Systems*, ed. Scott F. Marion, James W. Pellegrino, and Amy I. Berman (National Academy of Education, 2024): 48–92, https://doi.org/10.31094/2024/1.
36. Shepard, "Ambitious Teaching."
37. David P. Ausubel, *Educational Psychology: A Cognitive View* (Holt, Rinehart, and Winston, 1968); Paola Sztajn, Jere Confrey, P. Holt Wilson, and Cynthia Edgington, "Learning Trajectory Based Instruction: Toward a Theory of Teaching," *Educational Researcher* 41, no. 5 (2012): 147–56, https://doi.org/10.3102/0013189X12442801.
38. National Academies of Sciences, Engineering, and Medicine, *How People Learn II: Learners, Contexts, and Cultures* (The National Academies Press, 2018), https://doi.org/10.17226/24783.
39. Susan De La Paz, Chauncey Monte-Sano, Mark K. Felton, Robert G. Croninger, Cara Jackson, and Kelly Worland Piantedosi, "A Historical Writing Apprenticeship for Adolescents: Integrating Disciplinary Learning With Cognitive Strategies," *Reading Research Quarterly* 52, no. 1 (2017): 31–52, https://doi.org/10.1002/rrq.147.
40. Enrique Salmón, "Kincentric Ecology: Indigenous Perceptions of the Human-Nature Relationship," *Ecological Applications* 10, no. 5 (October 2000): 1327–32, https://jstor.org/stable/2641288.
41. Megan Bang, "Consequential Science Learning in the 21st Century: Cultivating Socio-Ecological Justice and Sustainability," presentation at the NCME Classroom Assessment Conference, Boulder, CO, 2018.
42. Carole Ames, "Classrooms: Goals, Structures, and Student Motivation," *Journal of Educational Psychology* 84, no. 3 (September 1992): 261–71, https://doi.org/10.1037/0022-0663.84.3.261; Mary Helen Immordino-Yang and Antonio Damasio, "We Feel, Therefore We Learn: The Relevance of Affective and Social Neuroscience to Education," *Mind, Brain, and Education* 1, no. 1 (March 2007): 3–10, https://doi.org/10.1111/j.1751-228X.2007.00004.x.

43. Nasir et al., *Rethinking Learning*; Jennifer Randall, "'Color-Neutral' Is Not a Thing: Redefining Construct Definition and Representation Through a Justice-Oriented Critical Antiracist Lens," *Educational Measurement: Issues and Practice* 40, no. 4 (Winter 2021): 82–90, https://doi.org/10.1111/emip.12429.
44. National Research Council, *Knowing What Students Know: The Science and Design of Educational Assessment* (The National Academies Press, 2001), https://doi.org/10.17226/10019.
45. Luis C. Moll and Stephen Diaz. "Change as the Goal of Educational Research," *Anthropology & Education Quarterly* 18, no. 4 (1987): 300–311, https://doi.org/10.1525/aeq.1987.18.4.04x0021u.
46. Angelique A. Aitken, Steve Graham, and Daniel McNeish, "The Effects of Choice Versus Preference on Writing and the Mediating Role of Perceived Competence," *Journal of Educational Psychology* 114, no. 8 (September 2022): 1844, https://doi.org/10.1037/edu0000765.
47. "Interpreting Multiplication and Division," Mathematics Assessment Project (Shell Center, University of Nottingham, 2015), https://map.mathshell.org/download.php?fileid=1592.
48. Randy E. Bennett, "Integrating Measurement Principles into Formative Assessment," in *Handbook of Formative Assessment in the Disciplines*, ed. Heidi L. Andrade, Randy E. Bennett, and Gregory J. Cizek (Routledge, 2019).
49. Randall, "Color-Neutral."
50. Harry West, Nicole Skidmore, Laura Bennett, Juliet Eve, Cathy Minett-Smith, and Luke Rudge, "The Language of Assessment: Identifying Challenging Terminology for Students and Exploring Implications for Practice," *Assessment & Evaluation in Higher Education* (September 2004): 1–15, https://doi:10.1080/02602938.2024.2402960.
51. Ames, "Classrooms"; Albert Bandura, "Self-Efficacy Mechanism in Human Agency," *American Psychologist* 37, no. 2 (1982): 122, https://doi.org/10.1037/0003-066X.37.2.122.
52. Dale H. Schunk, "Self-Efficacy, Motivation, and Performance," *Journal of Applied Sport Psychology* 7, no. 2 (1995): 112–37, https://doi.org/10.1080/10413209508406961.
53. James H. McMillan and Amanda B. Turner, "Understanding Student Voices About Assessment: Links to Learning and Motivation," paper presented at the Annual Meeting of the American Educational Research Association, Philadelphia, April 2014.
54. Quotations of Jerome S. Bruner, AZQuotes.com, accessed July 29, 2017, https://azquotes.com/quote/600207; Margaret Heritage and John Heritage, "Teacher Questioning: The Epicenter of Instruction and Assessment," *Applied Measurement in Education* 26, no. 3 (2013): 176–90, https://doi.org/10.1080/08957347.2013.793190.
55. E. Caroline Wylie and Margaret Heritage, "Assessment Literacy and Professional Learning," in *Reimagining Balanced Assessment Systems*, ed. Scott F. Marion, James W. Pellegrino, and Amy I. Berman (National Academy of Education, 2024), https://doi.org/10.31094/2024/1.
56. Kathryn H. Au and Alice J. Kawakami, "Cultural Congruence in Instruction," in *Teaching Diverse Populations: Formulating a Knowledge Base*, ed. Etta R. Hollins, Joyce E. King, and Warren C. Hayman (State University of New York Press, 1994); Megan Bang and Douglas Medin, "Cultural Processes in Science Education: Supporting the Navigation of Multiple Epistemologies," *Science Learning in Everyday Life* 94, no. 6 (November 2010): 1008–26, https://doi.org/10.1002/sce.20392; Bronwen Cowie, Christine Harrison, and Jill Willis, "Supporting Teacher Responsiveness in Assessment for Learning Through Disciplined Noticing," *The Curriculum Journal* 29, no. 4 (December 2018): 464–78, https://doi.org/10.1080/09585176.2018.1481442.
57. Cowie et al., "Supporting Teacher Responsiveness."

58. Django Paris, "Culturally Sustaining Pedagogy: A Needed Change in Stance, Terminology, and Practice," *Educational Researcher* 41, no. 3 (2012): 93–97, https://doi.org/10.3102/0013189X12441244.
59. Carol D. Lee, "Integrating Research on How People Learn and Learning Across Settings as a Window of Opportunity to Address Inequality in Educational Processes and Outcomes," *Review of Research in Education* 41, no. 1 (March 2017): 88–111, https://doi.org/10.3102/0091732X16689046.
60. Adapted from Karen Sloan, "Teaching Strategies for Culturally Inclusive Math," *Carnegie Learning* (blog), Carnegie Learning, Inc., December 11, 2023, https://carnegielearning.com/blog/culturally-responsive-math/ .
61. Richards et al., "Addressing Diversity in Schools."
62. Miho Taguma, Kelly Makowiecki, and Florence Gabriel, "OECD Learning Compass 2030: Implications for Mathematics Curricula," in *Mathematics Curriculum Reforms Around the World: The 24th ICMI Study*, ed. Yoshinori Shimizu and Renuka Vithal (Springer Cham, 2023), https://doi.org/10.1007/978-3-031-13548-4_32.
63. Paul R. Pintrich, "Understanding Self-Regulated Learning," *New Directions for Teaching and Learning* 1995, no. 63 (Autumn 1995): 3–12, https://doi.org/10.1002/tl.37219956304; Barry J. Zimmerman and Dale H. Schunk, "Reflections on Theories of Self-Regulated Learning and Academic Achievement," in *Self-Regulated Learning and Academic Achievement: Theoretical Perspectives*, 2nd ed., ed. Barry J. Zimmerman and Dale H. Schunk (Routledge, 2001).
64. Lorena Llosa, Scott Grapin, Alison Haas, and Okee Lee, "Integrating Science and Language for All Students with a Focus on English Language Learners," website of the New York State Education Department, updated September 12, 2023, https://www.nysed.gov/bilingual-ed/integrating-science-and-language-all-students-focus-english-language-learners.
65. Quotations from student work and teachers' written materials are presented without modification throughout the book and may contain nonstandard spelling or grammar.
66. "March on Washington," Digital Inquiry Group, https://inquirygroup.org/history-assessments/march-washington.
67. Source: Gabriela Cárdenas, Para Los Niños Charter Elementary School, in discussion with the authors.
68. As with written material, transcriptions of speech from our classroom data are provided as spoken and may contain nonstandard grammar or phonetic spellings (such as "cuz" for "[be]cause").
69. Scott F. Marion, James W. Pellegrino, and Amy I. Berman, "Reimagining Balanced Assessment Systems: An Introduction," in *Reimagining Balanced Assessment Systems*, ed. Scott F. Marion, James W. Pellegrino, and Amy I. Berman (National Academy of Education, 2024), https://doi.org/10.31094/2024/1.

Chapter 2

1. Stephen Hinds, Laura Tavares, Stephen Zrike, and Chelsea Banks, "How to Reduce Student Absenteeism," letter to the editor, *New York Times*, April 13, 2024, https://www.nytimes.com/2024/04/13/opinion/student-absenteeism.html.
2. Na'ilah Suad Nasir, Carol D. Lee, Roy Pea, and Maxine McKinney de Royston, "Rethinking Learning: What the Interdisciplinary Science Tells Us," *Educational Researcher* 50, no. 8 (2021): 557–65.

3. Maria Araceli Ruiz-Primo and Erin M. Furtak, "Classroom Activity Systems to Support Ambitious Teaching and Assessment," in *Reimagining Balanced Assessment Systems*, ed. Scott F. Marion, James W. Pellegrino, and Amy I. Berman (National Academy of Education, 2024), https://doi.org/10.31094/2024/1.
4. National Academies of Sciences, Engineering, and Medicine (NASEM), *How People Learn II: Learners, Contexts, and Cultures* (The National Academies Press, 2018), https://doi.org/10.17226/24783.
5. Susan R. Goldman and Carol D. Lee, "Human Learning and Development: Theoretical Perspectives to Inform Assessment Systems," in *Reimagining Balanced Assessment Systems*, ed. Scott F. Marion, James W. Pellegrino, and Amy I. Berman (National Academy of Education, 2024), https://doi.org/10.31094/2024/1.
6. National Research Council, *Next Generation Science Standards: For States, By States* (The National Academies Press, 2013).
7. Sarah Michaels, Catherine O'Connor, and Lauren B. Resnick, "Deliberative Discourse Idealized and Realized: Accountable Talk in the Classroom and in Civic Life," *Studies in Philosophy and Education* 27, no. 4 (July 2008): 283–97, https://doi.org/10.1007/s11217-007-9071-1.
8. Source: Kristy Walters, Corunna Public Schools, in discussion with the authors.
9. Jeremy Kilpatrick, Jane Swafford, and Bradford Findell, eds., *Adding It Up: Helping Children Learn Mathematics* (The National Academies Press, 2001), https://doi.org/10.17226/9822.
10. NASEM, *How People Learn II.*
11. "Frederick Douglass & Abraham Lincoln," Digital Inquiry Group, https://inquirygroup.org/history-lessons/frederick-douglass-abraham-lincoln.
12. Robin Alexander, "Developing Dialogic Teaching: Genesis, Process, Trial," *Research Papers in Education* 33, no. 5 (2018): 561–98.
13. Zaretta Hammond, "Liberatory Education: Integrating the Science of Learning and Culturally Responsive Practice," *American Educator* 45, no. 2 (Summer 2021): 4–11, 39, https://files.eric.ed.gov/fulltext/EJ1305167.pdf.
14. Linda Darling-Hammond, Lisa Flook, Channa Cook-Harvey, Brigid Barron, and David Osher, "Implications for Educational Practice of the Science of Learning and Development," *Applied Developmental Science* 24, no. 2 (2020): 97–140.
15. Aida Walqui, Lee Hartman, and Mary Schmida, *English Language Arts Curriculum* (National Center for Improving Outcomes of English Learners in Secondary Schools, 2022).
16. L. S. Vygotsky, *Mind in Society: Development of Higher Psychological Processes* (Harvard University Press, 1978).
17. Alexander, "Developing Dialogic Teaching."
18. Source: Gabriella Cárdenas, in discussion with the authors.
19. Source: Gabriella Cárdenas, UCLA (University of California, Los Angeles) Laboratory School.
20. Hammond, "Liberatory Education," 4.
21. Hammond, "Liberatory Education," 4.
22. Django Paris, "Culturally Sustaining Pedagogy: A Needed Change in Stance, Terminology, and Practice," *Educational Researcher* 41, no. 3 (2012): 93–97, https://doi.org/10.3102/0013189X12441244.
23. Source: Lindsey Howe, high school teacher and Annlyn McKenzie, career tech curriculum coordinator in discussion with the authors.

24. Norma Gonzalez, Luis C. Moll, and Cathy Amanti, eds., *Funds of Knowledge: Theorizing Practices in Households, Communities, and Classrooms* (Erlbaum, 2005); "Funds of Knowledge Survey," Reading Is Fundamental, https://www.rif.org/sites/default/files/documents/2023/03/20/Funds-of-Knowledge-Survey.pdf.
25. Zaretta Hammond, "The Power of Protocols for Equity," *Educational Leadership* 77, no. 7 (April 2020): 45–50.
26. Darling-Hammond et al., "Implications for Educational Practice."
27. Paul Black and Dylan Wiliam, "Assessment and Classroom Learning," *Assessment in Education: Principles, Policy & Practice* 5, no. 1 (1998): 7–74, https://dx.doi.org/10.1080/0969595980050102; Paul J. Black, Christine Harrison, Clare Lee, and Bethan Marshall, "Working Inside the Black Box: Assessment for Learning in the Classroom," *Phi Delta Kappan* 86, no. 1 (September 2004): 8–21, https://doi.org/10.1177/003172170408600105.
28. Source: Annlyn McKenzie, in discussion with the authors.
29. NASEM, *How People Learn II*, 133.
30. Peter C. Scales, Martin Van Boekel, Kent Pekel, Amy K. Syvertsen, and Eugene C. Roehlkepartain, "Effects of Developmental Relationships with Teachers on Middle-School Students' Motivation and Performance," *Psychology in the Schools* 57, no. 4 (April 2020): 646–77, https://doi.org/10.1002/pits.22350.
31. National Research Council, *Next Generation Science Standards.*
32. Carbon TIME, "What is Carbon TIME?," Environmental Literacy Project at Michigan State University, https://carbontime.create4stem.msu.edu/.
33. National Science Teaching Association, "Uncovering Student Ideas in Science Series," official NSTA website, https://www.nsta.org/book-series/uncovering-student-ideas-science.
34. Revathy Kumar, Stuart A. Karabenick, Jeffery H. Warnke, Susan Hany, and Nancy Seay, "Culturally Inclusive and Responsive Curricular Learning Environments (CIRCLEs): An Exploratory Sequential Mixed-Methods Approach," *Contemporary Educational Psychology* 57, no. 5 (April 2019): 87–105, https://doi.org/10.1016/j.cedpsych.2018.10.005.
35. cf. Carol S. Dweck, *Self-Theories: Their Role in Motivation, Personality, and Development* (Psychology Press, Taylor & Francis Group, 2000), https://doi.org/10.4324/9781315783048; Gloria Ladson-Billings, "Race Still Matters: Critical Race Theory in Education," in *The Routledge International Handbook of Critical Education*, ed. Michael W. Apple, Wayne Au, and Luis Armando Gandin (Routledge, 2009), https://doi.org/10.4324/9780203882993.
36. NASEM, *How People Learn II*, 160.
37. Francesca M. Forzani, "Understanding 'Core Practices' and 'Practice-Based' Teacher Education: Learning From the Past," *Journal of Teacher Education* 65, no. 4 (2014): 357–68.
38. Lorrie A. Shepard, "Ambitious Teaching and Equitable Assessment: A Vision for Prioritizing Learning, Not Testing," *American Educator* (Fall 2021): 28–48, https://files.eric.ed.gov/fulltext/EJ1321974.pdf.
39. Lorrie A. Shepard, "Assessment Lessons From K-12 Education Research: Knowledge Representation, Learning, And Motivation," *AIP Conference Proceedings* 1413, no. 1 (February 2012): 73–76, https://doi.org/10.1063/1.3679997.
40. Heidi L. Andrade, "Students as the Definitive Source of Formative Assessment: Academic Self-Assessment and the Self-Regulation of Learning," in *Handbook of Formative Assessment*, ed. Heidi L. Andrade and Gregory J. Cizek (Routledge, 2009), https://doi.org/10.4324/9780203874851.
41. Christine A. Tell, Francoise M. Bodone, and Karen L. Addie, "A Framework of Teacher Knowledge and Skills Necessary in a Standards-Based System: Lessons from High School

and University Faculty," paper presented at the American Educational Research Association Annual Meeting, New Orleans, LA, April 28, 2000, https://files.eric.ed.gov/fulltext/ED447206.pdf; Matthew Graham, Anthony Milankowski, and Jackson Miller, *Measuring and Promoting Inter-Rater Agreement of Teacher and Principal Performance Ratings* (Center for Educator Compensation Reform, 2012).

42. Heidi L. Andrade, Ying Du, and Kristina Mycek, "Rubric-Referenced Self-Assessment and Middle School Students' Writing," *Assessment in Education: Principles, Policy & Practice* 17, no. 2 (2010): 199–214, https://doi.org/10.1080/09695941003696172; Neil Mercer, Lyn Dawes, Rupert Wegerif, and Claire Sams, "Reasoning as a Scientist: Ways of Helping Children to Use Language to Learn Science," *British Educational Research Journal* 30, no. 3 (June 2004): 359–77, https://doi.org/10.1080/01411920410001689689; Barbara Y. White and John R. Frederiksen, "Inquiry, Modeling, and Metacognition: Making Science Accessible to All Students," *Cognition and Instruction* 16, no. 1 (1998): 3–118, https://doi.org/10.1207/s1532690xci1601_2.
43. Louise Bourgeois, "Supporting Students' Learning: From Teacher Regulation to Co-Regulation," in *Assessment for Learning: Meeting the Challenge of Implementation*, ed. Dany Laveault and Linda Allal (Springer, 2016), https://doi.org/10.1007/978-3-319-39211-0_20.

Chapter 3

1. Scott F. Marion, James W. Pellegrino, and Amy I. Berman, "Reimagining Balanced Assessment Systems: An Introduction," in *Reimagining Balanced Assessment Systems*, ed. Scott F. Marion, James W. Pellegrino, and Amy I. Berman (National Academy of Education, 2024), 2, 4, https://doi.org/10.31094/2024/1.
2. Carla Evans and Scott Marion, *Understanding Instructionally Useful Assessment* (Taylor & Francis, 2024).
3. Evans and Marion, *Understanding Instructionally*, 60.
4. Margaret Heritage, Molly Faulkner-Bond, and Aida Walqui, *A New Direction for Assessing English Learners in the Secondary Grades* (National Research and Development Center to Improve Education for Secondary English Learners at WestEd, 2021).
5. Norma González, Luis C. Moll, and Cathy Amanti, eds., *Funds of Knowledge: Theorizing Practices in Households, Communities, and Classrooms* (Routledge, 2006).
6. Evans and Marion, *Understanding Instructionally.*
7. Edward H. Haertel, "Tests, Test Scores, and Constructs," *Educational Psychologist* 53, no. 3 (2018), https://doi.org/10.1080/00461520.2018.1476868; cited in Evans and Marion, *Understanding Instructionally.*
8. Marion et al., "Reimagining Balanced Assessment."
9. Harry Torrance and John Pryor, "Developing Formative Assessment in the Classroom: Using Action Research to Explore and Modify Theory," *British Educational Research Journal* 27, no. 5 (2001): 615–31, https://doi.org/10.1080/01411920120095780.
10. Torrance and Pryor, "Developing Formative Assessment."
11. Bronwen Cowie and Christine Harrison, "The What, When & How Factors: Reflections on Classroom Assessment in the Service of Inquiry," *International Journal of Science Education* 43, no. 3 (2021): 449–65, https://doi.org/10.1080/09500693.2020.1824088.
12. Cowie and Harrison, "What, When & How."
13. Cowie and Harrison, "What, When & How," 454.
14. Randy E. Bennett, "Toward a Theory of Socioculturally Responsive Assessment," *Educational Assessment* 28, no. 2 (2023): 83–104, https://doi.org/10.1080/10627197.2023.2202312.

15. New York State Department of Environmental Conservation (NYDEC), "Weather and Climate," official NYDEC website, https://extapps.dec.ny.gov/docs/remediation_hudson_pdf/hrlpweatherclimatehs.pdf.
16. Educational Testing Service, *To Assess, To Teach, To Learn: A Vision for the Future of Assessment*, Technical Report: The Gordon Commission Final Report (2013), https://www.ets.org/Media/Research/pdf/gordon_commission_technical_report.pdf.
17. Source: Gabriella Cárdenas, UCLA [University of California, Los Angeles] Lab School, Los Angeles, videotaped by authors.
18. Lorena Llosa, Scott Grapin, and Alison Haas, "Integrating Science and Language for All Students with a Focus on English Language Learners: Science and Language Assessment Shifts," New York State Department of Education website, 2020, https://www.nysed.gov/sites/default/files/programs/bilingual-ed/brief-6-science-and-language-assessment-shifts-integrating-science-and-language-for-all-students-with-a-focus-on-english-language-learners-a.pdf.
19. Llosa et al., "Integrating Science and Language."
20. Lorena Llosa, personal communication with Margaret Heritage, spring 2023.
21. Heidi L. Andrade, "Students as the Definitive Source of Formative Assessment: Academic Self-Assessment and the Self-Regulation of Learning," in *Handbook of Formative Assessment*, ed. Heidi L. Andrade and Gregory J. Cizek (Routledge, 2009), https://doi.org/10.4324/9780203874851.
22. Joe Nelson, personal communication with Caroline Wylie, spring 2024.
23. Dylan Wiliam, "Designing Great Hinge Questions," *Educational Leadership* 73, no. 1 (September 2015): 40–44, https://ascd.org/el/articles/designing-great-hinge-questions.
24. Wiliam, "Designing Great Hinge Questions."
25. Aida Walqui, Lee Hartman, and Mary Schmida, *English Language Arts Curriculum*, (National Center for Improving Outcomes of English Learners in Secondary Schools, 2022).
26. Joe Feldman, *School Grading Policies are Failing Children: A Call to Action for Equitable Grading* (Crescendo Education Group, 2018).
27. Feldman, *School Grading Policies*; Susan M. Brookhart, Thomas R. Guskey, Alex J. Bowers, James H. McMillan, Jeffrey K. Smith, Lisa F. Smith, Michael T. Stevens, and Megan E. Welsh, "A Century of Grading Research: Meaning and Value in the Most Common Educational Measure," *Review of Educational Research* 86, no. 4 (2016): 803–48, https://doi.org/10.3102/0034654316672069.
28. Brookhart et al., "Century of Grading."
29. Paul L. Dressel, *Handbook of Academic Evaluation* (Jossey-Bass, 1976).
30. Brookhart et al., "Century of Grading."
31. Joe Feldman, *Grading for Equity, What It Is, Why It Matters, and How It Can Transform Schools and Classrooms* (Corwin, 2024).
32. Susan D. Blum, ed., *Ungrading: Why Rating Students Undermines Learning (and What to Do Instead)* (West Virginia University Press, 2020); Starr Sackstein, *Hacking Assessment: 10 Ways to Go Gradeless in a Traditional Grades School* (Times 10 Publications, 2015).
33. Feldman, *Grading for Equity*; Brookhart et al., "Century of Grading."
34. Feldman, *Grading for Equity*; Catherine S. Taylor and Susan Bobbitt Nolen, *Culturally and Socially Responsible Assessment: Theory, Research, and Practice* (Teachers College Press, 2022).
35. Feldman, *School Grading Policies*.
36. University of Oregon Center on Teaching and Learning, "What is DIBELS [Dynamic Indicators of Basic Early Literacy Skills]?," website of DIBELS, https://dibels.uoregon.edu/.

37. University of Oregon Center on Teaching and Learning, "DIBELS."
38. Timothy Shanahan, "Should We Test Reading or DIBELS?," *Reading Rockets* (blog), January 29, 2018, https://www.readingrockets.org/blogs/shanahan-on-literacy/should-we-test-reading-or-dibels.
39. Oregon Department of Education, *The Right Assessment for the Right Purpose Guiding Document*, August 2019, https://www.oregon.gov/ode/educator-resources/assessment/Documents/RightAssessmentRightPurpose.pdf.
40. Jan McArthur, "Reflections on Assessment for Social Justice and Assessment for Inclusion," in *Assessment for Inclusion in Higher Education: Promoting Equity and Social Justice in Assessment*, ed. Rola Ajjawi, Joanna Tai, David Boud, and Trina Jorre de St Jorre (Routledge, 2022), https://doi.org/10.4324/9781003293101-4.

Chapter 4

1. Jennifer Gonzalez, "Conquering National Board Certification (and Why It's Totally Worth It)," *Cult of Pedagogy* (blog), November 13, 2013, https://www.cultofpedagogy.com/nbct/.
2. David Charles Berliner, "Learning About and Learning From Expert Teachers," *International Journal of Educational Research* 35, no. 5 (December 2001): 463–82, https://doi.org/10.1016/S0883–0355(02)00004–6.
3. Eric A. Hanushek and Steven G. Rivkin, "Teacher Quality," in *Handbook of the Economics of Education*, ed. Eric A. Hanushek and Finis Welch (Elsevier, 2006), https://doi.org/10.1016/S1574–0692(06)02018–6.
4. Andrew Leigh, "Estimating Teacher Effectiveness From Two-Year Changes in Students' Test Scores," *Economics of Education Review* 29, no. 3 (June 2010): 480–88, https://doi.org/10.1016/j.econedurev.2009.10.010; K. Anders Ericsson, Neil Charness, Paul J. Feltovich, and Robert R. Hoffman, *The Cambridge Handbook of Expertise and Expert Performance* (Cambridge University Press, 2006), https://doi.org/10.1017/CBO9780511816796.
5. Lloyd Bond, Tracy Smith, Wanda K. Baker, and John Hattie, *The Certification System of the National Board for Professional Teaching Standards: A Construct and Consequential Validity Study* (Greensboro Center for Educational Research and Evaluation, University of North Carolina at Greensboro, 2000).
6. Berliner, "Learning."
7. Christopher DeLuca, Andrew Coombs, Stephen MacGregor, and Amirhossein Rasooli, "Toward a Differential and Situated View of Assessment Literacy: Studying Teachers' Responses to Classroom Assessment Scenarios," in *Frontiers in Education* 4 (2019): 94, https://doi.org/10.3389/feduc.2019.00094.
8. Miriam Gamoran Sherin, Victoria R. Jacobs, and Randolph A. Philipp, *Mathematics Teacher Noticing: Seeing Through Teachers' Eyes* (Routledge, 2011).
9. Michael J. Cleary and Shirley Groer, "Inflight Decisions of Expert and Novice Health Teachers," *Journal of School Health* 64, no. 3 (March 1994): 110–14.
10. Robert Glaser, "Changing the Agency for Learning: Acquiring Expert Performance," in *The Road to Excellence: The Acquisition of Expert Performance in the Arts and Sciences, Sports, and Games*, ed. K. Anders Ericsson (Erlbaum, 1996).
11. Margaret Heritage and E. Caroline Wylie, *Formative Assessment in the Disciplines: Framing a Continuum of Professional Learning* (Harvard Education Press, 2020).
12. Etienne Wenger, *Communities of Practice: Learning, Meaning, and Identity* (Cambridge University Press, 1998).

13. Jean Lave and Etienne Wenger, *Situated Learning: Legitimate Peripheral Participation* (Cambridge University Press, 1991); Etienne Wenger, "Communities of Practice: Learning as a Social System," *Systems Thinker* 9, no. 5 (1998): 2–3.
14. Lave and Wenger, *Situated Learning.*
15. Linda Darling-Hammond, Maria E. Hyler, and Madelyn Gardner, *Effective Teacher Professional Development* (Learning Policy Institute, 2017), https://learningpolicyinstitute.org/sites/default/files/product-files/Effective_Teacher_Professional_Development_REPORT.pdf; Mary M. Kennedy, "How Does Professional Development Improve Teaching?" *Review of Educational Research* 86, no. 4 (2016): 945–80, https://doi.org/10.3102/0034654315626800.
16. Sam Sims, Harry Fletcher-Wood, Alison O'Mara-Eves, Sarah Cottingham, Claire Stansfield, Josh Goodrich, Jo Van Herwegen, and Jake Anders, "Effective Teacher Professional Development: New Theory and a Meta-Analytic Test," *Review of Educational Research* (2023), https://doi.org/10.3102/00346543231217480.
17. Sims et al., "Effective Teacher Professional Development."
18. Larrissa Peru and Kasie Betten, personal communication with Caroline Wylie, spring 2024.
19. Heritage and Wylie, *Formative Assessment.*
20. Dylan Wiliam, "Teacher Expertise: Why It Matters, and How to Get More of It," in *Ten Essays on Improving Teacher Quality*, ed. Joe Hallgarten, Louise Bamfield, and Kenny McCarthy (The RSA, November 2014).
21. Wiliam, "Teacher Expertise."
22. Dylan Wiliam, Clare Lee, Christine Harrison, and Paul J. Black, "Teachers Developing Assessment for Learning: Impact on Student Achievement," *Assessment in Education: Principles, Policy & Practice* 11, no. 1 (March 2004): 49–65, https://doi.org/10.1080/0969594042000208994; Paul Black, Christine Harrison, Clare Lee, Bethan Marshall, and Dylan Wiliam, *Assessment for Learning: Putting It Into Practice* (Open University Press, 2003); Bruce Randel, Andrea D. Beesley, Helen Apthorp, Tedra F. Clark, Xin Wang, Louis F. Cicchinelli, and Jean M. Williams, *Classroom Assessment for Student Learning: Impact on Elementary School Mathematics in the Central Region. Final Report*, NCEE 2011–4005 (National Center for Educational Evaluation and Regional Assistance, Institute of Education, US Department of Education, 2011); Hansol Lee, Huy Q. Chung, Yu Zhang, Jamal Abedi, and Mark Warschauer, "The Effectiveness and Features of Formative Assessment in US K-12 Education: A Systematic Review," *Applied Measurement in Education* 33, no. 2 (2020): 124–40, https://doi.org/10.1080/08957347.2020.1732383.
23. Heritage and Wylie, *Formative Assessment.*
24. Pam Grossman, Christa Compton, Danielle Igra, and Matthew Ronfeldt, "Teaching Practice: A Cross-Professional Perspective," *Teachers College Record* 111, no. 9 (2009), 2058, https://doi.org/10.1177/016146810911100905. See also, B. Duckor and C. Holmberg, *Feedback for Continuous Improvement in the Classroom: New Perspectives, Practices, and Possibilities* (Corwin, 2023).
25. Karl Ericsson, Ralf T. Krampe, and Clemens Tesch-Roemer, "The Role of Deliberate Practice in the Acquisition of Expert Performance," *Psychological Review* 100, no. 3 (July 1993): 363–406.
26. Ericsson et al., "Role of Deliberate Practice."
27. Marnie Thompson, *TLC Leader Handbook* (Educational Testing Service, 2009); E. Caroline Wylie, ed., *Tight But Loose: Scaling Up Teacher Professional Development in Diverse Contexts* (Educational Testing Service, 2008), https://doi.org/10.1002/j.2333-8504.2008.tb02115.x.
28. E. Caroline Wylie, Christine J. Lyon, and Laura Goe, *Teacher Professional Development Focused on Formative Assessment: Changing Teachers, Changing Schools* (Educational Testing Service, 2014), https://doi.org/10.1002/j.2333-8504.2009.tb02167.x.

29. Etienne Wenger, Richard McDermott, and William M. Snyder, *Cultivating Communities of Practice: A Guide to Managing Knowledge* (Harvard Business School Publishing, 2002).
30. Richard DuFour and Robert Eaker, *Professional Learning Communities at Work: Best Practices for Enhancing Student Achievement* (Solution Tree, 1998).
31. Laurie Calvert, "The Power of Teacher Agency: Why We Must Transform Professional Learning So That It Really Supports Educator Learning," *The Learning Professional* 37, no. 2 (April 2016): 51–56, https://learningforward.org/wp-content/uploads/2016/04/the-power-of-teacher-agency-april16.pdf; Auli Toom, Kirsi Pyhältö, and Frances O'Connell Rust, "Teachers' Professional Agency in Contradictory Times." *Teachers and Teaching* 21, no. 6 (2015): 615–623. See also, B. Duckor and D. Perlstein, "Assessing Habits of Mind: Teaching to the Test at Central Park East Secondary School," *Teachers College Record* 116, no. 2 (2014): 1–33.
32. Nick Smith, a high school data coach, in personal communication with the authors.
33. Caroline Wylie, participant comment at a professional learning session, spring 2024.
34. Christopher DeLuca, Michael Holden, and Nathan Rickey, "From Challenge to Innovation: A Grassroots Study of Teachers' Classroom Assessment Innovations," *British Educational Research Journal* (2024).
35. Christine Suurtamm and Martha J. Koch, "Navigating Dilemmas in Transforming Assessment Practices: Experiences of Mathematics Teachers in Ontario, Canada," *Educational Assessment, Evaluation and Accountability* 26, no. 3 (August 2014): 263–87, https://doi.org/10.1007/s11092-014-9195-0; Mark Windschitl, "Framing Constructivism in Practice as the Negotiation of Dilemmas: An Analysis of the Conceptual, Pedagogical, Cultural, and Political Challenges Facing Teachers," *Review of Educational Research* 72, no. 2 (2002): 131–75, https://doi.org/10.3102/00346543072002131.
36. Calvert, "Power of Teacher Agency."
37. Observation from an interview with district leaders following an assessment audit process, led by Caroline Wylie, spring 2024.
38. Personal communication with Caroline Wylie, fall 2023.
39. E. Caroline Wylie and Christine J. Lyon, "Developing a Formative Assessment Protocol to Support Professional Growth," *Educational Assessment* 25, no. 4 (2020): 314–30, https://doi.org/10.1080/10627197.2020.1766956.
40. E. Caroline Wylie, Christine J. Lyon, and Elizabeth P. O'Dwyer, "The Benefits of Peer Teacher Observations," in *Research Handbook on Classroom Observation*, ed. Sean Kelly (Edward Elgar Publishing Ltd., 2025).
41. Johann Hari, *Stolen Focus: Why You Can't Pay Attention—and How to Think Deeply Again* (Crown, 2023).
42. Personal communication with Caroline Wylie, spring 2024.

Chapter 5

1. Robert J. Mislevy and Geneva D. Haertel, "Implications of Evidence-Centered Design for Educational Testing," *Educational Measurement: Issues and Practice* 25, no. 4 (2006): 6–20.
2. Connie M. Moss, *Learning Targets and Success Criteria* (Routledge, 2022).
3. James W. Pellegrino,"Assessment as a Positive Influence on 21st Century Teaching and Learning: A Systems Approach to Progress," *Psicología Educativa* 20, no. 2 (2014): 65–77.
4. Dylan Wiliam, "Classroom Formative Assessment: Engaging Learners and Responding to Their Needs," presentation at the National Council of Teachers of Mathematics, Atlanta, July 14, 2014.
5. Scott F. Marion, James W. Pellegrino, and Amy I. Berman, "Reimagining Balanced Assessment Systems: An Introduction," in *Reimagining Balanced Assessment Systems*, ed.

Scott F. Marion, James W. Pellegrino, and Amy I. Berman (National Academy of Education, 2024), https://doi.org/10.31094/2024/1.

6. *College, Career, and Civic Life (C3) Framework for Social Studies State Standards: Guidance for Enhancing the Rigor of K-12 Civics, Economics, Geography, and History* (National Council for the Social Studies, 2013), https://www.socialstudies.org/system/files/2022/c3-framework-for-social-studies-rev0617.2.pdf.
7. Gabriela Cárdenas, personal communication with Margaret Heritage.
8. Adapted from Tracy J. Zager, *Becoming the Math Teacher You Wish You'd Had: Ideas and Strategies for Vibrant Classrooms* (Stenhouse, 2017).
9. Valentina Klenowski and Claire Wyatt-Smith, *Assessment for Education: Standards, Judgement and Moderation* (Sage, 2013), 77.
10. John D. Bransford, Ann L. Brown, and Rodney R. Cocking, eds., "Effective Teaching: Examples in History, Mathematics, and Science," in *How People Learn: Brain, Mind, Experience, and School* (National Academy Press, 2000), http://books.nap.edu/html/howpeople1.
11. Linda Darling-Hammond, Suzanne Orcutt, and Kim Austin, "Organizing What We Know: The Structure of the Disciplines," in *The Learning Classroom*, https://www.learner.org/wp-content/uploads/2019/02/The-Learning-Classroom_Organizing-What-We-Know.pdf.
12. Nathaniel L. Gage and David C. Berliner, *Educational Psychology* (Houghton Mifflin, 1998), cited in Darling-Hammond et al., "Organizing What We Know."
13. This school was the UCLA (University of California, Los Angeles) Lab School.
14. Michigan Assessment Consortium (MAC), "Early Literacy Assessment Systems That Support Learning: A Guide and Resources for Developing, Implementing, and Supporting District Assessment Systems," official website of the MAC, https://www.michiganassessmentconsortium.org/elas/.
15. Moisès Esteban-Guitart and Luis Moll, "Funds of Identity: A New Concept Based on the Funds of Knowledge Approach," *Culture & Psychology* 20, no. 1 (March 2014): 31–48, 37.
16. David Subero, Mariona Llopart, Carina Siqués, and Moisès Esteban-Guitart, "The Mediation of Teaching and Learning Processes Through *Identity Artefacts.* A Vygotskian Perspective," *Oxford Review of Education* 44, no. 2 (2018): 156–70, https://doi.org/10.1080/03054985.2017.1352501.
17. Subero et al., "Mediation of Teaching."
18. "My Compass Guide [Trailer]," posted May 26, 2023, by EL Education, Vimeo, https://vimeo.com/830628747.
19. Aspen Institute, *From a Nation at Risk to a Nation at Hope: Recommendations From the National Commision on Social, Emotional, and Academic Development* (Aspen Institute, 2019), https://learningpolicyinstitute.org/media/3962/download?inline&file=Aspen_SEAD_Nation_at_Hope.pdf.
20. Miho Taguma, Kelly Makowiecki, and Florence Gabriel, "OECD Learning Compass 2030: Implications for Mathematics Curricula," in *Mathematics Curriculum Reforms Around the World: The 24th ICMI Study*, ed. Yoshinori Shimizu and Renuka Vithal (Springer Cham, 2023), https://doi.org/10.1007/978-3-031-13548-4_32.
21. Barry J. Zimmerman and Dale H. Schunk, "Self-Regulated Learning and Performance: An Introduction and and Overview," in *Handbook of Self-Regulation of Learning and Performance*, ed. Barry J. Zimmerman and Dale H. Schunk (Routledge/Taylor & Francis Group, 2011), https://doi.org/10.4324/9780203839010.

22. Albert Bandura, *Exercise of Personal and Collective Efficacy in Changing Societies* (Cambridge University Press, 1995); Barry J. Zimmerman, "Self-Regulation Involves More Than Metacognition: A Social Cognitive Perspective," *Educational Psychologist* 30, no. 4 (June 2010): 217–21.
23. National Academies of Sciences, Medicine, Division of Behavioral, Social Sciences, Board on Science Education, Board on Behavioral, Sensory Sciences, Committee on How People Learn II, The Science, and Practice of Learning. *How people learn II: Learners, Contexts, and Cultures.* National Academies Press, 2018.
24. E. Caroline Wylie and Margaret Heritage, "Assessment Literacy and Professional Learning," in *Reimagining Balanced Assessment Systems*, ed. Scott F. Marion, James W. Pellegrino, and Amy I. Berman (National Academy of Education, 2024): https://doi.org/10.31094/2024/1.
25. Patrick Griffin, "Teachers' Use of Assessment Data," in *Educational Assessment in the 21st Century: Connecting Theory and Practice*, ed. Claire M. Wyatt-Smith and J. Joy Cumming (Springer, 2009), 196.
26. Susan M. Brookhart, Thomas R. Guskey, Alex J. Bowers, James H. McMillan, Jeffrey K. Smith, Lisa F. Smith, Michael T. Stevens, and Megan E. Welsh, "A Century of Grading Research: Meaning and Value in the Most Common Educational Measure," *Review of Educational Research* 86, no. 4 (2016): 803–48, https://doi.org/10.3102/0034654316672069.
27. Connie M. Moss and Susan M. Brookhart, *Formative Classroom Walkthroughs: How Principals and Teachers Collaborate to Raise Student Achievement* (ASCD [formerly Association for Supervision and Curriculum Development], 2015), 121.
28. Margaret Heritage, *Formative Assessment: Making It Happen in the Classroom*, 2nd ed. (Corwin Press, 2022).
29. Heritage, *Formative Assessment.*

Chapter 6

1. Robert J. Mislevy, "Evidence and Inference in Educational Assessment," *Psychometrika* 59, no. 4 (1994): 439–83; James W. Pellegrino, "Assessment as a Positive Influence on 21st Century Teaching and Learning: A Systems Approach to Progress," *Psicología Educativa* 20, no. 2 (2014): 65–77.
2. Dylan Wiliam and Marnie Thompson, "Integrating Assessment with Instruction: What Will It Take to Make It Work?," in *The Future of Assessment: Shaping Teaching and Learning*, ed. Carol Anne Dwyer (Lawrence Erlbaum Associates, 2006).
3. Carla Evans and Scott Marion, *Understanding Instructionally Useful Assessment* (Taylor & Francis, 2024).
4. Lorena Llosa, Alison Haas, Scott Grapin, and Okhee Lee, "Integrating Science and Language for All Students with a Focus on English Language Learners," official website of the New York State Education Department, 2020, https://www.nysed.gov/sites/default/files/programs/bilingual-ed/brief-5-classroom-example-integrating-science-and-language-for-all-students-with-a-focus-on-english-language-learners-a.pdf.
5. New York State Education Department, *P-12 Science Learning Standards*, official website of the New York State Education Department, 2016, https://www.nysed.gov/sites/default/files/programs/curriculum-instruction/p-12-science-learning-standards.pdf.
6. This unit is available at nyusail.org for download and use.
7. Lorena Llosa, Scott Grapin, and Alison Haas, "Formative Assessment in the Science Classroom," official website of the New York State Education Department, 2020,

https://www.nysed.gov/sites/default/files/programs/bilingual-ed/brief-7-formative-assessment-in-the-science-classroom-a.pdf.

8. Llosa et al., "Formative Assessment."
9. Example taken from a video recorded lesson (using a pseudonym for the teacher) as part of a grant (R305A180149) awarded to ETS (Educational Testing Service) by the Institute of Education Sciences, US Department of Education, through Grant to ETS. For more details on the grant, see E. Caroline Wylie, Christine J. Lyon, and Elizabeth P. O'Dwyer, "The Benefits of Peer Teacher Observations," in *Research Handbook on Classroom Observation*, ed. Sean Kelly (Edward Elgar Publishing Ltd., 2025).
10. Ernesto Panadero, Anders Jönsson, and Jan-Willem Strijbos, "Scaffolding Self-Regulated Learning through Self-Assessment and Peer Assessment: Guidelines for Classroom Implementation," in *Assessment for Learning: Meeting the Challenges of Implementation*, ed. Dany Laveault and Linda Allal (Springer, 2016), https://doi.org/10.1007/978-3-319-39211-0_18.
11. Mathematics Assessment Resource Service (MARS), "About the Math Assessment Project," MARS website, Shell Center for Mathematical Education, https://www.map.mathshell.org/background.php.
12. Randy E. Bennett, "Integrating Measurement Principles into Formative Assessment," in *Handbook of Formative Assessment in the Disciplines*, ed. Heidi L. Andrade, Randy E. Bennett, and Gregory J. Cizek (Routledge, 2019); Kris D. Gutiérrez and Barbara Rogoff, "Cultural Ways of Learning: Individual Traits or Repertoires of Practice," *Educational Researcher* 32, no. 5 (June–July 2003): 19–25; Na'ilah Suad Nasir, Carol D. Lee, Roy Pea, and Maxine McKinney de Royston, "Rethinking Learning: What the Interdisciplinary Science Tells Us," *Educational Researcher* 50, no. 8 (2021): 557–65, 557, https://doi.org/10.3102/0013189X211047251; Na'ilah Suad Nasir, Ann S. Rosebery, Beth Warren, and Carol D. Lee, "Learning as a Cultural Process. Achieving Equity Through Diversity," in *The Cambridge Handbook of the Learning Sciences*, 3rd ed., ed. R. K. Sawyer (Cambridge University Press, 2022).
13. Paul Black and Dylan Wiliam, "Assessment and Classroom Learning," *Assessment in Education: Principles, Policy & Practice* 5, no. 1 (1998): 7–74, https://dx.doi.org/10.1080/0969595980050102; Lorrie A. Shepard, "Ambitious Teaching and Equitable Assessment: A Vision for Prioritizing Learning, Not Testing," *American Educator* (Fall 2021): 28, https://files.eric.ed.gov/fulltext/EJ1321974.pdf.
14. Margaret Heritage and John Heritage, "Teacher Questioning: The Epicenter of Instruction and Assessment," *Applied Measurement in Education* 26, no. 3 (2013): 176–90, https://doi.org/10.1080/08957347.2013.793190; Margaret Heritage, E. Caroline Wylie, Molly Faulkner-Bond, and Aida Walqui, "A Vision for Using an Argument-Based Framework for Validity Applied to a System of Assessment for English learners in the Secondary Grades," *National Research and Development Center to Improve Education for Secondary English Learners* (WestEd, 2021).
15. Megan Bang and Douglas Medin, "Cultural Processes in Science Education: Supporting the Navigation of Multiple Epistemologies," *Science Learning in Everyday Life* 94, no. 6 (November 2010): 1008–26, https://doi.org/10.1002/sce.20392; Bronwen Cowie, Christine Harrison, and Jill Willis, "Supporting Teacher Responsiveness in Assessment for Learning Through Disciplined Noticing," *The Curriculum Journal* 29, no. 4 (December 2018): 464–78, https://doi.org/10.1080/09585176.2018.1481442.

16. Geneva Gay, *Educating for Equity and Excellence: Enacting Culturally Responsive Teaching* (Teachers College Press, 2023); Lorrie A. Shepard, "The Role of Assessment in a Learning Culture," *Educational Researcher* 29, no. 7 (October 2000): 4–14, https://doi.org/10.3102/0013189X029007004.
17. Mirko Chardin and Katie R. Novak, *Equity by Design: Delivering on the Power and Promise of UDL* (Corwin Press, Inc., 2021); Angelique A. Aitken, Steve Graham, and Daniel McNeish, "The Effects of Choice Versus Preference on Writing and the Mediating Role of Perceived Competence," *Journal of Educational Psychology* 114, no. 8 (September 2022), 1844, https://doi.org/10.1037/edu0000765.
18. Heidi L. Andrade, Ying Du, and Kristina Mycek, "Rubric-Referenced Self-Assessment and Middle School Students' Writing," *Assessment in Education: Principles, Policy & Practice* 17, no. 2 (2010): 199–214, https://doi.org/10.1080/09695941003696172; Louise Bourgeois, "Supporting Students' Learning: From Teacher Regulation to Co-Regulation," in *Assessment for Learning: Meeting the Challenge of Implementation*, ed. Dany Laveault and Linda Allal (Springer, 2016), https://doi.org/10.1007/978-3-319-39211-0_20; Geoff Munns and Helen Woodward, "Student Engagement and Student Self-Assessment: The REAL Framework," *Assessment in Education: Principles, Policy & Practice* 13, no. 2 (2006): 193–213, https://doi.org/10.1080/09695940600703969.
19. Frederick Erickson, "Practice in Classrooms, Schools, and Teacher Communities: Some Thoughts on 'Proximal' Formative Assessment of Student Learning," *Teachers College Record* 109, no. 13 (2007): 186–216, https://doi.org/10.1177/016146810710901304.
20. Shepard, "Ambitious Teaching and Equitable Assessment."
21. Jeffrey K. Smith, "Reconsidering Reliability in Classroom Assessment," *Educational Measurement Issues and Practice* 22, no. 4 (October 2005): 26–33, https://doi.org/10.1111/j.1745-3992.2003.tb00141.x.
22. Fritz Mosher, personal communication to author, October 2011.
23. Patrick Griffin, Leanne Murray, Esther Care, Amanda Thomas, and Pierina Perri, "Developmental Assessment: Lifting Literacy Through Professional Learning Teams," *Assessment in Education: Principles, Policy & Practice* 17, no. 4 (2010): 383–97, https://doi.org/10.1080/0969594X.2010.516628.
24. Don Klinger, Patricia McDivitt, Barbara Howard, Todd Rogers, Marco Munoz, and Caroline Wylie, *Classroom Assessment Standards for PreK-12 Teachers: Joint Committee on Standards for Educational Evaluation* (Kindle Direct Press, 2015); for the associated NCME ITEMS module, see E. Caroline Wylie, "Digital Module 20: Classroom Assessment Standards," *Educational Measurement: Issues and Practice* 39, no. 4 (2020): 135–36, https://doi.org/10.1111/emip.12407; Michigan Assessment Consortium (MAC), "Assessment Literacy Standards," website of the MAC, 2024, https://www.michiganassessmentconsortium.org/assessment-literacy-standards; The National Center for the Improvement of Educational Assessment (NCIEA), "Classroom Assessment Learning Modules," website of the NCIEA, June 26, 2022, https://www.nciea.org/library/classroom-assessment-learning-modules.
25. Morgan Polikoff, *Beyond Standards: The Fragmentation of Education Governance and the Promise of Curriculum Reform* (Harvard Education Press, 2021).
26. Carla Evans, "Eliminating Unnecessary District-Required Assessments," website of the NCIEA, August 14, 2024, https://www.nciea.org/blog/eliminating-unnecessary-tests.

Chapter 7

1. Jenelle Reeves, "Teacher Identity," in *The TESOL Encyclopedia of English Language Teaching*, ed. John I. Liontas (Wiley-Blackwell, 2018), https://doi.org/10.1002/9781118784235.eelt0268.
2. Ana Maria Villegas and Tamara Lucas, *Educating Culturally Responsive Teachers: A Coherent Approach* (State University of New York Press, 2002).
3. Catherine S. Taylor and Susan Bobbitt Nolen, *Culturally and Socially Responsible Assessment: Theory, Research, and Practice* (Teachers College Press, 2022); Joe Feldman, *Grading for Equity, What It Is, Why It Matters, and How It Can Transform Schools and Classrooms* (Corwin, 2023).
4. Aída Walqui and George C. Bunch, eds., *Amplifying the Curriculum: Designing Quality Learning Opportunities for English Learners* (Teachers College Press, 2019).
5. Christine Rubie-Davies, Kane Meissel, Mohamed Alansari, Penelope Watson, Annaline Flint, and Lyn McDonald, "Achievement and Beliefs Outcomes of Students with High and Low Expectation Teachers," *Social Psychology of Education* 23 (2020): 1173–1201, https://doi.org/10.1007/s11218-020-09574-y.
6. Facing History & Ourselves (FH&O), "Social Identity Wheel," website of FH&O, February 25, 2021, https://www.facinghistory.org/resource-library/social-identity-wheel.
7. Collaborative Discussion Project (CDP), "Culturally Responsive Collaboration," website of CDP, https://www.collaborativediscussionproject.com/activities/module-4.
8. Mary Helen Diegel, personal communication to authors, 2024.
9. Videotaped lesson at Para Los Niños School, Los Angeles
10. "Quote Origin: We Do Not Inherit the Earth from Our Ancestors; We Borrow It from Our Children," Quote Investigator, January 22, 2013, https://quoteinvestigator.com/2013/01/22/borrow-earth/
11. Mathematics Assessment Resource Service (MARS), "Modeling Relationships: Car Skid Marks," *Mathematics Assessment Project* (Shell Center, University of Nottingham, 2015), www.map.mathshell.org/download.php?fileid=1600.
12. Margaret Heritage and John Heritage, "Teacher Questioning: The Epicenter of Instruction and Assessment," *Applied Measurement in Education* 26, no. 3 (2013): 176–90, https://doi.org/10.1080/08957347.2013.793190.
13. Cultures of Thinking Project, "Looking at Student Thinking Protocol," website of Project Zero, Harvard School of Education, 2005, https://pz.harvard.edu/sites/default/files/LAST+protocol_New.pdf.
14. L. Brown Easton, "Protocols for Examining Student Work," in *Protocols for Professional Learning* (ASCD [formerly known as the Association for Supervision and Curriculum Development], 2009), https://pdo.ascd.org/LMSCourses/PD13OC010M/media/Leading_Prof_Learning_M5_Reading2.pdf.
15. Easton, "Protocols."
16. Joseph P. McDonald, Nancy Mohr, Alan Dichter, and Elizabeth C. McDonald, *The Power of Protocols: An Educator's Guide to Better Practice* (Teachers College Press, 2003).
17. Lee Shulman, "Knowledge and Teaching: Foundations of the New Reform," *Harvard Educational Review* 57, no. 1 (1987): 8, https://doi.org/10.17763/haer.57.1.j463w79r56455411.
18. Sam Sims, Harry Fletcher-Wood, Alison O'Mara-Eves, Sarah Cottingham, Claire Stansfield, Josh Goodrich, Jo Van Herwegen, and Jake Anders, "Effective Teacher Professional Development: New Theory and a Meta-Analytic Test," *Review of Educational Research* (2023), https://doi.org/10.3102/00346543231217480.

19. Margaret Heritage, *Formative Assessment: Making It Happen in the Classroom*, 2nd ed. (Corwin Press, 2021).
20. Jerome S. Bruner, "Good Teaching is Forever Being on the Cutting Edge of a Child's Competence," AZQuotes, azquotes.com/quote/600207.
21. Heritage and Heritage, "Teacher Questioning."
22. Sententiaeantique, "We Have Two Ears, One Mouth (And Many More Ascriptions . . .)," *Sententiae Antiquae* (blog), January 30, 2020, https://sententiaeantiquae.com/2020/01/30/we-have-two-ears-one-mouth-and-many-more-ascriptions/.

Chapter 8

1. Shane Safir and Jamila Dugan, *Street Data: A Next-Generation Model for Equity, Pedagogy, and School Transformation* (Corwin, 2021).
2. Network for College Success, "ATLAS-Looking at Data Protocol," *NCS Freshman On-Track Toolkit*, https://toandthrough.uchicago.edu/sites/default/files/uploads/documents/NCS_FOT_Toolkit_ISBT_SetB_ATLAS%20Data%20Protocol.pdf.
3. Laura Hamilton, Richard Halverson, Sharnell S. Jackson, Ellen Mandinach, Jonathan A. Supovitz, and Jeffrey C. Wayman, *Using Student Achievement Data to Support Instructional Decision Making*, NCEE 2009–4067 (National Center for Education Evaluation and Regional Assistance, Institute of Education Sciences, US Department of Education, 2009), https://ies.ed.gov/ncee/wwc/Docs/PracticeGuide/dddm_pg_092909.pdf.
4. No Child Left Behind Act of 2001 (NCLB), Pub. L. No. 107-10, 115 Stat. 1425 (2002); Every Student Succeeds Act of 2015 (ESSA), Pub. L. No. 114-95, 114 Stat. 1177 (2015–2016).
5. E. Caroline Wylie and Melissa Gholson, "U.S. Federal Assessment Policy Reforms in the Twenty First Century and Their Impacts," *International Encyclopedia of Education*, 4th ed. (Elsevier Science, 2023), https://doi.org/10.1016/B978-0-12-818630-5.09027-8.
6. Scott F. Marion, James W. Pellegrino, and Amy I. Berman, "Reimagining Balanced Assessment Systems: An Introduction," in *Reimagining Balanced Assessment Systems*, ed. Scott F. Marion, James W. Pellegrino, and Amy I. Berman (National Academy of Education, 2024), https://doi.org/10.31094/2024/1.
7. NCLB, 2002; Mike Fast, Steve Ferrara, and Dan Conrad, *Current Efforts in Developing English Language Proficiency Measures as Required by NCLB: Description of an 18-State Collaboration* (American Institutes for Research, 2004).
8. ESSA, 2015.
9. WIDA, "Individual Student Report 2024," ACCESS for ELLs, 2024, https://wida.wisc.edu/sites/default/files/resource/ACCESS-Sample-Individual-Score-Report-English.pdf.
10. National Center for Education Statistics, "English Learners in Public Schools," *Condition of Education* (Institute of Education Services, US Department of Education, 2024), https://nces.ed.gov/programs/coe/indicator/cgf.
11. Margaret Heritage, Aída Walqui, and Robert Linquanti, *English Language Learners and the New Standards: Developing Language, Content Knowledge, and Analytical Practices in the Classroom* (Harvard Education Press, 2015).
12. Heritage, Walqui, and Linquanti, 2015.
13. Elizabeth Burr, Eric Haas, and Karen Ferriere, *Identifying and Supporting English Learner Students with Learning Disabilities: Key Issues in the Literature and State Practice*, REL 2015–086 (Regional Educational Laboratory West, National Center for Education Evaluation and Regional Assistance, Institute of Education Sciences, US Department of Education, 2015), https://files.eric.ed.gov/fulltext/ED558163.pdf.

14. Margaret Heritage, Molly Faulkner-Bond, and Aída Walqui, *A New Direction for Assessing English Learners in the Secondary Grades* (WestEd, 2021), https://files.eric.ed.gov/fulltext/ED626107.pdf.
15. Rebecca M. Callahan, "Tracking and High School English Learners: Limiting Opportunity to Learn," *American Educational Research Journal* 42, no. 2 (2005): 305–28, https://doi.org/10.3102/00028312042002305; Yael Glick and Aída Walqui, "Affordances in the Development of Student Voice and Agency: The Case of Bureaucratically Labeled Long-Term English Learners," in *Reconceptualizing the Role of Critical Dialogue in American Classrooms: Promoting Equity through Dialogic Education*, ed. Amanda Kibler, Guadalupe Valdés, and Aída Walqui (Routledge, 2020); Angela Johnson, "A Matter of Time: Variations in High School Course-Taking by Years-as-EL Subgroup," *American Educational Research Journal* 41, no. 4 (2019): 461–82, https://doi.org/10.3102/0162373719867087; Robin Alexander, *A Dialogic Teaching Companion* (Routledge, 2020); Aída Walqui and George C. Bunch, eds., *Amplifying the Curriculum: Designing Quality Learning Opportunities for English Learners* (Teachers College Press, 2019); Amanda K. Kibler and Guadalupe Valdés, "Conceptualizing Language Learners: Socioinstitutional Mechanisms and Their Consequences," *The Modern Language Journal* 100, no. S1 (2016): 96–116, https://doi.org/10.1111/modl.12310.
16. Marianne Perie, Scott Marion, and Brian Gong, "Moving Toward a Comprehensive Assessment System: A Framework for Considering Interim Assessments," *Educational Measurement: Issues and Practice* 28, no. 3 (2009): 5–13, https://doi.org/10.1111/j.1745-3992.2009.00149.x.
17. Joseph Martineau and Scott Marion, *Wyoming's Statewide Assessment System: Recommendations from the Wyoming Assessment Task Force* (The National Center for the Improvement of Educational Assessment [NCIEA], October 15, 2015), http://www.nciea.org/wp-content/uploads/2021/11/Final-WY-ATF-Report-12-07-2015.pdf.
18. Hugh Morrison, John Healy, and Caroline Wylie, "Teacher Knows Best: A Solution to the Marks-to-Levels Problem in National Curriculum Testing," *British Educational Research Journal* 21, no. 2 (1995): 175–82, https://doi.org/10.1080/0141192950210204.
19. Plain English, "Expression: Stay in Your Lane," Plain English website, https://plainenglish.com/expressions/stay-in-your-lane.

Chapter 9

1. Helen Timperley, "Using Assessment Data for Improving Teaching Practice," paper presented at Assessment and Student Learning: Collecting, Interpreting, and Using Data to Inform Teaching, August 17, 2009, Australian Council for Educational Research, Perth, Australia, https://research.acer.edu.au/cgi/viewcontent.cgi?article=1036&context=research_conference. See, e.g., B. Duckor and C. Holmberg, "Deciding on 'Next Steps' Together: Using Progress Guides to Better Differentiate Feedback for All in Diverse Middle School Math and Science Classrooms," *Assessment Matters* 18 (2024): 25–51.
2. Timperley, "Using Assessment Data."
3. Tim Mazzarol and Sophie Reboud, "The Entrepreneurial Process," in *Entrepreneurship and Innovation: Theory, Practice and Context*, 4th ed. (Springer, 2020).
4. Anthony Birritteri, "Trade-Talk Roundtable—The Path of Business Ownership Truly Requires a Brave Heart!," *New Jersey Business Magazine*, July 24, 2017, https://njbmagazine.com/monthly-articles/35545-2.
5. Christopher Day and Pamela Sammons, *Successful School Leadership* (Education Development Trust, 2016), https://files.eric.ed.gov/fulltext/ED565740.pdf.
6. Stephanie Trovas, "Cultivate a Learning Culture Within Your Organization," Center for Creative Leadership, May 12, 2022, http://www.ccl.org/articles/leading-effectively-articles/cultivate-and-sustain-a-learning-culture-within-your-organization.

Acknowledgments

This book has its origins in our coauthored chapter for the National Academy of Education volume *Reimaging Balanced Assessment Systems*. We are grateful to the volume's editors, Scott Marion, James Pellegrino, and Amy Berman, for their invitation to contribute and for stimulating our thinking about teachers' assessment literacy. We are also grateful to reviewers of our chapter, especially Lorrie Shepard, for their thoughtful guidance and feedback.

We owe a huge debt of thanks to the many teachers from around the US whose classroom practice is illustrated in the examples throughout the book. In particular, we offer our gratitude to Kasie Betten, Gabriela Cárdenas, Mary Helen Diegel, Lindsey Howe, Olivia Lozano, Wendy Johnson, Annlyn McKenzie, Joe Nelson, Larrissa Peru, Nick Smith, and Kristy Walters, who have willingly shared their practice with us, and from whom we have learned so much about classroom assessment, ambitious teaching, and teachers' assessment literacy.

Our thanks to the Bell Burkhardt Daro Shell Centre Trust for permission to reproduce some of their mathematics tasks, to Lorena Llosa, Scott Grapin, and Alison Haas for permission to reproduce materials from two of the science units that they have developed, and to the Digital Inquiry Group for permission to reproduce two history assessments.

We are very grateful to Julie Park Haubner for her assistance in the preparation of our manuscript.

Our warm thanks to Karen Adler, our editor from Harvard Education Press, whose guidance from our initial thinking about a book proposal to the final manuscript has been invaluable. We have greatly benefited from her for her prompt reviews of each chapter and her careful editing and feedback.

Finally, Margaret thanks her husband, John, who has lived this book with her, for his support and patience. Caroline thanks Cassandra and Melissa, who provided encouragement for this book over weekend diner breakfasts.

Acknowledgments

About the Authors

Margaret Heritage is an independent consultant in education. Her entire career has spanned both research and practice. She spent twenty-two years at UCLA, first serving as principal of the laboratory school of the Graduate School of Education and Information Studies, and then as an Assistant Director at the National Center for Research on Evaluation, Standards and Student Testing. While at UCLA, she taught in the Teacher Education Program. She has also served as a Senior Scientist at WestEd. Prior to work in the US, she had several roles in education in her native England: classroom teacher, an elementary school principal, an adjunct professor in the Department of Education at the University of Warwick, and a County Inspector of Schools.

Her current work centers on formative assessment, including how formative assessment contributes to educational equity goals, and on the development of teachers' assessment literacy knowledge and skills. Her most recent writing is a chapter coauthored with Caroline Wylie on teachers' assessment literacy for a volume on Balanced Assessment Systems published by the National Academy of Education.

E. Caroline Wylie is a senior associate at the National Center for the Improvement of Educational Assessment. Having completed her preservice teacher education with a focus on mathematics in Belfast, Northern Ireland, her focus shifted to classroom-based research. Her primary research interests include the design, implementation, and evaluation of balanced assessment systems, with a focus on the use of formative assessment to improve classroom teaching and learning. She has led studies related to the creation of effective, scaleable and sustainable teacher professional development, on the formative use of diagnostic questions for classroom-based assessment, assessment literacy, and on the role of learning progressions to support formative assessment in mathematics and science. She serves as a co-advisor for the CCSSO Balanced Assessment Systems Collaborative.

About the Authors

Index